PROFESSIONAL CLOJURE

PROFESSIONAL

Clojure

Jeremy Anderson
Michael Gaare
Justin Holguín
Nick Bailey
Timothy Pratley

wrox™
A Wiley Brand

Professional Clojure

Published by
John Wiley & Sons, Inc.
10475 Crosspoint Boulevard
Indianapolis, IN 46256
www.wiley.com

Copyright © 2016 by John Wiley & Sons, Inc., Indianapolis, Indiana

Published by John Wiley & Sons, Inc., Indianapolis, Indiana

Published simultaneously in Canada

ISBN: 978-1-119-26727-0
ISBN: 978-1-119-26728-7 (ebk)
ISBN: 978-1-119-26729-4 (ebk)

Manufactured in the United States of America

10 9 8 7 6 5 4 3 2 1

No part of this publication may be reproduced, stored in a retrieval system or transmitted in any form or by any means, electronic, mechanical, photocopying, recording, scanning or otherwise, except as permitted under Sections 107 or 108 of the 1976 United States Copyright Act, without either the prior written permission of the Publisher, or authorization through payment of the appropriate per-copy fee to the Copyright Clearance Center, 222 Rosewood Drive, Danvers, MA 01923, (978) 750-8400, fax (978) 646-8600. Requests to the Publisher for permission should be addressed to the Permissions Department, John Wiley & Sons, Inc., 111 River Street, Hoboken, NJ 07030, (201) 748-6011, fax (201) 748-6008, or online at http://www.wiley.com/go/permissions.

Limit of Liability/Disclaimer of Warranty: The publisher and the author make no representations or warranties with respect to the accuracy or completeness of the contents of this work and specifically disclaim all warranties, including without limitation warranties of fitness for a particular purpose. No warranty may be created or extended by sales or promotional materials. The advice and strategies contained herein may not be suitable for every situation. This work is sold with the understanding that the publisher is not engaged in rendering legal, accounting, or other professional services. If professional assistance is required, the services of a competent professional person should be sought. Neither the publisher nor the author shall be liable for damages arising herefrom. The fact that an organization or Web site is referred to in this work as a citation and/or a potential source of further information does not mean that the author or the publisher endorses the information the organization or Web site may provide or recommendations it may make. Further, readers should be aware that Internet Web sites listed in this work may have changed or disappeared between when this work was written and when it is read.

For general information on our other products and services please contact our Customer Care Department within the United States at (877) 762-2974, outside the United States at (317) 572-3993 or fax (317) 572-4002.

Wiley publishes in a variety of print and electronic formats and by print-on-demand. Some material included with standard print versions of this book may not be included in e-books or in print-on-demand. If this book refers to media such as a CD or DVD that is not included in the version you purchased, you may download this material at http://booksupport.wiley.com. For more information about Wiley products, visit www.wiley.com.

Library of Congress Control Number: 2016934964

Trademarks: Wiley, the Wiley logo, Wrox, the Wrox logo, Programmer to Programmer, and related trade dress are trademarks or registered trademarks of John Wiley & Sons, Inc. and/or its affiliates, in the United States and other countries, and may not be used without written permission. All other trademarks are the property of their respective owners. John Wiley & Sons, Inc., is not associated with any product or vendor mentioned in this book.

ABOUT THE AUTHORS

 JEREMY ANDERSON is a developer at Code Adept, a West Michigan–based software consultancy focused on delivering high-quality software through providing software development, agile coaching, and training services. He is a Clojure enthusiast and contributor to a few different Clojure libraries. He is very passionate about teaching others how to program and volunteers to help teach computer science to area high-school and middle-school students.

 MICHAEL GAARE is the platform technical lead at Nextangles, a financial technology startup. He's been using Clojure professionally since 2012 to build web services, data processing systems, and various libraries—not frameworks! In his spare time, he enjoys spending time with his wife and two daughters, and his hobby is opera singing.

 JUSTIN HOLGUÍN is a software engineer at Puppet Labs, where he specializes in Clojure back-end services. Justin has a passion for functional programming and a special interest in technologies that improve software reliability, such as advanced type systems and property-based testing.

 NICK BAILEY is a Clojure enthusiast and the maintainer of the Clojure java.jmx library. He is a software architect at DataStax, where he uses Clojure to build enterprise-level software for managing distributed databases. He was introduced to Clojure in 2010 and has been a fan ever since.

 TIMOTHY PRATLEY is a Clojure contributor and advocate. Clojure has been his language of choice since 2008. He develops solutions in Clojure, ClojureScript, and Clojure-Android at his current role at Outpace Systems, Inc. He has 15 years of professional software development experience during which he has used many languages, frameworks, and databases. He loves Clojure, Datomic, pair programming, and thinking.

ABOUT THE TECHNICAL EDITORS

JUSTIN SMITH is a full-time Clojure developer who is active in the online Clojure community. His day job is 100% Clojure development.

ZUBAIR QURAISHI is a UX/Design and marketing hacker based in Denmark who has sold 2 startups and invested in over 30 startups over the last 20 years. He has been using Clojure and ClojureScript for the last 5 years. He has worked in many startups and Fortune 500 companies based in the United States, Europe, and Asia. You can find his blog is at www.zubairquraishi.com.

ALEX OTT is a software architect in Intel Security (formerly McAfee), based in Paderborn, Germany. He works in the area of information security and has been using Clojure since release 1.0 (2009) to build prototypes, internal services, and open source projects, like Incanter.

DOUG KNIGHT has been programming computers professionally for 18 years, using Microsoft technologies for most of that time. He switched to Ruby on Rails in 2014 when he joined LivingSocial, and in 2015 he added Clojure as part of his work for the company.

CREDITS

PROJECT EDITOR
Charlotte Kughen

TECHNICAL EDITOR
Justin Smith
Zubair Quraishi
Alex Ott
Doug Knight

PRODUCTION EDITOR
Barath Kumar Rajasekaran

COPY EDITOR
Troy Mott

MANAGER OF CONTENT DEVELOPMENT AND ASSEMBLY
Mary Beth Wakefield

PRODUCTION MANAGER
Kathleen Wisor

MARKETING MANAGER
Carrie Sherrill

PROFESSIONAL TECHNOLOGY & STRATEGY DIRECTOR
Barry Pruett

BUSINESS MANAGER
Amy Knies

EXECUTIVE EDITOR
Jim Minatel

PROJECT COORDINATOR, COVER
Brent Savage

PROOFREADER
Nancy Bell

INDEXER
Nancy Guenther

COVER DESIGNER
Wiley

COVER IMAGE
©d8nn/Shutterstock

ACKNOWLEDGMENTS

JEREMY WOULD LIKE TO THANK God, first and foremost, for granting him the gifts that he has in order to do the things that he loves. Secondly, Jeremy thanks his family for being so supportive and understanding of him locking himself in his office to frantically write on evenings and weekends. Next, thanks to Christina Rudloff and Troy Mott for all the hard work they've done to put this project together and for inviting him onto this writing team, and thanks also to all the authors who helped make this project a reality. Finally, thanks to all the technical reviewers for taking the time to read and provide valuable feedback in the early stages of this book.

NICK WOULD LIKE TO THANK EVERYONE involved in making this book a reality: Troy and Christina for organizing, his fellow authors for writing and reviewing, and the technical reviewers for great feedback. He would also like to thank DataStax for giving him a chance to write Clojure professionally.

MICHAEL WOULD LIKE TO THANK LARA, Charlotte, and Juliette for their love, support, and understanding; Keith for his valuable assistance; Christina and Troy for their patience and the opportunity to write about a terrific subject; and Rich for creating something so interesting to write about—not to mention work with.

JUSTIN WOULD LIKE TO THANK HIS FAMILY for bootstrapping him and, among countless other things, encouraging his love of books and computers. He would also like to thank his many brilliant friends and colleagues at Puppet Labs, where he has been inspired and challenged to master Clojure bit by bit, day by day.

TIMOTHY WOULD LIKE TO THANK SHIN Nee for being the ultimate collaborator. He would like to thank you, the reader, for exploring how programming can be better; the Clojure community for providing a friendly, helpful, and pleasant ecosystem to exist in; and his parents for the many opportunities they crafted into his life.

CONTENTS

INTRODUCTION

WHAT IS CLOJURE?

Clojure is a dynamic, general-purpose programming language, combining the approachability and interactive development of a scripting language with an efficient and robust infrastructure for multithreaded programming. Clojure is a compiled language, yet remains completely dynamic—every feature supported by Clojure is supported at runtime. Clojure provides easy access to the Java frameworks, with optional type hints and type inference, to ensure that calls to Java can avoid reflection.

Clojure is a dialect of Lisp, and shares with Lisp the code-as-data philosophy and a powerful macro system. Clojure is predominantly a functional programming language, and features a rich set of immutable, persistent data structures. When mutable state is needed, Clojure offers a software transactional memory system and reactive Agent system that ensure clean, correct, multithreaded designs.

—Rich Hickey, author of Clojure

This quote from Rich Hickey, the creator of Clojure, captures what Clojure is. Many people equate Clojure with functional programming, but much like Lisp, its predecessor, it's a general-purpose language that will support you no matter what paradigm you decide to program in.

Clojure is, however, very opinionated and offers great support for programming in a functional manner, with its focus on immutable values and persistent data structures. You may be surprised to know that Clojure also offers the ability to do object-oriented programming, which we cover in this book.

WHO IS THIS BOOK FOR?

This book was written with the professional programmer in mind. This means you should have experience programming in a language, and you should know the basic syntax and concepts in Clojure, and be ready to take Clojure programming to the next level. Our goal is to take you from a Clojure beginner to being able to think like a Clojure developer. Learning Clojure is much more than just learning a new syntax. You must use tools and constructs much differently than anything you may be familiar with.

> **DEMO APPLICATION SOURCE CODE**
>
> You can access the source code from the Wiley website at `www.wiley.com/go/ professionalclojure` or at our demo application via Github at `https://github .com/backstopmedia/clojurebook`.

A powerful programming language is more than just a means for instructing a computer to perform tasks. The language also serves as a framework within which we organize our ideas about processes.

—STRUCTURE AND INTERPRETATION OF COMPUTER PROGRAMS

This book assumes some prior knowledge of Clojure and programming in general, but does not assume proficiency in Clojure. It will cover a broad scope of topics from changing the way you think and approach programming to how you integrate the REPL into your normal development routine to how you build real world applications using Ring and ClojureScript.

WHAT WILL YOU LEARN?

Our goal is to provide you with some real world examples of how to apply your Clojure knowledge to your day-to-day programming, not just theory and academia.

Chapter 1

In Chapter 1, you will learn about Clojure's unique view on designing programs. You'll discover some of the things that set Clojure apart from other languages, for example, how immutability is the default, and how Clojure qualifies as object-oriented programming.

Chapter 2

In Chapter 2, you will learn how to become proficient with the REPL and various tips and techniques for interacting with your actual application through the REPL. You'll learn how to run your code and tests from the REPL as well as how to write code that is easily reloaded from the REPL without having to restart it.

Chapter 3

In Chapter 3, you learn about building web services with Compojure, and the various concepts involved such as routes, handlers, and middleware. You will build a complete web service, and then learn various techniques for deploying your new application.

Chapter 4

Chapter 4 covers testing in Clojure, focusing primarily on the `clojure.test` testing library. You'll learn various techniques for many common testing scenarios, along with tools to help measure the quality of your code.

Chapter 5

In Chapter 5, you will learn how to build a task management web application similar to the popular Trello application in ClojureScript. You'll also learn the techniques for sharing functions between both your server-side and client-side applications.

Chapter 6

Chapter 6 takes a look at Datomic and how it applies the concept of immutability to databases. You'll learn the basics of how to model data in a Datomic database and how to extract that information. Then you'll apply this knowledge to building a database to support the task management application from Chapter 5.

Chapter 7

In Chapter 7, you'll take a look at performance and how to make your Clojure code execute faster. You'll discover how with a little work you can tweak your Clojure code to be as fast as Java code.

TOOLS YOU WILL NEED

Just as in any good adventure or journey, having the right tools makes things go much smoother. Fortunately, to work through the examples in this book, you only need three things: Java, Leiningen, and a good text editor.

Java

Most computers these days come with Java pre-installed, but in order to run the examples contained in this book you need to make sure you have installed a recent version. The code examples in this book were written with and confirmed to work with JDK 1.8.0_25. For instructions on how to download and install the proper JDK for your platform, see the documentation at Oracle's JDK download page: (`http://www.oracle.com/technetwork/java/javase/downloads/index.html`).

Leiningen

Leiningen, according to their website (`http://leiningen.org`), is the most contributed-to Clojure project. For those of you coming from a background in Java, Leiningen fills a similar role that

Maven does for the Java world, only without all of the XML, and you can avoid wanting to pull your hair out. It helps you manage the dependencies for your project and declaratively describe your project and configuration, and provides access to a wealth of plugins for everything from code analysis to automation, and more. Leiningen makes your Clojure experience much more enjoyable.

Fortunately, getting Leiningen up and running is a fairly simple task. You'll want to install the latest version available, which at the time of this writing is 2.5.3. Please refer to the Leiningen website for instructions particular to your programming environment.

Editors

Once you have Leiningen installed, the only thing left to do is to make sure you have a good text editor to efficiently edit your Clojure code. If you have a favorite editor, just use what you're already comfortable with. However, if your editor doesn't support basic things like parentheses balancing, integration with the REPL, syntax highlighting, or properly indenting Clojure code, you may want to consider one of the editors below.

Emacs

Emacs is the favored editor of many grizzled veterans. It has a long history with Lisp. Even though it has a steep learning curve, it is considered by many to be very powerful, and no other editor is as extensible. There are many custom Emacs configurations designed to help ease the learning curve, such as Emacs Prelude (`https://github.com/bbatsov/prelude`), which also contains a sensible default configuration for developing in many languages, including Clojure.

LightTable

LightTable (`http://lighttable.com`) began life as a Kickstarter project with a unique new vision of how to integrate the code editor, REPL, and documentation browser for Clojure. It has delivered on those promises and then some and has gained popularity among many in the Clojure community.

Cursive (IntelliJ)

If you're already comfortable with using any of the various JetBrains IDEs, you'll be happy to know that there is a plugin for IntelliJ called Cursive (`https://cursive-ide.com`). Besides having good integration with nREPL, it also stays true to its reputation and contains excellent refactoring support, as well as debugging and Java interop.

Counterclockwise (Eclipse)

For those who are familiar with Eclipse, there is Counterclockwise (`http://doc.ccw-ide.org`), which can be installed as either an Eclipse plugin or a standalone product. Counterclockwise boasts many of the same features as the previous editors, integration with the REPL, and ability to evaluate code inline.

CONVENTIONS

To help you get the most from the text and keep track of what's happening, we've used a number of conventions throughout the book.

> **NOTE** *Notes indicates notes, tips, hints, tricks, and/or asides to the current discussion.*

As for styles in the text:

➤ We *highlight* new terms and important words when we introduce them.

➤ We show code within the text like so: `persistence.properties`.

➤ We show all code snippets in the book using this style:

```
FileSystem fs = FileSystem.get(URI.create(uri), conf);
InputStream in = null;
try {
```

➤ URLs in text appear like this: `http://<Slave Hostname>:50075`.

SOURCE CODE

As you work through the examples in this book, you may choose either to type in all the code manually, or to use the source code files that accompany the book. All of the source code used in this book is available for download at `www.wiley.com`. Specifically for this book, the code download is on the Download Code tab at:

`www.wiley.com/go/professionalclojure`

You can also search for the book at `www.wrox.com` by ISBN (the ISBN for this book is 9781119267171 to find the code. And a complete list of code downloads for all current Wrox books is available at `www.wiley.com/dynamic/books/download.aspx`.

> **NOTE** *Because many books have similar titles, you may find it easiest to search by ISBN; this book's ISBN is 978-1-119-26727-0.*

Once you download the code, just decompress it with your favorite compression tool. Alternately, you can go to the main Wrox code download page at `www.wrox.com/dynamic/books/download.aspx` to see the code available for this book and all other Wrox books.

ERRATA

We make every effort to ensure that there are no errors in the text or in the code. However, no one is perfect, and mistakes do occur. If you find an error in one of our books, like a spelling mistake or faulty piece of code, we would be very grateful for your feedback. By sending in errata, you may save another reader hours of frustration, and at the same time, you will be helping us provide even higher quality information.

To find the errata page for this book, go to `www.wiley.com/go/` and click the Errata link. On this page you can view all errata that has been submitted for this book and posted by Wrox editors.

If you don't spot "your" error on the Book Errata page, go to `www.wrox.com/contact/techsupport .shtml` and complete the form there to send us the error you have found. We'll check the information and, if appropriate, post a message to the book's errata page and fix the problem in subsequent editions of the book.

P2P.WROX.COM

For author and peer discussion, join the P2P forums at `http://p2p.wrox.com`. The forums are a web-based system for you to post messages relating to Wrox books and related technologies and interact with other readers and technology users. The forums offer a subscription feature to e-mail you topics of interest of your choosing when new posts are made to the forums. Wrox authors, editors, other industry experts, and your fellow readers are present on these forums.

At `http://p2p.wrox.com`, you will find a number of different forums that will help you, not only as you read this book, but also as you develop your own applications. To join the forums, just follow these steps:

1. Go to `http://p2p.wrox.com` and click the Register link.
2. Read the terms of use and click Agree.
3. Complete the required information to join, as well as any optional information you wish to provide, and click Submit.
4. You will receive an e-mail with information describing how to verify your account and complete the joining process.

> **NOTE** *You can read messages in the forums without joining P2P, but in order to post your own messages, you must join.*

Once you join, you can post new messages and respond to messages other users post. You can read messages at any time on the web. If you would like to have new messages from a particular forum e-mailed to you, click the Subscribe to This Forum icon by the forum name in the forum listing.

For more information about how to use the Wrox P2P, be sure to read the P2P FAQs for answers to questions about how the forum software works, as well as many common questions specific to P2P and Wrox books. To read the FAQs, click the FAQ link on any P2P page.

1

Have a Beginner's Mind

WHAT'S IN THIS CHAPTER?

➤ Understanding the differences between imperative and functional programming

➤ Learning how to think more functionally

➤ Discovering Clojure's unique perspective on object-oriented programming

If your mind is empty, it is always ready for anything, it is open to everything. In the beginner's mind there are many possibilities, but in the expert's mind there are few.

—Shunryu Suzuki

Over the past thirty years many popular programming languages have more in common with each other than they have differences. In fact, you could argue that once you have learned one language, it's not difficult to learn another. You merely have to master the subtle differences in syntax, and maybe understand a new feature that isn't present in the language that you're familiar with. It's not difficult to call yourself a polyglot programmer when many of the top languages in use today are all so similar.

Clojure, on the other hand, comes from a completely different lineage than most of the popular languages in use today. Clojure belongs to the Lisp family of programming languages, which has a very different syntax and programming style than the C-based languages you are probably familiar with. You must leave all of your programming preconceptions behind in order to gain the most from learning Clojure, or any Lisp language in general.

Forget everything you know, or think you know about programming, and instead approach it as if you were learning your very first programming language. Otherwise, you'll just be learning a new syntax, and your Clojure code will look more like Java/C/Ruby and less like Clojure is designed to look. Learning Clojure/Lisp will even affect the way you write in other languages, especially with Java 8 and Scala becoming more popular.

FUNCTIONAL THINKING

C, C++, C#, Java, Python, Ruby, and even to some extent Perl, all have very similar syntax. They make use of the same programming constructs and have an emphasis on an imperative style of programming. This is a style of programming well suited to the von Neumann architecture of computing that they were designed to execute in. This is probably most apparent in the C language, where you are responsible for allocating and de-allocating memory for variables, and dealing directly with pointers to memory locations. Other imperative languages attempt to hide this complexity with varying degrees of success.

> In computer science, **imperative programming** is a **programming** paradigm that uses statements that change a program's state.

This C-style of programming has dominated the programming scene for a very long time, because it fits well within the dominant hardware architectural paradigm. Programs are able to execute very efficiently, and also make efficient use of memory, which up until recently had been a very real constraint. This efficiency comes at the cost of having more complex semantics and syntax, and it is increasingly more difficult to reason about the execution, because it is so dependent upon the state of the memory at the time of execution. This makes doing concurrency incredibly difficult and error prone. In these days of cheap memory and an ever growing number of multiple core architectures, it is starting to show its age.

Functional programming, however, is based on mathematical concepts, rather than any given computing architecture. Clojure, in the spirit of Lisp, calls itself a general-purpose language; however, it does provide a number of functional features and supports the functional style of programming very well. Clojure as a language not only offers simpler semantics than its imperative predecessors, but it also has arguably a much simpler syntax. If you are not familiar with Lisp, reading and understanding Clojure code is going to take some practice. Because of its heavy focus on immutability, it makes concurrency simple and much less error prone than having to manually manage locks on memory and having to worry about multiple threads reading values simultaneously. Not only does Clojure provide all of these functional features, but it also performs object-oriented programming better than its Java counterpart.

Value Oriented

Clojure promotes a style of programming commonly called "value-oriented programming." Clojure's creator, Rich Hickey, isn't the first person to use that phrase to describe functional programming, but he does an excellent job explaining it in a talk titled *The Value of Values* that he gave at Jax Conf in 2012 (https://www.youtube.com/watch?v=-6BsiVyC1kM).

By promoting this style of value-oriented programming, we are focused more on the values than mutable objects, which are merely abstractions of places in memory and their current state. Mutation belongs in comic books, and has no place in programming. This is extremely powerful, because it allows you to not have to concern yourself with worrying about who is accessing your data and when. Since you are not worried about what code is accessing your data, concurrency now becomes much more trivial than it ever was in any of the imperative languages.

One common practice when programming in an imperative language is to defensively make a copy of any object passed into a method to ensure that the data does not get altered while trying to use it. Another side effect of focusing on values and immutability is that this practice is no longer necessary. Imagine the amount of code you will no longer have to maintain because you'll be using Clojure.

In object-oriented programming, we are largely concerned with information hiding or restricting access to an object's data through encapsulation. Clojure removes the need for encapsulation because of its focus on dealing with values instead of mutable objects. The data becomes semantically transparent, removing the need for strict control over data. This level of transparency allows you to reason about the code, because you can now simplify complex functions using the substitution model for procedure application as shown in the following canonical example. Here we simplify a function called sum-of-squares through substituting the values:

```
(defn square [a] (* a a))
(defn sum-of-squares [a b] (+ (square a) (square b))

; evaluate the expression (sum-of-squares 4 5)

(sum-of-squares 4 5)
(+ (square 4) (square 5))
(+ (* 4 4) (* 5 5))
(+ 16 25)
41
```

By favoring functions that are referentially transparent, you can take advantage of a feature called memorization. You can tell Clojure to cache the value of some potentially expensive computation, resulting in faster execution. To illustrate this, we'll use the Fibonacci sequence, adapted for Clojure, as an example taken from the classic MIT text *Structure and Interpretation of Computer Programs (SICP)*.

```
(defn fib [n]
  (cond
    (= n 0) 0
    (= n 1) 1
    :else (+ (fib (- n 1))
             (fib (- n 2)))))
```

If you look at the tree of execution and evaluate the function for the value of 5, you can see that in order to calculate the fifth Fibonacci number, you need to call (fib 4) and (fib 3). Then, to calculate (fib 4), you need to call (fib 3) and (fib 2). That's quite a bit of recalculating values that you already know the answer to (see Figure 1-1).

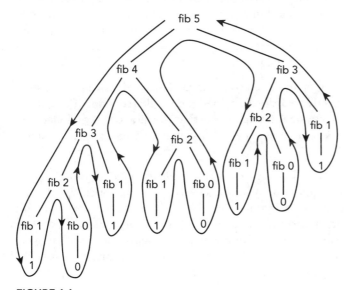

FIGURE 1-1

Calculating for (fib 5) executes quickly, but when you try to calculate for (fib 42) you can see that it takes considerably longer.

```
(time (fib 42))
"Elapsed time: 11184.49583 msecs"
267914296
```

You can rewrite a function to leverage memorization to see a significant improvement in the execution time. The updated code is shown here:

```
(def memoized-fib
  (memoize (fn [n]
            (cond
              (= n 0) 0
              (= n 1) 1
              :else (+ (fib (- n 1))
                       (fib (- n 2))))))))
```

When you first run this function, you'll see how the execution doesn't happen any faster; however, each subsequent execution instantaneously happens.

```
user> (time (memoized-fib 42))
"Elapsed time: 10586.656667 msecs"
```

```
267914296
user> (time (memoized-fib 42))
"Elapsed time: 0.10272 msecs"
267914296
user> (time (memoized-fib 42))
"Elapsed time: 0.066446 msecs"
267914296
```

This is a risky enhancement if you do this with a function that relies on a mutable shared state. However, since our functions are focused on values, and are referentially transparent, you can leverage some cool features provided by the Clojure language.

Thinking Recursively

Recursion is not something that is taught much in most imperative languages. Contrast this with most functional languages, and how they embrace recursion, and you will think more recursively. If you are unfamiliar with recursion, or struggle to understand how to think recursively, you should read *The Little Schemer*, by Daniel P. Friedman and Matthias Felleisen. It walks you through how to write recursive functions using a Socratic style of teaching, where the two authors are engaged in a conversation and you get to listen in and learn.

Let's take a look at a trivial example of calculating a factorial. A typical example in Java might look like the code shown below. You start by creating a local variable to store the ultimate result. Then, loop over every number, one-by-one, until you reach the target number, multiplying the last result by the counter variable defined by the for loop, and mutating the local variable.

```
public long factorial(int n) {
  long product = 1;
  for ( int i = 1; i <= n; i++ ) {
    product *= i;
  }
  return product;
}
```

Because of Clojure's focus on values and immutable structures, it relies on recursion for looping and iteration. A naïve recursive definition of a factorial in Clojure may look like the following:

```
(defn factorial [n]
    (if (= n 1)
        1
        (* n (factorial (- n 1)))))
```

If you trace the execution of the factorial program with an input of 6, as shown next, you see that the JVM needs to maintain each successive operation on the stack as n increases, until the factorial reaches a point where it returns a value instead of recurring. If you're not careful, you'll likely end up with a stack overflow. This style of recursion is often called linear recursion.

```
(factorial 6)
(* 6 (factorial 5))
(* 6 (* 5 (factorial 4)))
```

```
(* 6 (* 5 (* 4 (factorial 3))))
(* 6 (* 5 (* 4 (* 3 (factorial 2)))))
(* 6 (* 5 (* 4 (* 3 (* 2 (factorial 1))))))
(* 6 (* 5 (* 4 (* 3 (* 2 1)))))
(* 6 (* 5 (* 4 (* 3 2))))
(* 6 (* 5 (* 4 6)))
(* 6 (* 5 24))
(* 6 120)
720
```

To resolve this dilemma, rewrite your function in a tail recursive style using the special operator called `recur`, which according to the documentation, "does constant-space recursive looping by rebinding and jumping to the nearest enclosing loop or function frame." This means that it tries to simulate a tail call optimization, which the JVM doesn't support. If you rewrite the preceding factorial example using this style, it looks something like the following:

```
(defn factorial2 [n]
    (loop [count n acc 1]
       (if (zero? count)
           acc
         (recur (dec count) (* acc count)))))
```

In this version of the factorial function, you can define an anonymous lambda expression using the `loop` construct, thus providing the initial bindings for the local variables `count` to be the value passed into the factorial function to start the accumulator at 1. The rest of the function merely consists of a conditional that checks the base case and returns the current accumulator, or makes a recursive call using `recur`. Notice how in the tail position of the function this program doesn't require the runtime to keep track of any previous state, and can simply call `recur` with the calculated values. You can trace the execution of this improved version of the factorial as seen here:

```
(factorial2 6)
(loop 6 1)
(loop 5 6)
(loop 4 30)
(loop 3 120)
(loop 2 360)
(loop 1 720)
720
```

The call to `factorial2` take fewer instructions to finish, but it doesn't need to place new calls on the stack for each iteration, like the first version of `factorial` did.

But what happens if you need to perform mutual recursion? Perhaps you want to create your own version of the functions for determining if a number is odd or even. You could define them in terms of each other. A number is defined as being even if the decrement of itself is considered odd. This will recursively call itself until it reaches the magic number of 0, so at that point if the number is even it will return true. If it's odd it will return false. The code for the mutually recursive functions for `my-odd?` and `my-even?` are defined here:

```
(declare my-odd? my-even?)

(defn my-odd? [n]
```

```
  (if (= n 0)
    false
    (my-even? (dec n))))

(defn my-even? [n]
  (if (= n 0)
    true
    (my-odd? (dec n))))
```

This example suffers from the same issue found in the first example, in that each successive recursive call needs to store some sort of state on the stack in order to perform the calculation, resulting in a stack overflow for large values. The way you avoid this problem is to use another special operator called trampoline, and modify the original code to return functions wrapping the calls to your recursive functions, like the following example:

```
(declare my-odd? my-even?)

(defn my-odd? [n]
  (if (= n 0)
    false
    #(my-even? (dec n))))

(defn my-even? [n]
  (if (= n 0)
    true
    *(my-odd? (dec n))))
```

Notice the declare function on the first line. We can call the function using the trampoline operator as shown here:

```
(trampoline my-even? 42)
```

If the call to a function, in this case my-even?, would return another function, trampoline will continue to call the returned functions until an atomic value gets returned. This allows you to make mutually recursive calls to functions, and not worry about blowing the stack. However, we're still left with one problem. If someone wishes to use the version of my-even? and my-odd?, they must have prior knowledge to know they must call them using trampoline. To fix that you can rewrite the functions:

```
(defn my-even? [n]
  (letfn [(e? [n]
             (if (= n 0)
               true
               #(o? (dec n))))
          (o? [n]
             (if (= n 0)
               false
               #(e? (dec n))))]
    (trampoline e? n)))

(defn my-odd? [n]
  (not (my-even? n)))
```

We've effectively hidden away the knowledge of having to use trampoline from our users.

Higher Order Functions

One of the many qualities that define a language as being functional is the ability to treat functions as first class objects. That means functions can not only take values as parameters and return values, but they can also take functions as parameters as well. Clojure comes with a number of commonly used higher order functions such as map, filter, reduce, remove and iterate, as well as providing you with the tools to create your own.

In Java, for example, if you want to filter a list of customers that live in a specific state, you need to create a variable to hold the list of filtered customers, manually iterate through the list of customers, and manually add them to the local variable you created earlier. You have to specify not only what you want to filter by, but also how to iterate through the list.

```
public List<Customer> filterByState(List<Customer> input, String state) {
    List<Customer> filteredCustomers = new ArrayList<>();

    for(Customer customer : input) {
        if (customer.getState().equals(state)) {
            filteredCustomers.put(customer);
        }
    }

    return filteredCustomers;
}
```

This Clojure example deals less with how to do the filtering, and is a bit more concise and declarative. The syntax may look a little strange, but you are simply calling the filter function with an anonymous function telling what you should filter on and finally the sequence you want to filter with.

```
(def customers [{:state "CA" :name "Todd"}
                {:state "MI" :name "Jeremy"}
                {:state "CA" :name "Lisa"}
                {:state "NC" :name "Rich"}])
(filter #(= "CA" (:state %)) customers)
```

One common design pattern that exists in object-oriented programming, the Command pattern, exists as a way to cope with the lack of first class functions and higher order functions. To implement the pattern, you first define an interface that defines a single method for executing the command, a sort of pseudo-functional object. Then you can pass this Command object to a method to be called at the appropriate time. The downfall of this is that you need to either define several concrete implementations to cover every possible piece of functionality you would need to execute, or define an anonymous inner class wrapping the functionality.

```
public void wrapInTransaction(Command c) throws Exception {
    setupDataInfrastructure();
    try {
        c.execute();
        completeTransaction();
    } catch (Exception condition) {
        rollbackTransaction();
        throw condition;
    } finally {
```

```
            cleanUp();
        }
    }

    public void addOrderFrom(final ShoppingCart cart, final String userName,
                             final Order order) throws Exception {
        wrapInTransaction(new Command() {
            public void execute() {
                add(order, userKeyBasedOn(userName));
                addLineItemsFrom(cart, order.getOrderKey());
            }
        });
    }
```

In Clojure you have the ability to pass functions around the same as any other value, or if you just need to declare something inline you can leverage anonymous lambda expressions. You can rewrite the previous example in Clojure to look like this code:

```
(defn wrapInTransaction [f]
    (do
        (startTransaction)
        (f)
        (completeTransaction)))

(wrapInTransaction #(
    (do
        (add order user)
        (addLineItemsFrom cart orderKey))))
```

To put it another way, with imperative languages you usually have to be more concerned with how you do things, and in Clojure you're able to focus more on the what you want to do. You can define abstractions at a different level than what is possible in most imperative languages.

Partials

In object-oriented programming there are many patterns for building up objects in steps by using the Builder Pattern, or many related types of objects using the Abstract Factory Pattern. In Clojure, since the primary method of abstraction is the function, you also have a mechanism to build new functions out of existing ones with some of the arguments fixed to a value by using partial.

The canonical example of how to use partial, shown here is a bit trivial.

```
(def add2 (partial + 2))
```

For a better example, we'll take a look at the clojure.java.jdbc library. In the following listing is an example showing a typical pattern for defining the connection properties for your database, and a few simple query wrappers. Notice how every call to jdbc/query and jdbc/insert! takes the spec as its first parameter.

```
(ns sampledb.data
  (:require [clojure.java.jdbc :as jdbc]))

(def spec {:classname "org.postgresql.Driver"
```

```
              :subprotocol "postgresql"
              :subname "//localhost:5432/sampledb"})

    (defn all-users []
      (jdbc/query spec ["select * from login order by username desc"])))

    (defn find-user [username]
      (jdbc/query spec ["select * from login where username = ?" username]))

    (defn create-user [username password]
      (jdbc/insert! spec :login {:username username :password password :salt
        "some_salt"}))
```

There is a bit too much repetition in this example, and it only contains three functions for querying the database. Imagine how many times this occurs in a non-trivial application. You can remove this duplication by using `partial`, and creating a new function with this first parameter already bound to the `spec` variable as shown here:

```
    (ns sampledb.data
      (:require [clojure.java.jdbc :as jdbc]))

    (def spec {:classname "org.postgresql.Driver"
               :subprotocol "postgresql"
               :subname "//localhost:5432/sampledb"})

    (def query (partial jdbc/query spec))
    (def insert! (partial jdbc/insert! spec))

    (defn all-users []
      (query ["select * from login order by username desc"])))

    (defn find-user [username]
      (query ["select * from login where username = ?" username]))

    (defn create-user [username password]
      (insert! :login {:username username :password password :salt "some_salt"}))
```

Another useful way to use `partial` is for one of the higher order functions such as `map`, which expects a function with exactly one argument to apply to the objects in a collection. You can use `partial` to easily take a function that would normally require more than one argument and create a new one specifying any number of them so that it now only requires one. For example, the `*` function used for multiplying numbers doesn't make much sense with only one argument, but you can use `partial` to specify what you want to multiply each item by as shown here:

```
    (defn apply-sales-tax [items]
      ((map (partial * 1.06) items)))
```

The only real downside to `partial` is that you are only able to bind values to parameters in order, meaning that the parameter order is important. If you want to bind the last parameter to a function, you can't leverage `partial`. Instead, you can define another function that wraps the original function call or leverages a lambda expression.

Function Composition

Another useful piece of functionality is the ability to compose multiple functions together to make a new function. Once again, Clojure shows its functional roots based in mathematics. As an example, if you had a function called f and another called g, you could compose them together such that the output from f is fed as the input to g, in the same way you can leverage pipes and redirects on the Unix command line and compose several functions together. More specifically, if you have a function call that looks like (g (f (x)), you can rewrite it to read as ((comp g f) x).

To provide a more practical example, say you wanted to minify some JavaScript, or read in a JavaScript file and remove all of the new lines and extra whitespace, so that it requires less information to transfer from the server to the browser. You can accomplish this task by composing the common string functions provided by Clojure, str/join, str/trim, str/split-lines, as shown here:

```
(defn minify [input]
  (str/join (map str/trim (str/split-lines input))))
```

This can then be rewritten using the comp function to look like the following:

```
(def minify (comp str/join (partial map str/trim) str/split-lines))
```

Notice how the ordering of the functions passed to comp retain their original order of the last function being applied first, working your way back to the beginning of the list. Also we modified it a bit to leverage partial with the map and str/trim functions, to create a function that operates on a collection, since str/trim only operates on a single string.

Embracing Laziness

Clojure itself is not considered to be a lazy language in the same sense that a language like Haskell is; however, it does provide support for creating and using lazy sequences. In fact, most of the built in functions like map, filter, and reduce generate lazy sequences for you without you probably even knowing it. You can see this here:

```
user> (def result (map (fn [i] (println ".") (inc i)) '[0 1 2 3]))
#'user/result

user> result
.
.
.
.
(1 2 3 4)
```

When you evaluate the first expression, you don't see any output printed to the console. Had this been a non-lazy sequence, you would have seen the output printed to the screen immediately, because it would have evaluated the println expression at the time of building the sequence. Instead, the output is not printed until you ask Clojure to show you what is in the result symbol, and it has to fully realize what's inside the sequence. This is exceptionally useful, because the computation inside the function that you pass to map may contain some fairly expensive operation, and that expensive operation by itself may not be an issue. Yet, when the operation is executed, the execution of your application can be slowed by several or even hundreds of times.

Another useful example of a lazy sequence in action is when representing an infinite set of numbers. If you have a set of all real numbers, or a set of all prime numbers, you can set all of these numbers in the Fibonacci sequence as shown here.

```
(def fib-seq
     (lazy-cat [1 1] (map + (rest fib-seq) fib-seq)))

(take 10 fib-seq)
-> (1 1 2 3 5 8 13 21 34 55)
```

This sequence is defined using a lazy sequence, and next you will ask Clojure to give you the first 10 numbers in a sequence. In a language that did not support this level of laziness, this type of data modeling would simply not be possible.

Another example of how this can be useful is by infinitely cycling through a finite collection. For example, if you want to assign an ordinal value to every value in a collection for an example group of a list of people into four groups, you can write something similar to the following:

```
(def names '["Christia" "Arline" "Bethann" "Keva" "Arnold" "Germaine"
             "Tanisha" "Jenny" "Erma" "Magdalen" "Carmelia" "Joana"
             "Violeta" "Gianna" "Shad" "Joe" "Justin" "Donella"
             "Raeann" "Karoline"])

user> (mapv #(vector %1 %2) (cycle '[:first :second :third :fourth]) names)
[[:first "Christia"] [:second "Arline"] [:third "Bethann"] [:fourth "Keva"]
  [:first "Arnold"] [:second "Germaine"] [:third "Tanisha"] [:fourth "Jenny"]
  [:first "Erma"] [:second "Magdalen"] [:third "Carmelia"] [:fourth "Joana"]
  [:first "Violeta"] [:second "Gianna"] [:third "Shad"] [:fourth "Joe"]
  [:first "Justin"] [:second "Donella"] [:third "Raeann"] [:fourth "Karoline"]]
```

If you map over multiple collections, you will apply the function provided to the first item in the first collection, the first item in each successive collection, and then the second and so forth, until one of the collections is completely exhausted. So, in order to map the values :first, :second, :third, and :fourth repeatedly over all the names, without having to know how many names exist in the collection, you must find a way to cycle over and over repeatedly through the collection. This is what cycle and infinite lazy collections excel at.

When You Really Do Need to Mutate

Just because Clojure favors dealing with values doesn't mean you completely do away with mutable state. It just means you greatly limit mutable state, and instead use quarantine in your specific area of code. Clojure provides a few mechanisms to manage mutable state.

Atoms

Using Atoms is the first and simplest mechanism for handling mutable state provided by Clojure. Atoms provide you with a means to manage some shared state in a synchronous, uncoordinated, or independent manner. So, if you need to only manage a single piece of mutable state at a time, then Atoms are the tool you need.

Up to this point, we've primarily focused on values; however, Atoms are defined and used in a different way. Since Atoms represent something that can potentially change, out of necessity they must represent some reference to an immutable structure. An example of how to define an Atom is shown here.

```
user> (def app-state (atom {}))
#'user/app-state
user> app-state
#atom[{} 0x1f5b7bd9]
```

We've defined an Atom containing an empty map with a stored reference in `app-state`. As you can see by the output in the `repl`, the Atom stores a memory location to the map. Right now it doesn't do a whole lot, so let's associate some values into the map.

```
user> (swap! app-state assoc :current-user "Jeremy")
{:current-user "Jeremy"}
user> app-state
#atom[{:current-user "Jeremy"} 0x1f5b7bd9]
user> (swap! app-state assoc :session-id "some-session-id")
{:current-user "Jeremy", :session-id "some-session-id"}
user> app-state
#atom[{:current-user "Jeremy", :session-id "some-session-id"} 0x1f5b7bd9]
```

To modify `app-state`, Clojure provides you with two different functions called `swap!` and `reset!`, both of which atomically modify the value pointed to by the `app-state` reference. The `swap!` function is designed to take a function that will operate on the value stored in the reference, and will swap out the value with the value returned as a result of executing the function. In the preceding example we provided `swap!` with the `assoc` function to associate a new value into the map for a given keyword.

To simply replace the value referenced in `app-state` you can use the `reset!` function, and provide it with a new value to store in the Atom as shown here:

```
user> (reset! app-state {})
{}
user> app-state
#atom[{} 0x1f5b7bd9]
```

You can see that the app-state now references an empty map again.

Now that you know how to store the shared state in your Atom, you may be wondering how you get the values back out. In order to access the state stored in your Atom, use the `deref/@` reader macro as shown here:

```
user> (swap! app-state assoc :current-user "Jeremy" :session-id "some-session-id")
{:current-user "Jeremy", :session-id "some-session-id"}
user> (:current-user @app-state)
"Jeremy"
user> (:session-id @app-state)
```

```
"some-session-id"
user> (:foo @app-state :not-found)
:not-found
```

Once you de-reference your Atom using the `deref`/`@` reader macro, you can then interact with your `app-state`, just as if it were a map again.

Refs

While Atoms provide you with a means to manage some shared mutable state for a single value, they are limited by the fact that if you need to coordinate changes between multiple objects, such as the classic example of transferring money from one account to another, you need to use transaction references or Refs for short. Transaction references operate similar to how you would expect database transactions to use a concurrency model called Software Transactional Memory, or STM. In fact, Refs fulfill the first three parts required for ACID compliancy: Atomicity, Consistency, and Isolation. Clojure does not concern itself with Durability, however, since the transactions occur in memory.

To illustrate why you can't just use Atoms for coordinated access, consider the following example.

```
user> (def savings (atom {:balance 500}))
#'user/savings
user> (def checking (atom {:balance 250}))
#'user/checking
user> (do
        (swap! checking assoc :balance 700)
        (throw (Exception. "Oops..."))
        (swap! savings assoc :balance 50))
Exception Oops...  user/eval9580 (form-init1334561956148131819.clj:66)
user> (:balance @checking)
700
user> (:balance @savings)
500
```

Here two Atoms called `savings` and `checking` are defined, and we attempt to modify both of them in a `do` block. We are, however, throwing an exception in between updating the two Atoms. This causes our two accounts to get out of sync. Next, let's look at the same example using Refs.

```
user> (def checking (ref {:balance 500}))
#'user/checking
user> (def savings (ref {:balance 250}))
#'user/savings
user> (dosync
        (commute checking assoc :balance 700)
        (throw (Exception. "Oops..."))
        (commute savings assoc :balance 50))
Exception Oops...  user/eval9586/fn--9587 (form-init1334561956148131819.clj:6)
user> (:balance @checking)
500
user> (:balance @savings)
250
```

As you can see, you create Refs and read values out of them similar to how we did that with Atoms earlier. There are a few minor differences, however, in how you update the value stored in the Ref.

We use `commute` rather than `swap!`, and all update operations must perform on the Refs within a `dosync` block.

Nil Punning

If you're at all experienced in Java, you are very familiar with the dreaded `NullPointerException`. It's probably one of the most prolific errors encountered when developing in Java, so much so that the inventor of the Null reference, Tony Hoare, even gave a talk several years ago stating how big of a mistake it was (http://www.infoq.com/presentations/Null-References-The-Billion-Dollar-Mistake-Tony-Hoare). It seems odd that everything else, with the exception of primitive values, is an Object, except for `null`. This has led to several workarounds in languages, such as `Optional` in Java, null safe object navigation in Groovy, and even in Objective-C you send messages to `nil` and then just happily ignore them.

Clojure, being a Lisp, adopts the philosophy of `nil` punning. Unlike Java, `nil` has a value, and it simply means "no answer." It can also mean different things in different contexts.

When evaluated as a Boolean expression, like many other dynamic typed languages, it will be equivalent to `false`.

```
user> (if nil "true" "false")
"false"
```

`nil` can also be treated like an empty `Seq`. If you call `first` on `nil`, you get a returned `nil`, because there is no first element. If you then call `last` on `nil`, you also unsurprisingly get `nil`. However, don't assume that `nil` is a `Seq`, because when you call `seq` on `nil` you will get a `false` return.

```
user> (first nil)
nil
user> (last nil)
nil
user> (second nil)
nil
user> (seq? nil)
false
```

Unlike many other Lisps, Clojure does not treat empty lists, vectors, and maps as `nil`.

```
user> (if '() "true" "false")
"true"
user> (if '[] "true" "false")
"true"
user> (if '{} "true" "false")
"true"
```

Because `nil` can take on many meanings, you must be mindful to know when `nil` means false and when it means `nil`. For example, when looking for a value in a map, the value for a key can be `nil`. To determine whether or not it exists in the map, you have to return a default value.

```
user> (:foo {:foo nil :bar "baz"})
nil
user> (:foo {:foo nil :bar "baz"} :not-found)
nil
user> (:foo {:bar "baz"} :not-found)
:not-found
```

Unlike Java, `nil` is everywhere and `for` functions return `nil`. Most functions are/should be written to handle a passed in `nil` value. "Using `nil` where it doesn't make sense in Clojure code is *usually* a type error, not a `NullPointerException`, just as using a number as a function is a type error." (http://www.lispcast.com/nil-punning)

The Functional Web

It's interesting to see how web programming has evolved over the years. Many different paradigms have come and gone, with some better than others, and yet we haven't seen the end of this evolution. In the early days of the dynamic web back in the 1990s we saw technologies such as CGI, and languages such as Perl, PHP, and ColdFusion come into popularity. Then, with the rise of object-oriented programming, distributed object technologies such as CORBA and EJB rose up, along with object-centric web service technology such as SOAP, as well as object-focused web programming frameworks such as ASP.NET and JSF.

Recent years have seen a shift toward a more RESTful, micro-service based architecture. Nobody uses CORBA anymore, and even SOAP is a dirty word in many circles. Instead, web programming has started to embrace HTTP and its stateless nature and focus on values. Similar to how functional programming has gained popularity because of the rise in number of cores in modern day computers and the necessity of concurrent programming, the web also needs ways to deal with scaling horizontally rather than just vertically.

So what qualities, if any, does web programming in recent years share with functional programming? At its heart, your endpoints can be thought of as functions that take an HTTP request and transform them into an HTTP response. The HTTP protocol itself is also stateless in nature. True, there are things like cookies and sessions, but those merely simulate some sort of state through a shared secret between the client and server. For the most part, the REST endpoints can be thought of as being referentially transparent, which is why caching technologies are so prevalent.

That's not to say there aren't aspects of web programming that are not very functional. Obviously, it would be very difficult to get anything done without modifying some state somewhere. However, it seems like web programming shares as much if not more in common with functional programming than it does with object-oriented programming. In fact, you may find that there's much more opportunity for composability and reuse than with the component-based technologies that have fallen out of favor.

DOING OBJECT-ORIENTED BETTER

Object-oriented programming promised reusable components, and in many ways failed to deliver. Functional programming delivers on this promise where object-oriented programming couldn't. It may surprise you, but Lisp has been doing object-oriented programming since before Java existed. Most object-oriented languages, by definition, define everything as being an object. The problem is that, by forcing everything to fit into this mold of everything being an object, you end up with objects that exist only to "escort" methods, as cleverly explained in the excerpt from Steve Yegge's post *Execution in the Kingdom of Nouns* below.

> *In Javaland, by King Java's royal decree, Verbs are owned by Nouns. But they're not mere pets; no, Verbs in Javaland perform all the chores and manual labor in the entire kingdom. They are, in effect, the kingdom's slaves, or at very least the serfs and indentured servants. The residents of Javaland are quite content with this situation, and are indeed scarcely aware that things could be any different.*
>
> *Verbs in Javaland are responsible for all the work, but as they are held in contempt by all, no Verb is ever permitted to wander about freely. If a Verb is to be seen in public at all, it must be escorted at all times by a Noun.*
>
> *Of course "escort," being a Verb itself, is hardly allowed to run around naked; one must procure a VerbEscorter to facilitate the escorting. But what about "procure" and "facilitate?" As it happens, Facilitators and Procurers are both rather important Nouns whose job is the chaperonement of the lowly Verbs "facilitate" and "procure," via Facilitation and Procurement, respectively.*
>
> *The King, consulting with the Sun God on the matter, has at times threatened to banish entirely all Verbs from the Kingdom of Java. If this should ever to come to pass, the inhabitants would surely need at least one Verb to do all the chores, and the King, who possesses a rather cruel sense of humor, has indicated that his choice would be most assuredly be "execute."*
>
> *The Verb "execute," and its synonymous cousins "run," "start," "go," "justDoIt," "makeItSo," and the like, can perform the work of any other Verb by replacing it with an appropriate Executioner and a call to execute(). Need to wait? Waiter.execute(). Brush your teeth? ToothBrusher(myTeeth).go(). Take out the garbage? TrashDisposalPlanExecutor.doIt(). No Verb is safe; all can be replaced by a Noun on the run.*
>
> http://steve-yegge.blogspot.com/2006/03/execution-in-kingdom-of-nouns.html

At the heart of object-oriented programming is the concept of organizing your programs through creating classes containing the interesting things about a particular object and the things your objects can do. We call these things classes. We can then create more specialized versions of a class through inheritance. The canonical example of this is describing a program that is responsible for describing shapes (see Figure 1-2).

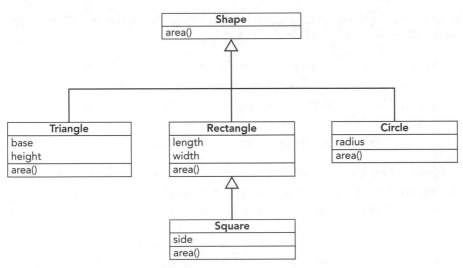

FIGURE 1-2

In the diagram in Figure 1-2 you can see that a generic class of shape is defined, and then several classes that inherit from shape are created, with each defining their own implementation of area(). The drawing application sends a message to each of the shapes asking for the area, so at runtime the application determines which implementation to call based on what type of shape it is. This is more commonly known as polymorphism. The key takeaways here are that the behavior belongs to and is defined by the classes themselves, and the methods are invoked on a particular object, and the specific implementation is then decided by the class of the object.

Polymorphic Dispatch with defmulti

Clojure, like many Lisps before it, takes a radically different approach to polymorphism by leveraging a concept called generic functions. This opens up a whole world of possibilities that just were not possible, and for the most part are still not possible, in object-oriented languages. In Clojure, you are not limited to runtime polymorphism on types alone, but also on values, metadata, and relationships between one or more arguments and more.

To rewrite our example above you would start by defining a generic function for area as shown here.

```
(defmulti area (fn [shape & _]
                 shape))
```

The generic function consists of first a name for the generic function, then a dispatch function to help Clojure figure out which implementation to call. In this case it's going to inspect the value of the first argument to our function. Then you can implement the various area functions for our different types of shapes like the following.

```
(defmethod area :triangle
  [_ base height]
  (/ (* base height) 2))
```

```
(defmethod area :square
  [_ side]
  (* side side))

(defmethod area :rectangle
  [_ length width]
  (* length width))

(defmethod area :circle
  [_ radius]
  (* radius radius Math/PI))
```

Here you've defined four implementations for the `area` function. You do this by, instead of defining them using `defn`, using the special form `defmethod`, followed by the name of the generic function, and the value from the dispatch function that you would like to match on. Notice how in the parameter lists for each of these functions, you can safely ignore the first parameter being passed in because it was only used for purposes of dispatch. You can see the actual usage of these below.

```
user> (area :square 5)
25
user> (area :triangle 3 4)
6
user> (area :rectangle 4 6)
24
user> (area :circle 5)
78.53981633974483
```

So, you may be wondering how this is any better than what we already have in object-oriented programming. Let's take a look at another example. Suppose you were creating a function that needed to apply a 5% surcharge if a customer lives in New York and a 4.5% surcharge if they live in California. You could model a very simplistic invoice as shown here.

```
{:id 42
 :issue-date 2016-01-01
 :due-date 2016-02-01
 :customer {:name "Foo Bar Industries"
            :address "123 Main St"
            :city "New York"
            :state "NY"
            :zipcode "10101"}
 :amount-due 5000}
```

Writing a similar method that handles this logic in Java would look something like the following.

```
public BigDecimal calculateFinalInvoiceAmount(Invoice invoice) {
    if (invoice.getCustomer().getState().equals("CA")) {
        return invoice.getAmount() * 0.05;
    } else if (invoice.getCustomer.getState().equals("NY")) {
        return invoice.getAmount() * 0.045;
    } else {
        return invoice.getAmount();
    }
}
```

In order to add another state that is needed to add a surcharge for, you must modify this method and add another `else if` conditional. If you wrote this example in Clojure, it would look like the following.

```
(defmulti calculate-final-invoice-amount (fn [invoice]
                                           (get-in invoice [:customer :state])))

(defmethod calculate-final-invoice-amount "CA" [invoice]
  (let [amount-due (:amount-due invoice)]
    (+ amount-due (* amount-due 0.05))))

(defmethod calculate-final-invoice-amount "NY" [invoice]
  (let [amount-due (:amount-due invoice)]
    (+ amount-due (* amount-due 0.045))))

(defmethod calculate-final-invoice-amount :default [invoice]
  (:amount-due invoice))
```

Now, if sometime in the future you decide to add a surcharge to another state, you can simply add another `defmethod` to handle the logic specific to that case.

Defining Types with deftype and defrecord

If you come from a background in object-oriented languages, you may feel compelled to immediately start defining a bunch of custom types to describe your objects, just as you would if you were designing an application in an object-oriented language. Clojure strongly encourages sticking to leveraging the built in types, but sometimes it's beneficial to define the data type so you can leverage things like type-driven polymorphism. In most programs written in object-oriented languages, the classes you define generally fall into one of two categories: classes that do interesting things, and classes that describe interesting things.

For the first of these things Clojure provides you with the `deftype`, and for the latter you can use `defrecord`. Types and records are very similar in how they're defined and used, but there are some subtle differences (see Table 1-1).

TABLE 1-1: deftypes and defrecords

DEFTYPE	DEFRECORD
Supports mutable fields.	Does not support mutable fields.
Provides no functionality other than constructor.	Behaves like a `PersistentMap` and provides default implementations for: ➤ Value based `hashCode` and `equals` ➤ Metadata support ➤ Associative support ➤ Keyword accessors for fields

DEFTYPE	DEFRECORD
Provides reader syntax for instantiating objects using a fully qualified name and argument vector. Passes argument vector directly to constructor. For example: `#my.type[1 2 "a"]`.	Provides additional reader syntax to instantiate objects using a fully qualified name and argument map. For example: `#my.type{:a "foo" :b "bar"}`.
Provides a special function `->YourType`, where `YourType` is the name of your custom type, that passes its arguments to the constructor of your custom type.	Provides a special function, `map->YourRecord`, where `YourRecord` is the name of your custom record, that takes a map and uses it to construct a record from it.

Before looking at how to define and use `deftype` and `defrecord`, you must first look at protocols.

Protocols

If you're at all familiar with Java, you can think of protocols as being very similar to interfaces. They are a named set of functions and their arguments. In fact, Clojure will generate a corresponding Java interface for each of the protocols you define. The generated interface will have methods corresponding to the functions defined in your protocol.

So, let's revisit the Shapes example from earlier. If you create a protocol for Shapes, it looks something like the following.

```
(defprotocol Shape
  (area [this])
  (perimeter [this]))
```

Next, create records for `Square` and `Rectangle` that implement the protocol for Shape as shown here.

```
(defrecord Rectangle [width length]
  Shape
  (area [this] (* (:width this) (:length this)))
  (perimeter [this] (+ (* 2 (:width this)) (* 2 (:length this)))))

(defrecord Square [side]
  Shape
  (area [this] (* (:side this) (:side this)))
  (perimeter [this] (+ (* 4 (:side this)))))
```

Then create and call the functions to calculate the area as shown here.

```
user> (def sq1 (->Square 4))
#'user/sq1
user> (area sq1)
16
user> (def rect1 (->Rectangle 4 2))
```

```
#'user/rect1
user> (area rect1)
8
```

Alternatively, you can also create your records using the `map->Rectangle` and `map->Square` functions as shown here.

```
user> (def sq2 (map->Square {:side 3}))
#'user/sq2
user> (def rect2 (map->Rectangle {:width 4 :length 7}))
#'user/rect2
user> (into {} rect2)
{:width 4, :length 7}
user> rect2
#user.Rectangle{:width 4, :length 7}
user> (into {} rect2)
{:width 4, :length 7}
user> (:width rect2)
4
user> (:length rect2)
7
user> (:foo rect2 :not-found)
:not-found
```

Also, recall that earlier records were discussed, which are basically wrappers around `PersistentMap`. This of course means that you can interact with your records as if they were maps in Clojure. You can access the members of your `Rectangle` object just as if it were a map, and you can even construct new maps from it using `into`.

Reify

Sometimes you want to implement a protocol without having to go through the trouble of defining a custom type or record. For that, Clojure provides `reify`. A quick example of this can be seen here.

```
(def some-shape
  (reify Shape
    (area [this] "I calculate area")
    (perimeter [this] "I calculate perimeter")))

user> some-shape
#object[user$reify__8615 0x221f1bd "user$reify__8615@221f1bd"]
user> (area some-shape)
"I calculate area"
user> (perimeter some-shape)
"I calculate perimeter"
```

You can think of `reify` as the Clojure equivalent of doing anonymous inner classes in Java. In fact, you can use `reify` to create anonymous objects that extend Java interfaces as well.

PERSISTENT DATA STRUCTURES

With most imperative languages, the data structures you use are destructive by nature, replacing values in place. This becomes problematic because if you use destructive data structures, you cannot long pass them around with the confidence that nothing else has come along and modified the values.

For example, if you update the second index of the list L1, shown above, in a language such as Java, you see that the value is updated in place and the list L1 is no longer the same list as before. So anything that may have been using L1 for calculations will have changed as well (see Figure 1-3).

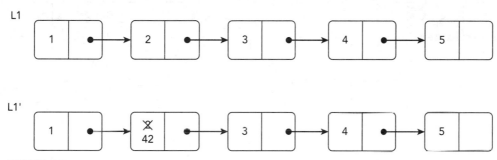

FIGURE 1-3

Clojure, on the other hand, continues with its tradition of focusing on values, and implements many of its data collections in a persistent manner, meaning that any time you do something to modify a collection, it returns a shiny new collection that may also share some of its structure with the original. You may be thinking to yourself that sharing elements between structures like this would be problematic, but because the elements themselves are immutable, you don't need to be concerned.

The example in Figure 1-4 shows a similar update using a persistent list data structure. Notice how when you update the second index in the list L1, you instead create a new list L2, thus creating new copies of all the nodes up to the point where we're updating. This then shares structure with the rest of the original list.

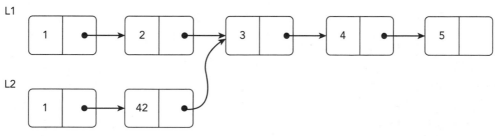

FIGURE 1-4

If you were to append a list L2 to the end of L1, it would be returned L3, which is basically a copy of L1 with the exception of the last node that then points to the beginning of L2. This maintains the integrity of both L1 and L2, so any function that was previously using them can continue to do so without worrying about the data being changed out from under them.

Let's take a look at another example (see Figure 1-5), but this time we'll look at a simplistic binary search tree. If you start with a tree L1 and attempt to add the value 6 to the tree, you see that copies of all the nodes are made containing the path to where you want to add the new node. Then in the new root node (L2), you simply point to the right sub-tree from L1.

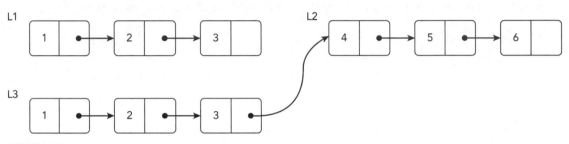

FIGURE 1-5

Next, let's take a look at how to implement the binary tree in Clojure. Start by defining a protocol called INode as shown here.

```
(defprotocol INode
  (entry [_])
  (left [_])
  (right [_])
  (contains-value? [_ _])
  (insert-value [_ _]))
```

Let's examine a few pieces of functionality for the example. Let's look at functions that retrieve the left and right sub-trees, regardless of whether the value exists in our tree, with the ability to add new values to the tree. Once you have the protocol defined, you can begin to implement the binary search tree by defining a new type using deftype as shown below.

```
(deftype Node [value left-branch right-branch]
  INode
  (entry [_] value)
  (left [_] left-branch)
  (right [_] right-branch)
  (contains-value? [tree v]
    (cond
      (nil? tree) false
      (= v value) true
      (< v value) (contains-value? left-branch v)
      (> v value) (contains-value? right-branch v)))
  (insert-value [tree v]
    (cond
      (nil? tree) (->Node v nil nil)
      (= v value) tree
      (< v value) (->Node value (insert-value left-branch v) right-branch)
      (> v value) (->Node value left-branch (insert-value right-branch v)))))
```

So let's try out the new code.

```
user> (def root (Node. 7 nil nil))
#'user/root
user> (left root)
nil
user> (right root)
nil
user> (entry root)
7
user> (contains-value? root 7)
true
```

So far so good. Now let's see if the tree contains 5.

```
user> (contains-value? root 5)
IllegalArgumentException No implementation of method: :contains-value? of protocol:
    #'user/INode found for class: nil  clojure.core/-cache-protocol-fn
    (core_deftype.clj:554)
```

What happened? If you investigate the error message it's trying to tell you that `nil` doesn't implement the protocol and thus it doesn't know how to call the function `contains-value?` on `nil`. You can fix this by extending the protocol onto `nil` as shown here.

```
(extend-protocol INode
  nil
  (entry [_] nil)
  (left [_] nil)
  (right [_] nil)
  (contains-value? [_ _] false)
  (insert-value [_ value] (Node. value nil nil)))
```

This now allows you to refactor the Node type to remove the redundant checks for `nil` to look like the following.

```
(deftype Node [value left-branch right-branch]
  INode
  (entry [_] value)
  (left [_] left-branch)
  (right [_] right-branch)
  (contains-value? [tree v]
    (cond
      (= v value) true
      (< v value) (contains-value? left-branch v)
      (> v value) (contains-value? right-branch v)))
  (insert-value [tree v]
    (cond
      (= v value) tree
      (< v value) (Node. value (insert-value left-branch v) right-branch)
      (> v value) (Node. value left-branch (insert-value right-branch v)))))
```

Now that we have that fixed, let's try this out again.

```
user> (contains-value? root 5)
false
```

Excellent. Now let's create a tree with a few more nodes.

```
user> (def root (Node. 7 (Node. 5 (Node. 3 nil nil) nil) (Node. 12
  (Node. 9 nil nil) (Node. 17 nil nil))))
#'user/root
```

The above code should produce a tree with the same structure as L1 shown in Figure 1-6.

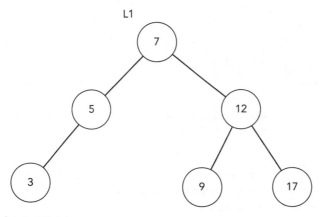

FIGURE 1-6

You can validate that assumption with the following commands.

```
user> (left root)
#object[user.Node 0x5cedcfe8 "user.Node@5cedcfe8"]
user> (entry (left root))
5
user> (entry (left (left root)))
3
user> (entry (right root))
12
user> (entry (right (right root)))
17
```

As you can see, when you ask for the value of the left sub-tree from root, you get the value 5, and when you ask for the left of that sub-tree, you get the value 3. Now, let's take a look at the identity value for the left and right sub-trees from `root` respectively.

```
user> (identity (left root))
#object[user.Node 0x5cedcfe8 "user.Node@5cedcfe8"]
user> (identity (right root))
#object[user.Node 0x124ee325 "user.Node@124ee325"]
```

Your values may differ slightly from above, but they should look similar. Next, let's add a new value of 6 to the tree, which should be inserted to the right of the 5 node. After you insert the new value, take a look at the identity values again from the root node of the new tree you just created.

```
user> (def l (insert-value root 6))
#'user/l
```

```
user> (identity (left 1))
#object[user.Node 0x167286ec "user.Node@167286ec"]
user> (identity (right 1))
#object[user.Node 0x124ee325 "user.Node@124ee325"]
```

You should see that a new Node for the left sub-tree of our tree is created, but the new list is pointing at the same instance of the right sub-tree as the original tree did. The result of the inserts should now produce the structure shown in Figure 1-7. With the original list still intact, the new list shares some structure with the original.

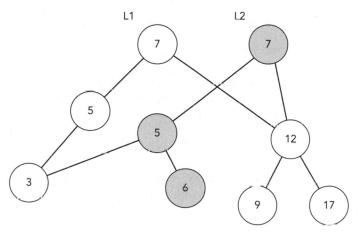

FIGURE 1-7

If you want to read more about the way that Clojure implements some of its persistent data structures, there are a pair of great articles explaining the implementation details found at http://blog.higher-order.net/2009/02/01/understanding-clojures-persis tentvector-implementation and http://blog.higher-order.net/2009/09/08/ understanding-clojures-persistenthashmap-deftwice.

SHAPING THE LANGUAGE

You may have heard at one point in time Lisp being described as a "programmable programming language," and that Lisp is homoiconic, or even how "code is data, data is code." What does this really mean for you as a programmer though? If you have a background in C, you may be familiar with the term "macro"; however, as stated earlier in this chapter, forget everything you think you know about macros. Macros in Clojure are a much more powerful construct than what is available in any imperative language. This is so powerful that entire books have been written on macros alone (see *Let Over Lambda* and *Mastering Clojure Macros*).

Macros in Clojure allow you to rewrite the normal syntax rules of Clojure in order to shape the language to fit your problem domain. While some languages offer some sort of mechanism to do metaprogramming, and the ability to modify default behavior, none of them exhibit quite the power of Clojure's macro system. Many frameworks in other languages seem to abuse this power, and this often leads to tricky to find bugs and confusion about where certain functionality comes from. So, you must exercise caution when deciding whether or not to use a macro.

So, what exactly constitutes a good use of macros and what doesn't? One exemplary example of how you can leverage macros to create a powerful and expressive DSL is the routes library in the Compojure framework. The routes library defines macros for creating ring handler mappings using a grammar that make perfect sense in this context. We see an example of the `defroutes` macro coupled with the various macros that map to the HTTP verbs:

```
(defroutes app-routes
  (GET "/" [] (index))
  (GET "/books" [] (get-books))
  (GET "/books/:id" [id] (find-book id))
  (POST "/books" [title author] (add-book title author)))
```

By leveraging macros, Compojure is able to change the semantics of how the language works. It allows you to define the mapping between URL and handler in a more natural fashion. The `defroutes` macro allows you to create a named set of routes, in this case called `app-routes`. Then a list of routes is provided that is evaluated by Ring until it finds one that matches. The routes themselves are defined using a macro that allows you to specify the HTTP verb, followed by the route, with the ability to define path variable bindings. Next we list any variables that will be bound. These can come from URL parameters, or in the case of the POST route, from the form parameters in the request. Finally, you are able to either define the actual handler inline, if it's simple enough, or have the route dispatch to a function defined elsewhere.

Another fine example of the power of macros and how you can build a natural fluent API is the Honey SQL library found at `https://github.com/jkk/honeysql`. It allows you to define SQL queries using Clojure's built in data structures and then provides a multitude of functions and macros that transform them into `clojure.java.jdbc`, and compatible parameterized SQL that you can then pass directly to `jdbc/query`, `jdbc/insert!`, and the like. Let's take a look at one of the examples from their documentation.

```
(def sqlmap {:select [:a :b :c]
             :from [:foo]
             :where [:= :f.a "baz"]})
(sql/format sqlmap)

=> ["SELECT a, b, c FROM foo WHERE (f.a = ?)" "baz"]
```

Honey SQL even defines a helper function called `build` that helps you define these map objects as shown below.

```
(sql/build :select :*
           :from :foo
           :where [:= :f.a "baz"])

=> {:where [:= :f.a "baz"], :from [:foo], :select [:*]}
```

Leveraging the build function allows you to still use the same style of specifying the query; however, it doesn't require all of the extra brackets as before, making it just that much more concise.

Clojure also offers some really nice metaprogramming abilities through `defprotocol`. Protocols are similar to Java interfaces in that they define a specific set of functions and their signatures, and even generate a corresponding interface that you can use in Java, which we'll cover later. The other thing you can do with protocols, though, is extend existing types, including final classes in Java. This means that you can add new methods to things like Java's `String` class as shown here.

```
(defprotocol Palindrome (is-palindrome? [object]))

(extend-type java.lang.String
  Palindrome
  (is-palindrome? [s]
    (= s (apply str (reverse s)))))

(is-palindrome? "tacocat")

=> true
```

You can see how to define a protocol called `Palindrome`, and define it as having a single function called `is-palindrome?`. Next, extend the `java.lang.String` class to add functionality to Java's built-in String class. Then, show it in action by calling `is-palindrome?` with the value `"tacocat"`.

As mentioned before, this level of modifying the language and types should be carefully considered before you decide to use it. It often leads to the same problems mentioned before with overuse of metaprogramming facilities and a lack of clarity about where things may be defined, especially when you can get by with just defining a regular function.

Clojure offers some very powerful ways to shape the language to the way you want to work. How you decide to use it is mostly a matter of personal preference.

SUMMARY

In this chapter you have seen how Clojure is different than most other mainstream languages in use today. As defined at the beginning of the chapter, if you don't come at it with a clear mind and learn how to do things the Clojure way, you'll simply be writing the same old code in a different syntax. Enlightenment will not come overnight; however, if you do approach it with an open mind it will likely fundamentally change the way you think about programming in general. As stated by Eric Raymond, "Lisp is worth learning for the profound enlightenment experience you will have when you finally get it; that experience will make you a better programmer for the rest of your days, even if you never actually use Lisp itself a lot."

Rapid Feedback Cycles with Clojure

WHAT'S IN THIS CHAPTER?

➤ Understanding why rapid feedback cycles are important

➤ Achieving rapid feedback with Clojure's built-in tools

➤ Leveraging your existing tool set to speed up the feedback process

Hopefully you found Chapter 1 to be a good overview of Clojure and why it is an ideal choice for your development language. Clojure's approach to functional programming, laziness, mutability, and other concepts make it a good candidate for web development. You've likely chosen Clojure for many of these reasons, but an important part of being successful with any language is being productive.

There are multiple aspects that factor into your productivity with a given language, but perhaps one of the most important aspects is feedback. Decreasing the amount of time spent waiting on feedback is a critical part of improving your productivity in any language. Shortening the feedback cycle is a problem that is addressed not only by specific languages and the tooling for that language but by development methodologies in general. Ideas like agile programming, continuous integration, and test-driven development have shorter feedback cycles as one of their goals.

Of course, high-level approaches to developing projects like these are outside the scope of this book. This chapter dives into how you can be more productive with Clojure in your day-to-day work—specifically, how you can decrease the length of your feedback cycle with Clojure both by how you approach development with Clojure and by leveraging the tools provided by Clojure and its ecosystem.

REPL-DRIVEN DEVELOPMENT

A *REPL* is a tool found in many programming languages and is commonly used for quick feedback while developing. Even if you haven't heard the term REPL before, you've almost certainly used one before without knowing it. Any time you've used a command line, you've used a REPL.

> **NOTE** *REPL stands for read-eval-print loop and is a tool common to various programming languages.*

When you hear the term REPL-driven development, you may think of it similarly to other development methodologies, such as test-driven development. REPL-driven development, however, is not so much a strict set of practices and guidelines for development as it is a recognition that the REPL is a useful tool to leverage regardless of your development process. Even if you are already following a methodology like test-driven development, leveraging the REPL to speed your feedback leads to more productivity. This section covers the basics of working with the REPL in a Clojure project as well as how you can integrate a REPL with some tools you may already be familiar with.

Basic REPL Usage with Leiningen

If you are familiar with Clojure, then you are also likely very familiar with one of its more popular build tools: leiningen. Otherwise, you should visit `http://leiningen.org/` and make sure you have leiningen installed on your machine before you continue. Let's go ahead and create a new leiningen project so you can play with the REPL (lein is the script used within leiningen).

```
lein new compojure chapter2
cd chapter2
lein repl
nREPL server started on port 61908 on host 127.0.0.1 - nrepl://127.0.0.1:61908
REPL-y 0.3.5, nREPL 0.2.6
Clojure 1.7.0
Java HotSpot(TM) 64-Bit Server VM 1.8.0_45-b14
    Docs: (doc function-name-here)
          (find-doc "part-of-name-here")
  Source: (source function-name-here)
 Javadoc: (javadoc java-object-or-class-here)
    Exit: Control+D or (exit) or (quit)
 Results: Stored in vars *1, *2, *3, an exception in *e

user=>
```

Now you've created a new Clojure project named `chapter2` and started a REPL within that project. Already, the REPL has conveniently provided some clues as to how you can quickly start developing the application. You can see that there are useful tools available for looking up Clojure documentation, Clojure source code, and even Java documentation. Let's go ahead and try a few of them out.

```
user=> (doc map)
-------------------------
```

```
clojure.core/map
([f] [f coll] [f c1 c2] [f c1 c2 c3] [f c1 c2 c3 & colls])
  Returns a lazy sequence consisting of the result of applying f to
  the set of first items of each coll, followed by applying f to the
  set of second items in each coll, until any one of the colls is
  exhausted.  Any remaining items in other colls are ignored. Function
  f should accept number-of-colls arguments. Returns a transducer when
  no collection is provided.
nil
user=> (find-doc #"map.*parallel")
------------------------
clojure.core/pmap
([f coll] [f coll & colls])
  Like map, except f is applied in parallel. Semi-lazy in that the
  parallel computation stays ahead of the consumption, but doesn't
  realize the entire result unless required. Only useful for
  computationally intensive functions where the time of f dominates
  the coordination overhead.
nil
```

Not only can you easily find the documentation for functions and macros that you already know but you can use find-doc to look up things in the documentation for which you have forgotten the function or macro name. In this example, we couldn't remember what the parallel version of map was called, but passing a simple regular expression to find-doc helped us quickly find what we needed. We were able to use source to quickly look and see how pmap works under the hood:

```
user-> (source pmap)
(defn pmap
  "Like map, except f is applied in parallel. Semi-lazy in that the
  parallel computation stays ahead of the consumption, but doesn't
  realize the entire result unless required. Only useful for
  computationally intensive functions where the time of f dominates
  the coordination overhead."
  {:added "1.0"
   :static true}
  ([f coll]
   (let [n (+ 2 (.. Runtime getRuntime availableProcessors))
         rets (map #(future (f %)) coll)
         step (fn step [[x & xs :as vs] fs]
                (lazy-seq
                  (if-let [s (seq fs)]
                    (cons (deref x) (step xs (rest s)))
                    (map deref vs))))]
     (step rets (drop n rets))))
  ([f coll & colls]
   (let [step (fn step [cs]
                (lazy-seq
                  (let [ss (map seq cs)]
                    (when (every? identity ss)
                      (cons (map first ss) (step (map rest ss)))))))]
     (pmap #(apply f %) (step (cons coll colls))))))
nil
```

You can see from the line rets (map #(future (f %)) coll) that each invocation of the function passed to map is being run in a separate thread. Given the overhead of creating new threads, pmap probably isn't useful unless the function you are applying is intensive. Of course, the documentation states that, but being able to dive in and understand why is incredibly useful.

Lastly, look at the `javadoc` function. As mentioned in Chapter 1, Clojure's interoperability with Java means that you often use Java objects and methods directly rather than use a Clojure interface. It is incredibly useful to be able to quickly open relevant documentation in these situations. In the source for `pmap`, you can see the use of the Java class `Runtime` to get the number of processors, so this example looks up the Java documentation for that class (see Figure 2-1).

```
user=> (javadoc Runtime)
true
```

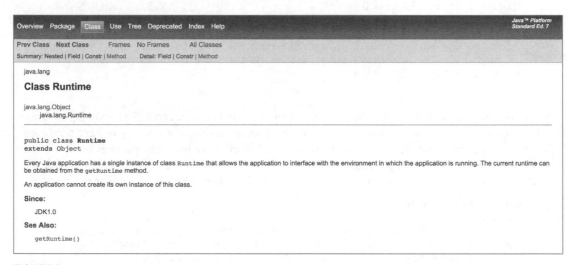

FIGURE 2-1

As you can see the, the `javadoc` function automatically launched the configured default browser and loaded the documentation for the specified class. This will prove invaluable as you are developing Clojure code, especially if you are coming from a background with limited Java experience.

Remote REPLs with nREPL

When you start a REPL with lein, there is actually a lot more going on behind the scenes than may be immediately obvious. Rather than just starting a single REPL process, lein is actually starting a REPL server in the background and is also starting a client to connect to that server. In the previous section, you may have noticed the following line printed when we started our REPL.

```
nREPL server started on port 61908 on host 127.0.0.1 - nrepl://127.0.0.1:61908
```

First, you can see that something called an `nREPL server` is starting, which uses the Clojure library `tools.nrepl` (https://github.com/clojure/tools.nrepl). The `tools.nrepl` library provides an easy interface for starting, stopping, and interacting with a REPL over the network (the *n* in nREPL stands for network). So you can see that when we started our REPL earlier with lein an nREPL server was started automatically on a randomly picked port. When we are working in our REPL, we aren't actually evaluating our code in the client process; we are submitting it to the nREPL server for evaluation and displaying the result. It's easy to verify this by connecting two REPLs to the same server. First an initial REPL is started and a hello world function is created:

```
lein repl :start :host localhost :port 60000
nREPL server started on port 60000 on host localhost - nrepl://localhost:60000
...
user=> (defn hello-world [name]
  #_=>   (println (format "Hello %s!" name)))
#'user/hello-world
```

Then a second REPL pointed at the same server is started and the hello world function is called:

```
lein repl :connect localhost:60000
Connecting to nREPL at localhost:60000
...
user=> (hello-world "Nick")
Hello Nick!
```

As you can see, the function defined in the first REPL is also available in the second REPL instance because they are connected to the same server. In practice, connecting to a single REPL server simultaneously from multiple clients while developing may not be particularly useful. In fact, it may even lead to confusion if one client is changing code in use by another client. Simply having a REPL that runs remotely is rather useful, though. For one thing, you can start a REPL in the background without a client and connect to it on demand without needing to start a server again. Running `lein repl :headless :host localhost :port 60000` starts a REPL server without a client whereas `lein repl :connect localhost:60000` connects to that server.

In addition to simply running a REPL server in the background, you can also embed a REPL into your applications. This allows you to debug your application interactively while it is running. Starting a REPL server programmatically with the `tools.nrepl` library is simple:

```
user=> (use '[clojure.tools.nrepl.server :only (start-server stop-server)])
nil
user=> (start-server :port 7888)
#'user/server
```

Generally speaking, though, it's not wise to run a REPL server in a production application. Because that would pose potential security concerns, you generally want to run a REPL server in your application only while you are developing.

The next section of this chapter describes an example of configuring an application to start a REPL server automatically during development.

REPL Usage with a Real Application

At this point we've covered the REPL and some simple applications. Now, let's build a simple application to demonstrate leveraging the REPL in a more realistic scenario. Earlier you created a lein project named "chapter2" by running `lein new compojure chapter2`. This created a new project using the `compojure` (`https://github.com/weavejester/compojure`) project template. If you open `src/chapter2/handler.clj` in your editor of choice, you should see the following:

```
(ns chapter2.handler
  (:require [compojure.core :refer :all]
            [compojure.route :as route]
            [ring.middleware.defaults :refer [wrap-defaults site-defaults]]))

(defroutes app-routes
  (GET "/" [] "Hello World")
  (route/not-found "Not Found"))

(def app
  (wrap-defaults app-routes site-defaults))
```

At the moment this application is just a sample hello world app. But, let's build a to-do list application with a simple REST based interface. For now, the to-do list will be fairly simple. Create the file `src/chapter2/core.clj` with the following contents:

```
(ns chapter2.core)

(def id-atom (atom 0))
(defn next-id [] (swap! id-atom inc))

(def tasks (atom (sorted-map)))

(defn get-tasks
  "Get all tasks on the to-do list"
  []
  @tasks)

(defn add-task
  "Add a task to the to-do list. Accepts a string describing the task."
  [task]
  (swap! tasks assoc (next-id) task))

(defn remove-task
  "Removes a task from the to-do list. Accepts the id of the task to remove."
  [task-id]
  (swap! tasks dissoc task-id))
```

You now have an extremely simple to-do list that stores the tasks on the list in memory. Of course, with a real application you'd want to use some sort of persistent storage for your tasks. Before you modify `src/chapter2/handler.clj` to define the REST API for the to-do list, let's test it out from the REPL. First, make some modifications to the lein project to make development easier. Tell lein what the main class of the application is by adding `:main chapter2.core`, and add some dependencies to make development and testing easier. Edit your `project.clj` so that it contains:

```
(defproject chapter2 "0.1.0-SNAPSHOT"
  :description "FIXME: write description"
  :url "http://example.com/FIXME"
  :min-lein-version "2.0.0"
  :dependencies [[org.clojure/clojure "1.7.0"]
```

```
                    [compojure "1.4.0"]
                    [ring/ring-defaults "0.1.5"]
                    [ring/ring-json "0.4.0"]]
  :plugins [[lein-ring "0.9.7"]]
  :ring {:handler chapter2.handler/app}
  :main chapter2.core
  :profiles
  {:dev {:dependencies [[clj-http "2.0.1"]
                        [javax.servlet/servlet-api "2.5"]
                        [ring/ring-mock "0.3.0"]]}})
```

Now, when you start a REPL, you'll notice that lein automatically puts you in the chapter2.core namespace. Let's test out the simple to-do list from the REPL.

```
lein repl
...
chapter2.core=> (doc add-task)
-------------------------
chapter2.core/add-task
([task])
  Add a task to the to-do list. Accepts a string describing the task.
nil
chapter2.core=> (add-task "Buy more milk.")
{1 "Buy more milk."}
chapter2.core=> (add-task "Take out the trash.")
{1 "Buy more milk.", 2 "Take out the trash."}
chapter2.core=> (add-task "File taxes.")
{1 "Buy more milk.", 2 "Take out the trash.", 3 "File taxes."}
chapter2.core=> (doc remove-task)
-------------------------
chapter2.core/remove-task
([task-id])
  Removes a task from the to-do list. Accepts the id of the task to remove.
nil
chapter2.core=> (remove-task 2)
{1 "Buy more milk.", 3 "File taxes."}
chapter2.core=> (get-tasks)
{1 "Buy more milk.", 3 "File taxes."}
chapter2.core=>
```

You can leverage the tools you learned about earlier in the chapter like doc to see your own internal documentation, and then easily check to see how the code works. Now that we've verified this simple to-do list is working, we'll modify our compojure app to provide a REST interface for interacting with the app. The updated src.chapter2.handler is:

```
(ns chapter2.handler
  (:require [chapter2.core :as tasks]
            [compojure.core :refer :all]
            [compojure.route :as route]
            [ring.middleware.defaults :refer [wrap-defaults api-defaults]]
            [ring.middleware.keyword-params :refer [wrap-keyword-params]]
            [ring.middleware.json :refer [wrap-json-response]]))
```

```clojure
(defroutes api-routes
  (GET "/api/tasks" []
    {:body (tasks/get-tasks)})
  (POST "/api/tasks" {{task :task} :params}
    {:body (tasks/add-task task)})
  (DELETE "/api/tasks/:task-id" [task-id]
    {:body (tasks/remove-task (Integer/parseInt task-id))})
  (route/not-found "Not Found"))

(def app
  (-> api-routes
      (wrap-defaults api-defaults)
      wrap-json-response))
```

All you need to do now to run the application is run `lein ring server-headless`. That will run the application on port 3000, and you can again head to the REPL to test things out. Let's use the `clj.http` library as a quick and easy way to test the REST API.

```clojure
chapter2.core=> (require '[clj-http.client :as client])
nil
chapter2.core=> (:body
         #_=>   (client/get "http://localhost:3000/api/tasks" {:as :json}))
{}
chapter2.core=> (:body
         #_=>   (client/post "http://localhost:3000/api/tasks"
         #_=>                 {:form-params {:task "Buy milk."} :as :json}))
{:1 "Buy milk."}
chapter2.core=> (:body
         #_=>   (client/post "http://localhost:3000/api/tasks"
         #_=>                 {:form-params {:task "Take out trash."} :as :json}))
{:1 "Buy milk.", :2 "Take out trash."}
chapter2.core=> (:body
         #_=>   (client/post "http://localhost:3000/api/tasks"
         #_=>                 {:form-params {:task "File taxes."} :as :json}))
{:1 "Buy milk.", :2 "Take out trash.", :3 "File taxes."}
chapter2.core=> (:body
         #_=>   (client/delete "http://localhost:3000/api/tasks/2" {:as :json}))
{:1 "Buy milk.", :3 "File taxes."}
chapter2.core=>
```

So far we've been using a REPL outside of the application to develop, but as covered earlier, you also have the option to embed a REPL directly inside of the application. The lein ring (`https://github.com/weavejester/lein-ring`) you've been using to start the application makes starting an embedded REPL extremely simple. Update `project.clj` to tell `lein ring` to also start a REPL server.

```clojure
(defproject chapter2 "0.1.0-SNAPSHOT"
  :description "FIXME: write description"
  :url "http://example.com/FIXME"
  :min-lein-version "2.0.0"
  :dependencies [[org.clojure/clojure "1.7.0"]
                 [compojure "1.4.0"]
                 [ring/ring-defaults "0.1.5"]
                 [ring/ring-json "0.4.0"]]
  :plugins [[lein-ring "0.9.7"]]
```

```
     :ring {:handler chapter2.handler/app
            :nrepl {:start? true
                    :port 60000}}
     :main chapter2.core
     :profiles
     {:dev {:dependencies [[clj-http "2.0.1"]
                           [javax.servlet/servlet-api "2.5"]
                           [ring/ring-mock "0.3.0"]]}})
```

Now when you run `lein ring server-headless`, you can connect the REPL to the running application. This allows you to directly inspect and modify the internal data structures and functions while the application is still running.

```
lein repl :connect localhost:60000
...
user=> (ns chapter2.core)
nil
chapter2.core=> (require '[clj-http.client :as client])
nil
chapter2.core=> (:body
          #_=>   (client/post "http://localhost:3000/api/tasks"
          #_=>                 {:form-params {:task "Buy milk."} :as :json}))
{:2 "Buy milk."}
chapter2.core=> (:body
          #_=>   (client/post "http://localhost:3000/api/tasks"
          #_=>                 {:form-params {:task "Take out trash."} :as :json}))
{:2 "Buy milk.", :3 "Take out trash."}
chapter2.core=> (defn clear-all-tasks [] (swap! tasks empty))
#'chapter2.core/clear-all-tasks
chapter2.core=> (clear-all-tasks)
{}
chapter2.core=> (:body (client/get "http://localhost:3000/api/tasks" {:as :json}))
{}
chapter2.core=>
```

By connecting a REPL to the running application, you can create a new function for clearing out the task list and verify that the function works without having to restart the application.

Connecting Your Editor to a REPL

So far we avoided calling out any specific editors or IDEs to use while writing the Clojure application. Generally speaking, any editor is a viable candidate to use while developing Clojure. Practically speaking though, making the right choice in an editor can drastically improve your experience and shorten your feedback loop. Of course, there are the normal concerns with language support for Clojure in your choice of editor. In addition to that, choosing an editor that provides REPL support out of the box or through plugins will prove invaluable during development.

The home page for `tools.nrepl` (https://github.com/clojure/tools.nrepl) handily lists the editors that are known to support `tools.nrepl` already. As you can see, there are plugins for popular editors like Emacs, Vim, Eclipse, IntelliJ, and Atom. Unsurprisingly, you can also see the top three development environments from the 2014 State of Clojure Survey (https://cognitect.wufoo.com/reports/state-of-clojure-2014-results/): Emacs, IntelliJ, and Vim.

The benefit of connecting your editor of choice to an nREPL server is gaining much of the same functionality that we've discussed so far directly inside your editor, rather than in a separate REPL process. By connecting your editor to a REPL you can easily look up documentation, view source, and evaluate code directly from the editor.

We won't go into the specifics of setting up each editor to connect to a REPL, but instead simply recommend that you take a moment to set up the editor you are most familiar with and configure nREPL support. The plugins for nREPL support for Emacs, IntelliJ, and Vim, are cider (`https://github.com/clojure-emacs/cider`), cursive (`https://cursive-ide.com/`), and fireplace (`https://github.com/tpope/vim-fireplace`).

RELOADING CODE

So far we've touched on leveraging the REPL for rapid feedback while developing new Clojure code, but in the real world it's much more common during your day-to-day development that you will modify existing code, rather than writing brand new code from scratch. As you've seen, the REPL is a great tool, but it isn't necessarily a replacement for your preferred editor or IDE.

As you've made changes in your editor, you've been forced to reload your application or REPL in order to view those changes. Ideally, you can develop code normally in your editor and reload changed code in other places without interrupting your workflow. Luckily, Clojure makes this process simple for all parts of the workflow, from your REPL to your tests. In this section you'll see the different ways code reloading can smooth your development process, as well as how best to structure your code for reloading.

Reloading Code from the REPL

For the first demonstration of reloading code, let's see how you can reload code from your external REPL process to avoid having to restart the REPL server when you want to see changes that have been made outside the REPL. Before you get started with the example, update your `project.clj` to pull in the dependencies you'll need for examples later in this section. Update your `project.clj` to:

```
(defproject chapter2 "0.1.0-SNAPSHOT"
  :description "FIXME: write description"
  :url "http://example.com/FIXME"
  :min-lein-version "2.0.0"
  :dependencies [[org.clojure/clojure "1.7.0"]
                 [compojure "1.4.0"]
                 [ring/ring-defaults "0.1.5"]
                 [ring/ring-json "0.4.0"]]
  :plugins [[lein-ring "0.9.7"]]
  :ring {:handler chapter2.handler/app
         :nrepl {:start? true
                 :port 60000}}
  :main chapter2.core
  :profiles
  {:dev {:dependencies [[clj-http "2.0.1"]
                        [javax.servlet/servlet-api "2.5"]
```

```
                          [org.clojure/tools.namespace "0.2.11"]
                          [ring/ring-mock "0.3.0"]]}})
```

Now, load your to-do list application from the previous section into the REPL.

```
lein repl
...
chapter2.core=> (add-task "Buy Milk.")
{1 "Buy Milk."}
chapter2.core=> (add-task "Take out the trash.")
{1 "Buy Milk.", 2 "Take out the trash."}
chapter2.core=> (get-tasks)
{1 "Buy Milk.", 2 "Take out the trash."}
```

Add some functionality to your to-do list application. Ideally, a to-do list application allows you to keep multiple lists of tasks that you want to track, rather than just a single list of all tasks. In your editor, update src/chapter2/core.clj to allow keeping separate lists of tasks.

```
(ns chapter2.core)

(def id-atom (atom 0))
(defn next-id [] (swap! id-atom inc))

(def tasks (atom (sorted-map)))

(defn get-task-lists
  "Get the names of all created task lists."
  []
  (keys @tasks))

(defn get-tasks
  "Get all tasks on the specified to-do list."
  [list-name]
  (get @tasks list-name))

(defn add-task
  "Add a task to the specified to-do list. Accepts the name of
  the list and a string describing the task."
  [list-name task]
  (swap! tasks assoc-in [list-name (next-id)] task))

(defn remove-task
  "Removes a task from the specified to-do list. Accepts the name
  of the list and the id of the task to remove."
  [list-name task-id]
  (swap! tasks update-in [list-name] dissoc task-id))
```

You can now track multiple lists to add and remove tasks from. If you go back to the REPL that you opened previously, however, you can see that the changes made aren't yet reflected in the REPL, so you can still use the previous versions of your functions.

```
chapter2.core=> (add-task "File Taxes.")
{1 "Buy Milk.", 2 "Take out the trash.", 3 "File Taxes."}
```

Luckily, the Clojure `require` function that you are already familiar with includes a flag for reloading a given namespace. Without leaving your REPL, reload the `chapter2.core` namespace and see the changes that have been made in your editor:

```
chapter2.core=> (require 'chapter2.core :reload)
nil
chapter2.core=> (add-task "Pay electric bill.")

ArityException Wrong number of args (1) passed to:
    core/add-task  clojure.lang.AFn.throwArity (AFn.java:429)
chapter2.core=> (doc add-task)
-----------------------
chapter2.core/add-task
([list-name task])
  Add a task to the to-do list. Accepts a string describing the task.
nil
chapter2.core=> (add-task "bills" "Pay electric bill.")
{"bills" {1 "Pay electric bill."}}
chapter2.core=> (get-tasks "bills")
{1 "Pay electric bill."}
```

Unfortunately, using `require` to reload namespaces can often present problems. Simply passing `:reload` to `require` will only reload the namespace(s) specified. If you make changes to multiple files that depend on each other, you need to remember to reload all of the namespaces you changed, or you will see compilation errors. There is also the `:reload-all` option that you can pass to `require`, which will not only reload the namespace specified, but the namespaces it depends on. Even that isn't necessarily perfect though. If you change the public method signatures of a namespace, you still need to remember to reload every namespace that depended on the one you changed. There is no way for `require` to automatically know which namespaces need to be reloaded.

Luckily, there is a Clojure library named `tools.namespace` (`https://github.com/clojure/tools.namespace`) that you can leverage to solve these problems. You may have noticed, that `tools.namespace` was the dependency added to `project.clj` in the beginning of this section. Before we demonstrate using `tools.namespace`, let's add some more functionality to the application and see how simply reloading with `require` can go wrong. You've already updated `chapter2.core` to allow the application to create and track multiple task lists, but you haven't updated the API yet. Also, since you've added the ability to create multiple lists, but not the ability to remove lists, let's add that functionality as well. The function to remove lists to add to `chapter2.core.clj` is:

```
(defn remove-list
  "Delete an entire list of tasks at a time. Accepts the name of
  the list to delete."
  [list-name]
  (swap! tasks dissoc list-name))
```

And the new `chapter2.handler.clj`:

```
(ns chapter2.handler
  (:require [chapter2.core :as tasks]
            [compojure.core :refer :all]
            [compojure.route :as route]
            [ring.middleware.defaults :refer [wrap-defaults api-defaults]]
```

```
              [ring.middleware.keyword-params :refer [wrap-keyword-params]]
              [ring.middleware.json :refer [wrap-json-response]]]))

(defroutes api-routes
  (GET "/api/tasks/:list-name" [list-name]
    {:body (tasks/get-tasks list-name)})
  (POST "/api/tasks/:list-name" {{list-name :list-name task :task} :params}
    {:body (tasks/add-task list-name task)})
  (DELETE "/api/tasks/:list-name" [list-name]
    {:body (tasks/remove-list list-name)})
  (DELETE "/api/tasks/:list-name/:task-id" [list-name task-id]
    {:body (tasks/remove-task list-name (Integer/parseInt task-id))})
  (route/not-found "Not Found"))

(def app
  (-> api-routes
      (wrap-defaults api-defaults)
      wrap-json-response))
```

You've now updated both `src/chapter2/core.clj` and `src/chapter2/handler.clj`. If you reload just the handler namespace, you'll immediately see a compilation error, because the compiler won't be able to find the `remove-list` function that was added.

```
chapter2.core=> (require 'chapter2.handler :reload)

CompilerException java.lang.RuntimeException:
    No such var: tasks/remove-list, compiling:(chapter2/handler.clj:15:12)
```

Of course, in this specific example, you can use `:reload-all` in order to reload the dependencies of `chapter2.handler`, but rather than remembering that ourselves, let's leverage `tools.namespace` instead.

```
chapter2.core=> (require '[clojure.tools.namespace.repl :refer [refresh]])
nil
chapter2.core=> (refresh)
:reloading (chapter2.core chapter2.handler chapter2.handler-test)
:ok
```

Behind the scenes, `tools.namespace` builds a graph of all the namespace dependencies in the project and uses that graph to reload everything in the correct order. You can see how useful this will be when developing larger Clojure applications, despite the current app being fairly simple. While `tools.namespace` is a handy tool to have, it certainly isn't a complete solution to every issue. Even the `refresh` function won't be able to successfully reload the project if you've accidentally introduced syntax errors into your code base during development. If you get REPL into an unknown state and you are uncertain what code is actually loaded or running, restarting your REPL completely and starting from scratch is a perfectly viable solution.

Automatically Reloading Code

So far when the act of reloading code has been a manual process. You first update the application through your editor, save the code, and then manually reload that code in your REPL. This is an incredibly useful way to rapidly get feedback about your development. In fact, this approach is so common that Clojure libraries and tools recognize this and make it even easier by removing the manual step.

Reloading a Running Application

Earlier in the chapter, you ran the REST API for the to-do list application by running `lein ring server-headless`. This automatically serves the API defined in `src/chapter2/handler.clj` on port 3000 on your local machine. In addition to serving the API though, the lein ring plugin automatically checks for changes in the local Clojure code when it receives new API requests, and reloads the application before processing those requests. Let's see this in action by expanding the functionality of your to-do list while the application is running. First, let's run the application:

```
lein ring server-headless
Started nREPL server on port 60000
2016-01-19 20:37:37.787:INFO:oejs.Server:jetty-7.6.13.v20130916
2016-01-19 20:37:37.818:INFO:oejs.AbstractConnector:Started
    SelectChannelConnector@0.0.0.0:3000
Started server on port 3000
...
```

Let's also verify that it's working the way it should using the `clj-http` library.

```
lein repl
...
chapter2.core=> (require '[clj-http.client :as client])
nil
chapter2.core=> (:body
        #_=>    (client/post "http://localhost:3000/api/tasks/chores"
        #_=>    {:form-params {:task "Take out the trash."} :as :json}))
{:chores {:1 "Take out the trash."}}
chapter2.core=> (:body
        #_=>    (client/post "http://localhost:3000/api/tasks/chores"
        #_=>                 {:form-params {:task "Mow the lawn."} :as :json}))
{:chores {:1 "Take out the trash.", :2 "Mow the lawn."}}
chapter2.core=> (:body
        #_=>    (client/get "http://localhost:3000/api/tasks/chores"
        #_=>                {:as :json}))
{:1 "Take out the trash.", :2 "Mow the lawn."}
```

Now, let's add some functionality to the to-do list. In addition to simply tracking a single task as a string describing the task, it might also be useful to track when a task was created. Let's start tracking when a task was created in addition to just the task. We'll create a Clojure `record` to represent tasks and give it a creation-time field. The new version of `src/chapter2/core.clj` is:

```
(ns chapter2.core)

(def id-atom (atom 0))
(defn next-id [] (swap! id-atom inc))

(def tasks (atom (sorted-map)))
(defrecord Task [task creation-time])
```

```
(defn now
  "Returns a java.util.Date object representing the current time."
  []
  (new java.util.Date))

(defn get-task-lists
  "Get the names of all created task lists."
  []
  (keys @tasks))

(defn get-tasks
  "Get all tasks on the specified to-do list."
  [list-name]
  (get @tasks list-name))

(defn add-task
  "Add a task to the specified to-do list. Accepts the name of
  the list and a string describing the task."
  [list-name task]
  (swap! tasks assoc-in [list-name (next-id)] (Task. task (now))))

(defn remove-list
  "Delete an entire list of tasks at a time. Accepts the name of
  the list to delete."
  [list-name]
  (swap! tasks dissoc list-name))

(defn remove-task
  "Removes a task from the specified to-do list. Accepts the name
  of the list and the id of the task to remove."
  [list-name task-id]
  (swap! tasks update-in [list-name] dissoc task-id))
```

While updating the to-do list application to also track task creation times, your application has continued running in the background. Let's test out the API again after making the changes.

```
chapter2.core=> (:body
         #_=>   (client/post "http://localhost:3000/api/tasks/chores"
         #_=>                     {:form-params {:task "Mow the lawn."}
         #_=>                      :as :json}))
{:chores {:1 {:task "Mow the lawn.", :creation-time "2016-01-20T03:23:55Z"}}}
chapter2.core=> (:body
         #_=>   (client/post "http://localhost:3000/api/tasks/chores"
         #_=>                     {:form-params {:task "Take out the trash"}
         #_=>                      :as :json}))
{:chores {:1 {:task "Mow the lawn.",
             :creation-time "2016-01-20T03:23:55Z"},
         :2 {:task "Take out the trash",
             :creation-time "2016-01-20T03:24:06Z"}}}
chapter2.core=> (:body
         #_=>   (client/get "http://localhost:3000/api/tasks/chores"
         #_=>                     {:as :json}))
{:1 {:task "Mow the lawn.", :creation-time "2016-01-20T03:23:55Z"},
 :2 {:task "Take out the trash", :creation-time "2016-01-20T03:24:06Z"}}
```

As you can see, the new version of `chapter2.core` has been automatically reloaded and added tasks now also have a creation-time.

Reloading Tests

One part of the development cycle that we haven't really touched on yet is testing. Testing is a broad subject both in general and from a Clojure perspective. Because of that, there is an entire chapter of this book dedicated to testing in Clojure. Chapter 4 provides an in depth look into testing libraries, writing tests, testing strategies, and more.

This chapter focuses on the development process and how you can shorten feedback cycles with Clojure. No matter what your thoughts are on testing, it's certainly an important part of the development cycle. You can also leverage Clojure's code reloading capabilities during the testing phase of the development cycle. This section focuses briefly on leveraging code reloading as part of testing, but for more on testing see Chapter 4.

Of course, in order to dive into testing as it relates to reloading, you first have to write some tests. Let's go ahead and add some tests for the `chapter.core` namespace. Create the file `test/chapter2/core_test.clj` and add the tests there.

```
(ns chapter2.core-test
  (:require [clojure.test :refer :all]
            [chapter2.core :refer :all]))

(defn clear-tasks-fixture [f] (swap! tasks empty) (f))
(use-fixtures :each clear-tasks-fixture)

(deftest test-get-task-lists
  (testing "No task lists."
    (is (empty? (get-task-lists))))
  (testing "Creating task lists."
    (add-task "list1" "task1")
    (is (= ["list1"] (get-task-lists)))
    (add-task "list2" "task2")
    (is (= ["list1" "list2"] (get-task-lists)))))

(deftest test-get-tasks
  (testing "Empty task list"
    (is (empty? (get-tasks "list1"))))
  (testing "Non-empty task lists."
    (add-task "list1" "task1")
    (is (= 1 (count (get-tasks "list1"))))
    (is (= "task1" (:task (second (first (get-tasks "list1"))))))
    (add-task "list1" "task2")
    (is (= 2 (count (get-tasks "list1")))))
  (testing "Duplicate tasks are allowed"
    (add-task "list2" "task1")
    (is (= 1 (count (get-tasks "list2"))))
    (add-task "list2" "task1")
    (is (= 2 (count (get-tasks "list2"))))))
```

For now, you've added two fairly simple test cases. Also, when you created the project, lein helpfully created a test file automatically for the handler namespace. Since we aren't concerned with testing that part of our application at the moment, let's delete the file `test/chapter2/handler_test.clj` in order to focus on the tests for the core namespace. After deleting `handler_test.clj` you can run tests with `lein test`, and you should see the tests pass.

```
lein test

lein test chapter2.core-test

Ran 2 tests containing 9 assertions.
0 failures, 0 errors.
```

Now, let's examine the reloading aspect of testing. There are actually multiple tools out there, but let's use the plugin `lein-test-refresh` (https://github.com/jakemcc/lein-test-refresh). The first step is to add the plugin to `project.clj`. Update the `:plugins` section of `project.clj` to add the `lein-test-refresh` plugin.

```
(defproject chapter2 "0.1.0-SNAPSHOT"
  :description "FIXME: write description"
  :url "http://example.com/FIXME"
  :min-lein-version "2.0.0"
  :dependencies [[org.clojure/clojure "1.7.0"]
                 [compojure "1.4.0"]
                 [ring/ring-defaults "0.1.5"]
                 [ring/ring-json "0.4.0"]]
  :plugins [[lein-ring "0.9.7"]
            [com.jakemccrary/lein-test-refresh "0.12.0"]]
  :ring {:handler chapter2.handler/app
         :nrepl {:start? true
                 :port 60000}}
  :main chapter2.core
  :profiles
  {:dev {:dependencies [[clj-http "2.0.1"]
                        [javax.servlet/servlet-api "2.5"]
                        [org.clojure/tools.namespace "0.2.11"]
                        [ring/ring-mock "0.3.0"]]}})
```

Now, you can run the plugin with `lein test-refresh`.

```
lein test-refresh
Retrieving com/jakemccrary/lein-test-refresh/0.12.0/lein-test-refresh-0.12.0.pom
    from clojars
Retrieving jakemcc/clojure-gntp/0.1.1/clojure-gntp-0.1.1.pom from clojars
Retrieving com/jakemccrary/lein-test-refresh/0.12.0/lein-test-refresh-0.12.0.jar
    from clojars
Retrieving jakemcc/clojure-gntp/0.1.1/clojure-gntp-0.1.1.jar from clojars
************************************************
*************** Running tests ***************
:reloading (chapter2.core chapter2.handler chapter2.core-test)

Testing chapter2.core-test

Ran 2 tests containing 9 assertions.
0 failures, 0 errors.

Passed all tests
Finished at 22:39:24.091 (run time: 1.806s)
```

The plugin starts up, runs the tests, and instead of exiting, continues watching your project files for changes so that as you make changes to your source code, your tests will run automatically. Let's test it out by letting `lein test-refresh` continue running and updating the behavior of your application slightly. Currently, your to-do list allows adding the same task to a list multiple times. The current test case explicitly tests that this behavior works. Instead, it might be more useful to ignore an attempt to add a duplicate task to a list. In the spirit of test driven development, let's update the tests to reflect the new desired behavior before you update the application. The new `test/chapter2/core_test.clj` is:

```
(ns chapter2.core-test
  (:require [clojure.test :refer :all]
            [chapter2.core :refer :all]))

(defn clear-tasks-fixture [f] (swap! tasks empty) (f))
(use-fixtures :each clear-tasks-fixture)

(deftest test-get-task-lists
  (testing "No task lists."
    (is (empty? (get-task-lists))))
  (testing "Creating task lists."
    (add-task "list1" "task1")
    (is (= ["list1"] (get-task-lists)))
    (add-task "list2" "task2")
    (is (= ["list1" "list2"] (get-task-lists)))))

(deftest test-get-tasks
  (testing "Empty task list"
    (is (empty? (get-tasks "list1"))))
  (testing "Non-empty task lists."
    (add-task "list1" "task1")
    (is (= 1 (count (get-tasks "list1"))))
    (is (= "task1" (:task (second (first (get-tasks "list1"))))))
    (add-task "list1" "task2")
    (is (= 2 (count (get-tasks "list1")))))
  (testing "Duplicate tasks are not allowed"
    (add-task "list2" "task1")
    (is (= 1 (count (get-tasks "list2"))))
    (add-task "list2" "task1")
    (is (= 1 (count (get-tasks "list2"))))
    (add-task "list2" "task1")
    (is (= 1 (count (get-tasks "list2"))))))
```

As soon as you save this new version of the test, you should notice how the running `lein test-refresh` process detects the changes and re-runs the tests, but this time with failures.

```
...
Finished at 22:39:24.091 (run time: 1.806s)
*********************************************
************** Running tests **************
:reloading (chapter2.core-test)

Testing chapter2.core-test

FAIL in (test-get-tasks) (core_test.clj:30)
```

```
  Duplicate tasks are allowed
  expected: (= 1 (count (get-tasks "list2")))
    actual: (not (= 1 2))

  FAIL in (test-get-tasks) (core_test.clj:32)
  Duplicate tasks are not allowed
  expected: (= 1 (count (get-tasks "list2")))
    actual: (not (= 1 3))

  Ran 2 tests containing 10 assertions.
  2 failures, 0 errors.

  Failed 2 of 10 assertions
  Finished at 22:50:42.699 (run time: 0.032s)
```

Immediately you see that the tests have failed as expected. Given that the startup time of the JVM can approach 10s of seconds in some cases when calling `lein test` manually, this approach of automatically reloading code and running tests can greatly help your productivity. Now that you've updated the tests with the desired behavior, go ahead and fix the currently broken code. The updated add-task function looks like:

```
(defn add-task
  "Add a task to the specified to-do list. Accepts the name of
  the list and a string describing the task."
  [list-name task]
  (letfn [(maybe-add-task [current-list]
            (if (some #(= task (:task (second %1))) current-list)
              current-list
              (assoc current-list (next-id) (Task. task (now)))))]
    (swap! tasks update list-name maybe-add-task)))
```

The new function scans your list of tasks and verifies that there isn't an existing task by that name already in your task list before adding it. This approach isn't particularly elegant, but it suits this simple application, and as you can see from the updated output of `lein test-refresh`, it satisfies your updated test case.

```
  ...
  Finished at 22:50:42.699 (run time: 0.032s)
  **********************************************
  *************** Running tests ***************
  :reloading (chapter2.core chapter2.handler chapter2.core-test)

  Testing chapter2.core-test

  Ran 2 tests containing 10 assertions.
  0 failures, 0 errors.

  Passed all tests
  Finished at 23:58:22.477 (run time: 0.048s)
```

Writing Reloadable Code

The final topic on reloading code relates to how you develop and structure the code you are writing, rather than the tools available for reloading it. Even if you are using intelligent tooling for reloading code, it is possible to write code that is not particularly reload friendly. The current to-do list application already falls into this trap by creating a global state in the `chapter2.core` namespace. Both `id-atom` and `tasks` in `src/chapter2/core.clj` represent a global state that is not reload friendly. Let's demonstrate what we mean via the REPL.

```
lein repl
...
chapter2.core=> tasks
#object[clojure.lang.Atom 0x36d0c4df {:status :ready, :val {}}]
chapter2.core=> (add-task "chores" "Mow lawn.")
{"chores"
  {1 #chapter2.core.Task{:task "Mow lawn.",
                         :creation-time #inst "2016-01-20T06:49:55.503-00:00"}}}
chapter2.core=> (add-task "chores" "Take out trash.")
{"chores"
  {1 #chapter2.core.Task{:task "Mow lawn.",
                         :creation-time #inst "2016-01-20T06:49:55.503-00:00"},
   2 #chapter2.core.Task{:task "Take out trash.",
                         :creation-time #inst "2016-01-20T06:50:02.155-00:00"}}}
chapter2.core=> tasks
#object[clojure.lang.Atom 0x36d0c4df
{:status :ready,
 :val
   {"chores"
     {1 #chapter2.core.Task{:task "Mow lawn.",
                            :creation-time #inst "2016-01-20T06:49:55.503-00:00"},
      2 #chapter2.core.Task{:task "Take out trash.",
                            :creation-time #inst "2016-01-20T06:50:02.155-00:00"}}}}]
chapter2.core=> (require 'chapter2.core :reload)
nil
chapter2.core=> tasks
#object[clojure.lang.Atom 0x779599ec {:status :ready, :val {}}]
```

In this example you add some tasks to your task list and then see that reloading your namespace erases the list of tasks, because `(def tasks (atom (sorted-map)))` is re-evaluated when you reload the namespace. When developing in the REPL, this behavior isn't particularly harmful or confusing. If code is being reloaded outside of the REPL, though, this can be problematic. If you add multiple tasks to your task list via the REST API, and then change the documentation on one of your functions in `chapter2.core`, you will be unpleasantly surprised when the next API request returns an empty task list because the namespace was reloaded. One potential solution is to use `defonce`, which only evaluates if the specified `var` doesn't exist. However, while that solution helps the problem when reloading with `require`, it does not when reloading with `tools.namespace`. When reloading with `tools.namespace`, you are actually unloading the previous versions of your namespaces, and then loading them completely from scratch. If you switch `chapter2.core` to use `defonce` instead of `def`, you see the following:

```
lein repl
...
chapter2.core=> tasks
#object[clojure.lang.Atom 0x13312d27 {:status :ready, :val {}}]
chapter2.core=> (add-task "chores" "Mow the lawn.")
{"chores"
  {1 #chapter2.core.Task{:task "Mow the lawn.",
```

```
                           :creation-time #inst "2016-01-20T07:06:10.705-00:00"}}}
chapter2.core=> (add-task "chores" "Take out the trash.")
{"chores"
  {1 #chapter2.core.Task{:task "Mow the lawn.",
                         :creation-time #inst "2016-01-20T07:06:10.705-00:00"},
   2 #chapter2.core.Task{:task "Take out the trash.",
                         :creation-time #inst "2016-01-20T07:06:22.358-00:00"}}}
chapter2.core=> (require 'chapter2.core :reload)
nil
chapter2.core=> tasks
#object[clojure.lang.Atom 0x13312d27
{:status :ready,
 :val
   {"chores"
     {1 #chapter2.core.Task{:task "Mow the lawn.",
                            :creation-time #inst "2016-01-20T07:06:10.705-00:00"},
      2 #chapter2.core.Task{:task "Take out the trash.",
                            :creation-time #inst "2016-01-20T07:06:22.358-00:00"}}}}]
chapter2.core=> (require '[clojure.tools.namespace.repl :refer [refresh]])
nil
chapter2.core=> (refresh)
:reloading (chapter2.core chapter2.handler chapter2.core-test)
:ok
chapter2.core=> tasks
#object[clojure.lang.Atom 0x27eab9ff {:status :ready, :val {}}]
chapter2.core=>
```

When you reloaded your namespace with `require` you avoided wiping out `tasks`, but reloading with `tools.namespace` again wiped it out. Really your only foolproof approach to writing completely reloadable code is to avoid global state altogether. The homepage for `tools.namespace` even describes some approaches to avoiding global state (https://github.com/clojure/tools .namespace#reloading-code-preparing-your-application). Luckily there is also a library called `component` (https://github.com/stuartsierra/component) that incorporates some of those concepts and provides a framework for structuring your application to avoid global state. We won't dive into the intricacies of components in this book; however, it is well worth investigating to help structure your code to avoid global state. Besides just the problems global state introduces for code reloading, it can also make your applications harder to understand.

Using a library like `component` and writing your application to avoid global state completely will require some additional effort and discipline in your development. You may decide in some of your applications that the extra cost isn't worth it, which may be valid. However, getting into the habit of avoiding global state while developing will eventually become easier and pay off over time.

SUMMARY

Getting feedback rapidly while developing is one of the most important factors in developer productivity. Clojure presents distinct advantages in this area, both in the design of the language and in the tooling in the Clojure ecosystem. In this chapter we dove into some basics for getting feedback while developing Clojure, some ways to leverage tooling in the Clojure ecosystem for rapid feedback, and some ways to approach structuring your code to make getting feedback easier. All of these will help make you a more productive Clojure developer.

3

Web Services

WHAT'S IN THIS CHAPTER?

➤ Understanding a project overview

➤ Mastering elements of a Clojure web service

➤ Crafting a link shortener example project

➤ Deploying a Clojure web service

Clojure is a great general-purpose language, but it really shines when it comes to web services. Clojure's characteristic focus on immutable data structures, safe concurrency, and code re-use allows you to write services that are composable, reliable, and expressive.

In this chapter, we'll introduce the fundamental abstractions common to virtually all Clojure services: HTTP handlers, middleware, and routing. You'll use the popular Compojure template, which is based on Ring for HTTP abstraction and Compojure for routing. After a tour of the building blocks of a web service, you'll actually write one from start to finish: a storage-backed link shortener. The service will let users submit a full URL and a short name, then redirect requests to that short name back to the original URL. Finally, we'll briefly cover some of the popular options for deploying Clojure web services in development or production, either locally or to the cloud.

PROJECT OVERVIEW

For this example project, you're going to use the standard `compojure` template:

```
lein new compojure example-project
```

The result is something very similar to the default template, but with a few extras:

1. An added dependency for Compojure, a popular request routing library
2. A development-only dependency on ring-mock for testing
3. The lein-ring plugin to easily start a server with `lein ring server`
4. Service-oriented example code and tests

At this point, it would be a good idea to take a few minutes to browse through the project, especially the `src/example_project/handler.clj` and `test/example_project/handler_test.clj` files, and see if you can examine what's going on. While you're exploring the code, keep the following questions in mind:

➤ What URLs will this web service handle, and what will the responses look like?

➤ Do you think the tests will pass?

➤ How do you think you might add a new endpoint?

Afterward, run `lein ring server` to start the example service and automatically open a browser (see Figure 3-1):

```
~/src/chapter3$ lein ring server
2016-01-30 13:43:11.821:INFO:oejs.Server:jetty-7.6.13.v20130916
2016-01-30 13:43:11.853:INFO:oejs.AbstractConnector:Started
  SelectChannelConnector@0.0.0.0:3000
Started server on port 3000
```

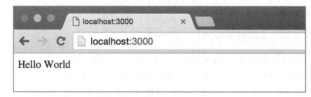

FIGURE 3-1

As a bonus challenge, try adding a `/film` endpoint that recommends your favorite movie, then add a test to make sure it works. Once you're done experimenting, continue on to read about namespace layout in a Clojure web service.

Namespace Layout

Like the default template, the `compojure` template sets up just one core namespace—`example-project.handler`. We'll get to handlers in an upcoming section, but let's cover now how to organize a web service into namespaces.

First, take a quick look at the `project.clj` file, and note the following line:

```
:ring {:handler example-project.handler/app}
```

It's important that `:handler` be associated with a reference to a ring handler. For now, the important thing to remember is that you'll always want to know where your default handler is to provide an accurate reference.

We'll go into more depth about namespace layout when working on the example project later in this chapter, but for the rest of this section think about what kinds of functions might belong in separate namespaces and why.

ELEMENTS OF A WEB SERVICE

Web services in Clojure are constructed differently than services in many other languages. First, the Clojure community has largely come to a consensus that heavy-duty web frameworks are unnecessary at best and harmful at worst. Instead, web services are made out of an *ad hoc* collection of libraries that handle common tasks like HTTP abstraction, routing, and serialization.

Let's examine some popular options for Clojure web services, focusing on a deep understanding of the fundamental abstractions that these services are built from. By the end of this section, you'll be able to tackle a real world example that makes use of everything you learn here.

Libraries, Not Frameworks

One thing you may notice about Clojure compared to other languages is that the community tends to shy away from heavy duty, opinionated web frameworks like Rails, Django, and Play. Instead, a Clojure project will typically make use of a number of smaller libraries that fill limited roles, like routing, database interactions, and templating.

Decoupling these distinct tasks allows you to combine the libraries that work for you, or substitute your own code at will, and build a project that doesn't require you to bend your logic to fit the assumptions made by the author of a given framework.

This flexibility does, of course, come at a cost. Using, say, four libraries instead of one framework means that you're going to have at least four times as many decisions to make. The still-growing Clojure community is also more fractured than other communities, with fewer experts per library to go around.

It's also possible that you'll run into compatibility issues between libraries, although this rarely happens in practice. In general, the separation of concerns between libraries makes it pretty easy to ensure that they all work together.

HTTP

On some level, a web service is really just a way to turn HTTP requests into HTTP responses. That's a gross oversimplification, but it's also a very helpful thing to remember. You've already seen how Clojure excels at turning input data into useful output data using (mostly) pure functions, so wouldn't it be nice to apply those same techniques to requests and responses?

Well, most Clojure web services use a library called Ring, which lets you treat requests like a normal hash map, with keys for the request method, URI, query string, etc. You write functions that take *request maps* and return *response maps*, which have keys for the status, body, and headers. A function from request to response is called a *handler*, which is an essential concept in Ring.

> **NOTE** *A handler is a function that takes an HTTP request and returns an HTTP response.*

Ring Requests

Here's an example GET request from `guest123` to `http://localhost/index.html`:

```
{:server-port 80,
 :server-name "localhost",
 :remote-addr "guest123",
 :uri "/index.html",
 :query-string nil,
 :scheme :http,
 :request-method :get,
 :headers {"host" "localhost"}}
```

We'll be talking a lot about Ring requests in upcoming sections, but for now the important thing is to get a general idea of what they look like. If you've written web services before, you should see what's going on in the example above. Remember, since this is a normal Clojure map, we can access these fields using the key as a function, such as `(:request-method request)` would return `:get`. If you want to get the value of the `host` header, you can use `(get-in request [:headers "host"])`, and so on.

Not all requests are that simple. Here's a POST request from localhost to `http://localhost/links` with a body:

```
{:remote-addr "localhost",
 :headers
 {"host" "localhost",
  "content-type" "application/x-www-form-urlencoded",
  "content-length" "28"},
 :server-port 80,
 :content-length 28,
 :content-type "application/x-www-form-urlencoded",
 :uri "/links",
 :server-name "localhost",
 :query-string nil,
 :body #object[java.io.ByteArrayInputStream]...,
 :scheme :http,
 :request-method :post}
```

Most of this example is fairly clear: You have some extra headers relating to the body (as expected), so the `:request-method` now says `:post`, the `:uri` key gives the path to the links endpoint, etc. What may be a bit surprising is that the `:body` key now points to a `java.io.ByteArrayInputStream`. This class has some gotchas covered later, in addition to a string and a native data structure.

Ring Responses

Ideally, every request should be met with a response, and Ring represents those with maps as well. Here's a simple Hello World response map:

```
{:status 200,
 :headers {"Content-Type" "text/html; charset=utf-8"},
           :body "Hello World"}
```

As you can see, HTTP responses are much simpler than requests—all you have to worry about are the status code, the headers, and the body. For some responses, the body is expected to be blank. Take a typical 302 redirect, such as:

```
{:status 302,
 :headers {"Location" "http://example.com"},
 :body ""}
```

Here, the important content is included under the "Location" header, rather than the body. Note that the body is still included, even though it's just the empty string. This is a practice that you should observe in your own responses, and Ring's built-in response helpers will add it for you where appropriate.

Now that you've seen both request and response maps, you can begin to think of your web service as a series of functions from the former to the latter. If you remember nothing else, remember that a function that takes a request and returns a response is called a *handler*.

Response Helpers

A 404 Not Found response from the example project will look something like this:

```
{:status 404,
 :headers
 {"Content-Type" "text/html; charset=utf-8",
  "Set-Cookie"
  ("ring-session=855650aa-6209-48af-944f-177cac7fad56;Path-/;HttpOnly"),
   "X-XSS-Protection" "1; mode=block",
   "X-Frame-Options" "SAMEORIGIN",
   "X-Content-Type-Options" "nosniff"},
  :body "Not Found"}
```

Although it's possible to write a response map by hand, it's usually not done that way. Instead, the process is typically broken down into two main phases:

1. Create the response using helpers from the `ring.util.response` namespace.
2. Apply middleware to outgoing responses to add common headers.

In the case of the `compojure` template, nearly all the preceding map is created by a combination of `compojure.route/not-found` and `ring.middleware.defaults/wrap-defaults`, both of which we'll cover later in this chapter.

For now, though, let's look at how to use the `ring.util.response` helpers to create a similar map:

```
(require '[ring.util.response :as ring-response])
(def my404
```

```
(-> (ring-response/response "Not found")
  ;; returns a basic response map with "Not found" in the body
  (ring-response/status 404)
  ;; updates the status of the response to 404
  (ring-response/content-type "text/html")
  ;; adds the Content-Type header to the response
  (ring-response/charset "utf-8")
  ;; extends the Content-Type header to include the character set
  ))
```

With the notable exception of `ring.util.response/response` (which takes only a body), most of the helper functions take a response map as their first argument. What this means in practice is that you'll almost always use them with the `->` (thread-first) macro, so you can read the whole expression as a series of updates to the immutable response map.

After evaluating the above forms, `my404` looks like this:

```
{:status 404,
 :headers {"Content-Type" "text/html; charset=utf-8"},
 :body "Not found"}
```

It's still missing a lot of the headers from the template's 404 response, but it's the job of the middleware to handle those.

You should take a moment to browse the `ring.util.response` namespace once or twice to get an idea of what you can do with Ring responses without having to reinvent the wheel, so to speak. You'll find that most of the functions are short and accomplish one task reliably, which makes them great examples for your own helpers.

Testing Ring Handlers

One of the great things about Ring is how easy it is to test. Recall how one of the added benefits of the `compojure` template is that it automatically adds a dependency on ring-mock. This section covers how ring-mock is used to test ring handlers without having to start a live HTTP server.

First of all, run `lein test` in the project directory (if you haven't already) to verify that they do pass. Once you're satisfied, look at how the tests actually work:

```
(ns chapter3.handler-test
  (:require [clojure.test :refer :all]
            [ring.mock.request :as mock]
            [chapter3.handler :refer :all]))

(deftest test-app
  (testing "main route"
          (let [response (app (mock/request :get "/"))]
            (is (= (:status response) 200))
            (is (= (:body response) "Hello World"))))

  (testing "not-found route"
          (let [response (app (mock/request :get "/invalid"))]
            (is (= (:status response) 404)))))
```

Notice that app is being called like a function (because handlers are functions), but it's being passed the mock/request thing. Let's see what happens if you evaluate (mock/request :get "/") in a REPL:

```
{:server-port 80,
 :server-name "localhost",
 :remote-addr "localhost",
 :uri "/",
 :query-string nil,
 :scheme :http,
 :request-method :get,
 :headers {"host" "localhost"}}
```

It's a Ring request map! Only this one has a lot of the boring stuff filled in for us, which makes the tests much easier to read. Let's continue by evaluating the whole expression (app (mock/request :get "/")):

```
{:status 200,
 :headers {"Content-Type" "text/html; charset=utf-8"},
            :body "Hello World"}
```

If you guessed that this is a Ring response map, you're absolutely correct. Once again, you can clearly see that Ring handlers are ordinary Clojure functions that take a (request) map as a parameter and return a (response) map. What's interesting is that these tests are avoiding actual HTTP transport by just calling the handlers directly—there's no network traffic involved.

The ring.mock.request/request function can just as easily generate a :post request, which will be very helpful later when we talk about ByteArrayInputStreams. Try it out with (mock/request :post "/foo" "Hello, this request has a body"):

```
{:remote-addr "localhost",
 :headers {"host" "localhost", "content-length" "30"},
 :server-port 80,
 :content-length 30,
 :uri "/foo",
 :server-name "localhost",
 :query-string nil,
 :body
 #object[java.io.ByteArrayInputStream 0x6e9da8f2 "java.io.ByteArrayInputStream..."],
 :scheme :http,
 :request-method :post}
```

Another thing that's worth remarking on is that there's only one handler for our entire (small) application: app. That's a result of Compojure doing its job, which is to compose handlers for various routes into a single handler that can answer any request it gets. This is covered more in the "Routing" section.

The ring-mock library only includes a few functions, most of which fine-tune the requests generated by ring.mock.request/request by updating headers, adding query parameters, and more. If you find yourself needing to create more sophisticated requests in your tests, have a quick look at the ring.mock.request namespace first to see if it has what you need.

Ring Middleware

Recall that handlers are functions that turn a request into a response, and they are the fundamental concept in Ring. The term middleware refers to a function that takes a handler and returns a handler. Because middleware has the same type for its parameter and return value, you can stack them indefinitely—middleware upon middleware upon middleware, until you get down to a basic handler.

Catching Exceptions

Let's say, for example, that you want to make sure that an uncaught exception in your service doesn't actually crash the whole thing. Instead, you'd probably prefer to return a 500 response and keep trying to service other requests. You could diligently add a try/catch to each individual handler and return the 500 there, but that would result in a lot of needless code duplication.

> **NOTE** *Thankfully, Ring won't really let an uncaught exception from a handler crash the service. But you probably won't want to use the built-in catchall anyway, so it's worth learning how to write your own.*

Using middleware for that purpose, separate that logic and apply it at whatever level in the application you want. Here's a plan for the 500 middleware, which is called `wrap-500-catchall`:

1. We take a handler as a parameter.

2. We're returning a new handler, so we'll need to start with something like `(fn [request] ...)`.

3. At this point, both the handler and the request are in scope, so we could just call `(handler request)`.

4. You want to wrap that in a `try/catch` expression.

5. The `catch` body should always return a 500 response and otherwise swallow the exception (although you would normally log it as well).

Middleware functions are usually named `wrap-x`, because each one is a sort of transparent layer around a handler. You can keep wrapping a handler with middleware indefinitely, and it's not uncommon to see ten or more layers, although that can be pretty unwieldy!

Here's one possible implementation of the `wrap-500-catchall` middleware:

```
(defn wrap-500-catchall
  "Wrap the given handler in a try/catch expression, returning a 500 response if
  any exceptions are caught."
  [handler] ;; we want to take a handler as a parameter
  (fn [request] ;; we're also returning a handler
    (try (handler request)
      ;; middleware almost always calls the handler that's passed in
      (catch Exception e
        (-> (ring-response/response (.getMessage e))
          ;; place the exception's message in the body
          (ring-response/status 500)
          ;; set the status code to 500
          (ring-response/content-type "text/plain")
```

```
;; there's no HTML here, so we'll use text/plain
(ring-response/charset "utf-8")
;; and update the character set
)))))
```

Let's add a new route that throws an exception for us. Routing is covered in more detail in the next section, but now you can get something working with just a single line in the `app-routes` definition in `handler.clj`:

```
(defroutes app-routes
  (GET "/" [] "Hello World")
  (GET "/trouble" [] (/ 1 0)) ;; this won't end well!
  (route/not-found "Not Found"))
```

Add the definition of `wrap-500-catchall` directly below `app-routes`, then use it to wrap `app`:

```
(def app
  (wrap-500-catchall (wrap-defaults app-routes site-defaults)))
```

This works because `app` is a handler, and all middleware takes a handler and returns a handler.

Let's verify that the middleware does what you might expect by writing a test.

```
(deftest catchall-test
  (testing "when a handler throws an exception"
    (let [response (app (mock/request :get "/trouble"))]
      (testing "the status code is 500"
        (is (= 500 (:status response))))
      (testing "and the body only contains the exception message"
        (is (= "Divide by zero" (:body response)))))))
```

If you want to see this for yourself in your browser, kill the Ring server process (if it's running) and run `lein ring server` again. Now, when you visit `http://localhost:3000/trouble`, you should see a "Divide by zero" message, while the other routes continue to work as usual.

Converting Request Bodies

The `wrap-500-catchall` middleware only affects the response, but you can also use middleware to prepare the request before the handlers even see it. Remember the Ring Request section above, where you saw that the `:body` key contains a `java.io.ByteArrayInputStream`? Well, run `lein repl` from the project directory so you can investigate that class a little bit:

```
user=> (require '[ring.mock.request :as mock])
nil
user=> (def request-with-body (mock/request :post "/" "This is the request body"))
#'user/request-with-body
user=> (:body request-with-body)
#object[java.io.ByteArrayInputStream 0x71e6fe51 "java.io.ByteArrayInputStream@..."]
```

At this point you can see that the body is a `java.io.ByteArrayInputStream`, but you can't see what its contents are. For that, you can call Clojure's `slurp` function.

```
user=> (slurp (:body request-with-body))
"This is the request body"
```

Slurping the body does indeed return the string. But what if you slurp it again?

```
user=> (slurp (:body request-with-body))
" "
```

That is disastrous. Slurping a `ByteArrayInputStream` also empties its contents. It turns out that, unlike almost everything else you deal with in Clojure, `java.io.ByteArrayInputStream` objects are mutable—simply reading their contents as a string leaves them blank. You can carefully work around that fact every time you process a request with a body, *or* you can write a new middleware so that you don't have to worry about it. Here's a plan:

1. It's middleware, thus taking a handler as a parameter.

2. Start with `(fn [request] ...)` for the return value.

3. If the request doesn't have a body, call `(handler request)`.

4. Otherwise, instead of just calling `(handler request)`, you will replace the request's `:body` with the `slurp`ed version, eliminating the need to ever worry about `ByteArrayInputStream`s in the rest of the application.

5. Finally, call the handler with the prepared version of the request.

Here's a basic implementation of the middleware, which you can call `wrap-slurp-body`:

```
(defn wrap-slurp-body
  [handler]
  (fn [request]
    (if (instance? java.io.InputStream (:body request))
      (let [prepared-request (update request :body slurp)]
        (handler prepared-request))
      (handler request))))
```

Note that you're checking for instances of `java.io.InputStream`, a superclass of `java.io.ByteArrayInputStream`. Although you've only seen `ByteArrayInputStream`s so far, the fact is that Ring will sometimes pass other subclasses of `InputStream`, but they can all be read with `slurp` and suffer from the same mutability issue, so this is a much safer approach.

Normally you would use a route that takes a body in order to test this, but it's not quite time to do that with Compojure (that's coming up in the next section). That said, there's nothing stopping you from writing a simpler handler and testing it. Let's write a handler that just echoes the body back:

```
(defn body-echo-handler
  [request]
  (if-let [body (:body request)] ;; remember, not all requests have bodies!
    (-> (ring-response/response body)
        (ring-response/content-type "text/plain")
        (ring-response/charset "utf-8"))
    ;; if there's no body, let's call this a 400 (Bad request)
    (-> (ring-response/response "You must submit a body with your request!")
        (ring-response/status 400))))
```

Now let's wrap the handler in some middleware to give you something to use for tests:

```
(def body-echo-app
(-> body-echo-handler
  wrap-500-catchall
  wrap-slurp-body))
```

And finally, add the tests themselves to `handler_test.clj`:

```
(deftest slurp-body-test
  (testing "when a handler requires a request body"
    (testing "and a body is provided"
      (let [response (body-echo-app (mock/request :post "/" "Echo!"))]
        (testing "the status code is 200"
          (is (= 200 (:status response)))
        (testing "with the request body in the response body"
          (is (- "Echo!" (:body response)))))))
    (testing "and a body is not provided"
      (let [response (body-echo-app (mock/request :get "/"))]
        (testing "the status code is 400"
          (is (= 400 (:status response))))))))
```

Even though you're not using it yet, you might as well wrap the main `app` in `wrap-slurp-body` as well. At the same time, let's clean it up a bit with the thread-first macro:

```
(def app
  (-> app-routes
    (wrap-defaults api-defaults)
    wrap-slurp-body
    wrap-500-catchall))
```

It can be a pain, but you often have to pay attention to the order in which you apply middleware. As each middleware function wraps the handler, that new middleware becomes the first thing to see the request. So, even though it's last in the list, `wrap-500-catchall` is the first thing to get called when a request is being answered. Let's consider a slightly different order for a moment:

```
(def app
  (-> app-routes
    wrap-500-catchall
    (wrap-defaults api-defaults)
    wrap-slurp-body))
```

In this case, the `wrap-500-catchall` middleware *only* applies to `app-routes` directly—it will never see exceptions thrown by `wrap-defaults` or `wrap-slurp-body`. That may or may not be what you would want in your own application, but the important thing is to be aware of the effect that ordering can have on your middleware.

Middleware is a powerful abstraction around both requests and responses. When your middleware is doing its job, your handlers can be smaller and more focused, which is key to writing clean, maintainable web services. It's easy to compose middleware by stacking it on top of your handlers, but remember that the last middleware you apply will be the first to be called when there's a request.

Routing

Imagine a simple web service with two endpoints: a /links endpoint that responds to GET and POST requests, and a /links/{ID} endpoint, which may support GET and DELETE. The routing library is responsible for examining an incoming request and passing it along (with any relevant data) to a function of your choosing.

If you look again at the request maps in the HTTP section, you can probably begin to imagine how this would work—examine the :request-method and :uri keys in the request map, and if they match an endpoint in your application then pass the request map along to the appropriate function to return a response.

You could do that manually, but hardly anybody does. Instead, by offloading that work to a *routing library*, you will keep your code much cleaner and easier to reason about. By far, the most popular Clojure routing library is Compojure. It's well documented, fairly straightforward, and very flexible.

Composing Routes

The chapter3.handler namespace already has three Compojure routes defined under app-routes:

```
(defroutes app-routes
  (GET "/" [] "Hello World")
  (GET "/trouble" [] (/ 1 0))
  (route/not-found "Not Found"))
```

The defroutes macro is purely a convenience around def (you've seen) and routes (will be covered in depth soon). Just to prove there's no other magic involved, let's revise this bit of code to eliminate the use of defroutes:

```
(def app-routes
  (routes
   (GET "/" [] "Hello World")
   (GET "/trouble" [] (/ 1 0))
   (route/not-found "Not Found")))
```

Now that the structure is easier to see, let's talk about what's going on here. Although it might not look much like it right now, remember that *app-routes is a handler.* That is, app-routes takes a Ring request map and returns a response map.

That fact alone gives you a good idea of what routes does: It takes some number of Compojure routes and turns them into a single handler. But what are the routes individually? Have a guess, then open up a REPL in the project directory:

```
user=> (require '[compojure.core :refer :all])
nil
user=> (def get-foo (GET "/foo" [] "Hello from foo"))
#'user/get-foo
user=> (require '[ring.mock.request :as mock])
nil
```

```
user=> (get-foo (mock/request :get "/foo"))
{:status 200,
 :headers {"Content-Type" "text/html; charset=utf-8"},
 :body "Hello from foo"}
```

As you can see, GET (and indeed, the PUT/POST/DELETE/etc.) returns a handler. In this case, you'll test it out with a request that the handler was ready for—a simple GET request to /foo. Let's jump back to the REPL and see what happens if the route *doesn't* match:

```
user=> (get-foo (mock/request :get "/"))
nil
```

Well, nil isn't a valid Ring response, so it would be a really bad idea to use this handler directly. Let's look again at app-routes:

```
(def app-routes
  (routes
   (GET "/" [] "Hello World")
   (GET "/trouble" [] (/ 1 0)) ;; this won't end well!
   (route/not-found "Not Found")))
```

Now that you know that each route is a handler that can return nil, you can fully deduce the purpose of the routes function: to combine multiple handlers, sending the request to each one until a valid response (not nil) is returned.

This is the first function that can turn two or more handlers into one, and it's about time! You don't want to write one huge handler all at once to represent the application; it's much more reasonable to split it up and handle one route at a time.

Writing Routes

Here again are some simple Compojure routes:

```
(defroutes app-routes
  (GET "/" [] "Hello World")
  (GET "/trouble" [] (/ 1 0)) ;; this won't end well!
  (route/not-found "Not Found"))
```

There's definitely a common structure here:

➤ HTTP verb, like GET, PUT, POST, DELETE

➤ A path

➤ A parameter vector

➤ The body of the response

Most of the time, Compojure routes resemble Clojure functions. Instead of defn, each route is introduced with the HTTP verb it responds to. Standing in for the function name is the path, which can contain abstract segments such as :id. Like an ordinary function, a route must have a (possibly empty) parameter vector, which supports the standard destructuring forms. Finally, you can define the result of matching the route by providing an expression to evaluate.

The routes above are extremely simple, which is good when trying not to dive too deep into routing, but now it's time to jump in with both feet. Let's bring the echo handler into Compojure:

```
(defroutes app-routes
  (GET "/" [] "Hello World")
  (GET "/trouble" [] (/ 1 0))
  (POST "/echo" [:as request] (body-echo-handler request))
  (route/not-found "Not Found"))
```

This finally gives you something more interesting to look at in the parameter vector, so let's focus on that first. You may recognize :as, which is part of Clojure's standard destructuring syntax. Normally, :as x would take all of the parameters and wrap them up in a collection called x. In Compojure specifically, :as is a nice shortcut to get the entire Ring request as a parameter so that it can be passed off to a handler. The request can have any name, but in this case it's hard to imagine a reason not to call it request. Once you have the request in scope, call the old body-echo-handler directly.

Let's revisit the tests for app-routes and add a couple for the newly integrated echo endpoint:

```
(deftest test-app
  (testing "main route"
    (let [response (app (mock/request :get "/"))]
      (is (= (:status response) 200))
      (is (= (:body response) "Hello World"))))

  (testing "echo route"
    (let [response (app (mock/request :post "/echo" "Echo!"))]
      (is (= 200 (:status response)))
      (is (= "Echo!" (:body response))))

    (let [response (app (mock/request :post "/echo"))]
      (is (= 400 (:status response)))))
  (testing "not-found route"
    (let [response (app (mock/request :get "/invalid"))]
      (is (= (:status response) 404)))))
```

This works for POST, but this handler is used to accepting any request that contains a body. You can work your way back up to the old functionality like this:

```
(defroutes app-routes
  (GET "/" [] "Hello World")
  (GET "/trouble" [] (/ 1 0))
  (POST "/echo" [:as request] (body-echo-handler request))
  (PUT "/echo" [:as request] (body-echo-handler request))
  (DELETE "/echo" [:as request] (body-echo-handler request))
  (route/not-found "Not Found"))
```

Or maybe this doesn't work. This amount of code duplication is unforgivable, even in this small example project. Let's take advantage of another routing function that Compojure provides:

```
(defroutes app-routes
  (GET "/" [] "Hello World")
  (GET "/trouble" [] (/ 1 0)) ;; this won't end well!
  (ANY "/echo" [:as request] (body-echo-handler request))
  (route/not-found "Not Found"))
```

Now you can match any HTTP request to the /echo path. Let's verify that by adding a few more requests to the tests for the echo route:

```
(deftest test-app
  (testing "main route"
    (let [response (app (mock/request :get "/"))]
      (is (= (:status response) 200))
      (is (= (:body response) "Hello World"))))

  (testing "echo route"
    (let [response (app (mock/request :post "/echo" "Echo!"))]
      (is (= 200 (:status response)))
      (is (= "Echo!" (:body response))))

    (let [response (app (mock/request :put "/echo" "Hello!"))]
      (is (= 200 (:status response)))
      (is (= "Hello!" (:body response))))

    (let [response (app (mock/request :patch "/echo" "Goodbye!"))]
      (is (= 200 (:status response)))
      (is (= "Goodbye!" (:body response))))

    (let [response (app (mock/request :post "/echo"))]
      (is (= 400 (:status response)))))
  (testing "not-found route"
    (let [response (app (mock/request :get "/invalid"))]
      (is (= (:status response) 404)))))
```

There's more to do here to clean up the echo handler. Although convenient, it's usually unnecessary to pass along the entire request to a Compojure route handler. In this case, all the echo handler actually needs is the body, which may be nil. Leave echo-body-handler in place, but write a new function that doesn't rely on any extraneous data:

```
(defn echo ;; based on echo-body-handler
  [body]
  (if (not-empty body) ;; excludes nil and the empty string
    (-> (ring-response/response body)
        (ring-response/content-type "text/plain")
        (ring-response/charset "utf-8"))
    ;; if there's no body, let's call this a 400 Malformed
    (-> (ring-response/response "You must submit a body with your request!")
        (ring-response/status 400))))
```

Notice how the function is renamed to echo. Since it no longer takes a full request map, it would be misleading to give it a name with *handler* in it. Also, since it only takes the body as a parameter, it doesn't make sense to also put *body* in the name. So that leaves you with echo. Unfortunately, the tests are also failing now, so you need to update app-routes to only pass the body along to this function:

```
(defroutes app-routes
  (GET "/" [] "Hello World")
  (GET "/trouble" [] (/ 1 0)) ;; this won't end well!
  (ANY "/echo" [:as {body :body}] (echo body))
  (route/not-found "Not Found"))
```

Notice how the request was replaced with {body :body}. The latter is also standard destructuring syntax, roughly translating to "take whatever's in the :body key and bind it to body." Leave the :as there to make sure that you're destructuring the request map; otherwise you'll get an error about an unexpected binding form. Go ahead and run the tests again to make sure everything's back in working order with the newly refactored handler.

Compojure Responses

You may have noticed that Compojure doesn't seem to mind if a string is returned instead of a proper ring response map. This is not practical most of the time because you need to add a bit more with the request. Still, it's worth taking note of exactly *how* Compojure is able to turn that string into a Ring response, since you can extend that behavior to other types that might be more useful.

Compojure uses the compojure.response/Renderable protocol for this purpose. The protocol defines a single method, render, which returns a proper Ring response. You can take a look at the compojure.response namespace to see how this method is defined for nil, strings, maps, etc.

Path Variables

At the beginning of this section, a route is mentioned with an abstract segment: /links/{ID}, where {ID} is an extra parameter that the handler can use. Compojure also makes this quite easy with a little bit of magic:

```
(defroutes app-routes
  (GET "/" [] "Hello World")
  (GET "/trouble" [] (/ 1 0))
  (GET "/links/:id" [id] (str "The id is: " id))
  (ANY "/echo" [:as {body :body}] (echo body))
  (route/not-found "Not Found"))
```

Here you have a new route, /links/:id, with just [id] for the parameter vector. When Compojure matches a route, any segments that start with a colon are treated as abstract path segments and added to the request map. You can access them through the request yourself, but Compojure also adds a more convenient way—providing the name of the segment in the parameter vector. That means that you can't use, say, [link-id] for the parameter name; it wouldn't have matched.

Let's write some tests to verify that the /links/:id endpoint actually works:

```
(deftest links-test
  (testing "the links/:id endpoint"
    (testing "when an id is provided"
      (let [response (app (mock/request :get "/links/foo123"))]
        (testing "returns a 200"
          (is (= 200 (:status response))))
        (testing "with the id in the body"
          (is (re-find #"foo123" (:body response)))))))
    (testing "when the id is omitted"
      (let [response (app (mock/request :get "/links"))]
        (testing "returns a 404"
          (is (= 404 (:status response))))))
    (testing "when the path is too long"
      (let [response (app (mock/request :get "/links/foo123/extra-segment"))]
```

```
(testing "returns a 404"
  (is (= 404 (:status response)))))))))
```

As the tests show, the route will only match if there is exactly one segment for `:id`—anything else will result in a 404.

Routes and Middleware

Using middleware to your advantage is always a good idea, but you don't always want to apply the same middleware to every route. For example, you don't actually need to apply the `wrap-slurp-body` middleware to all of the routes just because the `/echo` endpoint relies on it. Instead, you can group routes and apply middleware in multiple stages. First, split off the `/echo` route from the rest of `app-routes`:

```
(def body-routes
  (-> (routes
        (ANY "/echo" [:as {body :body}] (echo body)))
    (wrap-routes wrap-slurp-body)))

(defroutes non-body-routes
  (GET "/" [] "Hello World")
  (GET "/trouble" [] (/ 1 0)) ;; this won't end well!
  (GET "/links/:id" [id] (str "The id is: " id))
  (route/not-found "Not Found"))
```

Note that we're wrapping body-routes directly, rather than at a later stage. This works well conceptually, since any route that gets grouped under `body-routes` is going to need this middleware and other routes probably won't. This pattern isn't possible with the `defroutes` macro because there's no way to sneak in the middleware between `def` and `routes` in that case.

The other very important note here is that even though you can call wrap-slurp-body on the route, you'll instead pass it as an argument to `wrap-routes`. The rationale for this has to do with the way that Compojure combines handlers. When you pass multiple handlers to `routes`, they each get called with the request map until one of them returns a response. If one of those handlers somehow mutates the request map (which `wrap-slurp-body` does, because it consumes the original body), then subsequent handlers will see the mutated version.

The `wrap-routes` function is an essential workaround for this problem. It ensures that the given middleware is only applied when the route actually matches, meaning that it will only be called once per request. You should use `wrap-routes` whenever you're applying middleware with the `routes` function.

Moving on, instead of wrapping only `app-routes` in the remaining middleware, you can combine `body-routes` with `app-routes`. First, combine `body-routes` and `app-routes` into a single handler with the `routes` function:

```
(def app-routes
  (routes body-routes non-body-routes))
```

Next, remove `wrap-slurp-body` from the app, since it has already been applied to the routes that require it:

```
(def app
  (-> app-routes
```

```
wrap-500-catchall
(wrap-defaults api-defaults)))
```

It's very rare that all of your routes will need exactly the same middleware in exactly the same order, so always think about that when grouping routes together. You can always wrap handlers in middleware and you can always group handlers with routes, so you'll often see a sort of group-wrap-group-wrap-group-wrap pattern that slowly combines handlers into a single application.

JSON Endpoints

Most web services are going to produce and/or consume serialized data structures. Since JSON is by far the most common serialization format for modern web services, it is used in this chapter. Nonetheless, you can easily substitute XML (even on a per-request basis) or something more experimental like Cognitect's new Transit.

Although there's an official Clojure JSON library (clojure.data.json), you'll be using the much more popular Cheshire, which is more flexible and performant. Cheshire allows you to define JSON serialization methods for your own custom data types and it supports streaming, lazy decoding, and pretty-printed JSON output.

Let's add Cheshire as a dependency to the project so we can try it out. Update the :dependencies section in project.clj like so:

```
:dependencies [[org.clojure/clojure "1.7.0"]
               [compojure "1.4.0"]
               [ring/ring-defaults "0.1.5"]
               [cheshire "5.5.0"]] ;; new line
```

Then require it in handler.clj:

```
(ns chapter3.handler
  (:require [compojure.core :refer :all]
            [ring.util.response :as ring-response]
            [compojure.route :as route]
            [cheshire.core :as json] ;; new line
            [ring.middleware.defaults :refer [wrap-defaults site-defaults
              api-defaults]]))
```

And also require it in handler_test.clj:

```
(ns chapter3.handler-test
  (:require [clojure.test :refer :all]
            [ring.mock.request :as mock]
            [cheshire.core :as json] ;; new line
            [chapter3.handler :refer :all]))
```

Accepting JSON Data

Now that we're equipped to deal with JSON, let's write some middleware to handle parsing a JSON-encoded body, thus returning a 400 response if it's malformed:

```
(defn wrap-json
  [handler]
  (fn [request]
```

```
        (if-let [prepd-request (try (update request :body json/decode)
                                 (catch com.fasterxml.jackson.core.JsonParseException e
                                   nil))]
          (handler prepd-request)
          ;; we'll only get here if there's a parse error
          (-> (ring-response/response "Sorry, that's not JSON.")
            (ring-response/status 400)))))
```

One thing to note is that this middleware assumes that the body is going to be a string, which means it'll have to be applied before `wrap-slurp-body` (remember, applied first means called second). Let's write a handler that turns a JSON-encoded body into a Clojure map:

```
(defn handle-clojurefy
  [request]
  (-> (:body request) ;; extract the body of the request
    str ;; turn it into a string
    ring-response/response ;; wrap it in a response map
    (ring-response/content-type "application/edn"))) ;; set the Content-Type
```

Note the proper Ring handler is written here, rather than taking any of the shortcuts that Compojure opens up. This is usually the right thing to do—full Ring handlers are easier to test independently and they tend to be more explicit. In this case, returning a response map makes it possible to set the Content-Type to `application/edn`. If you're not familiar with EDN (Extensible Data Notation), it's essentially Clojure's built-in object serialization standard, and it can be a convenient way to pass data between Clojure services over HTTP.

Let's add the `/clojurefy` endpoint to `body-routes`, since it does require a body. You will wrap it with the `wrap-json` middleware right in the `route` definition:

```
(def body-routes
  (-> (routes
        (ANY "/echo" [:as {body :body}] (echo body))
        (POST "/clojurefy" [] (wrap-json handle-clojurefy)))
    wrap-slurp-body))
```

Remember the `compojure.response/Renderable` protocol? Well, it turns out that you can use it to skip the whole `[:as request]` bit. When you use a full-fledged Ring handler for the body of a route, Compojure assumes it's a handler and automatically passes it the request map. It looks a little strange, but it works, and the alternative looks even stranger:

```
(POST "/clojurefy" [:as request] ((wrap-json handle-clojurefy) request)) ;; weird!
```

Also note that `wrap-json` is placed where it can only see requests that have matched the `/clojurefy` route. This way it won't affect the `/echo` endpoint, which really doesn't care if the request contains valid JSON.

Finally, let's write some tests to see if this is successful:

```
(deftest json-test
  (testing "the /clojurefy endpoint"
    (testing "when provided with some valid JSON"
      (let [example-map {"hello" "json"}
            example-json (json/encode example-map)
            response (app (-> (mock/request :post "/clojurefy" example-json)
```

```
                         ;; note, we must set the content type of the request
                         (mock/content-type "application/json")))]
        (testing "returns a 200"
          (is (= 200 (:status response)))
          (testing "with a Clojure map in the body"
            (is (= (str example-map) (:body response)))))))))
    (testing "when provided with invalid JSON"
      (let [response (app (-> (mock/request :post "/clojurefy" ";!:")
                              (mock/content-type "application/json")))]
        (testing "returns a 400"
          (is (= 400 (:status response)))))))))
```

The tests pass, so all is good! Let's move on to returning JSON responses.

Returning JSON Data

Returning JSON is a bit easier than accepting it. You don't have to worry about problems with parsing; you just need to set the content type and encode the body. Here's a simple middleware function that should take care of this:

```
(defn wrap-json-response
  [handler]
  (fn [request]
    (-> (handler request) ;; call the handler first
        (update :body json/encode) ;; then encode the body
        (ring-response/content-type "application/json")))) ;; and set Content-Type
```

Most of the middleware written for this book so far alters incoming requests, so this is a little bit different. Instead of calling the handler last, you call it first. For the rest of the thread-first form let's work with the response map. Thread the response through update to encode the body, then use ring.util.response/content-type to apply the correct Content-Type header.

Now, let's write a handler that returns a JSON object with some basic information about the system it's running on:

```
(def handle-info
  (wrap-json-response
    (fn [_] ;; we don't actually need the request
      (-> {"Java Version" (System/getProperty "java.version")
           "OS Name" (System/getProperty "os.name")
           "OS Version" (System/getProperty "os.version")}
          ring-response/response))))
```

This is yet another way to wrap a handler. Since there is only one handler that returns JSON, there's no real problem with wrapping it this closely. If you had a few more routes like this, you'd want to compose them and then wrap the combined handler.

This handler uses the System/getProperty method to fetch some details about the host that the service is running on. You may not want to expose this information generally, but it's a useful thing to know about and a perfectly good source of structured data to encode.

Now let's add a route for the /info endpoint:

```
(defroutes non-body-routes
  (GET "/" [] "Hello World")
  (GET "/trouble" [] (/ 1 0)) ;; this won't end well!
  (GET "/links/:id" [id] (str "The id is: " id))
  (GET "/info" [] handle-info)
  (route/not-found "Not Found"))
```

In this case, it will be more interesting to run `lein ring server` and check out `http://localhost:3000/info`, but let's write some tests anyway:

```
(deftest json-response-test
  (testing "the /info endpoint"
    (let [response (app (mock/request :get "/info"))]
      (testing "returns a 200"
        (is (= 200 (:status response))))
      (testing "with a valid JSON body"
        (let [info (json/decode (:body response))]
          (testing "containing the expected keys"
            (is (= #{"Java Version" "OS Name" "OS Version"}
                   (set (keys info))))))))))
```

One thing to note here is that the `keys` function makes no guarantees about the order that the keys are in, so you'll use a set comparison to make sure that you don't need any such guarantees. As long as the map has exactly the keys "Java Version," "OS Name," and "OS Version" in any order, the test will pass.

Using ring-json

Writing your own JSON middleware is great practice, but the fact is that this has already been done for you. The ring-clojure organization maintains a very helpful library called `ring-json` (`https://github.com/ring-clojure/ring-json`). This library already provides a default 400 response, as well as middleware for JSON requests and JSON responses.

So, in the interest of not reinventing the wheel, let's refactor the code to use the `ring-json` library. First, add it as a dependency to `project.clj`:

```
:dependencies [[org.clojure/clojure "1.7.0"]
               [compojure "1.4.0"]
               [ring/ring-defaults "0.1.5"]
               [ring/ring-json "0.4.0"] ;; add this
               [cheshire "5.5.0"]]
```

Then require `ring.middleware.json` in `handler.clj`:

```
(ns chapter3.handler
  (:require [compojure.core :refer :all]
            [ring.middleware.json :as ring-json] ;; add this
            [ring.util.response :as ring-response]
            [ring.util.request :as ring-request]
            [compojure.route :as route]
            [cheshire.core :as json]
            [ring.middleware.defaults :refer [wrap-defaults api-defaults]]))
```

We have a slightly different middleware situation right now because `ring-json`'s version of `wrap-json-body` stringifies the request body for us; making `wrap-slurp-body` obsolete for JSON routes. Let's go ahead and move the /clojurefy endpoint out of body-routes and into its own json-routes var while you replace wrap-json with ring-json/wrap-json-body:

```
(def json-routes
  (routes
    (POST "/clojurefy" [] (ring-json/wrap-json-body handle-clojurefy))))

(def body-routes
  (-> (routes
        (ANY "/echo" [:as {body :body}] (echo body)))
    (wrap-routes wrap-slurp-body)))
```

You'll also need to update app-routes to include json-routes:

```
(def app-routes
  (routes json-routes body-routes non-body-routes))
```

Next, you'll replace wrap-json-response middleware with ring-json/wrap-json-response:

```
(def handle-info
  (ring-json/wrap-json-response
    (fn [_] ;; we don't actually need the request
      (-> {"Java Version" (System/getProperty "java.version")
           "OS Name" (System/getProperty "os.name")
           "OS Version" (System/getProperty "os.version")}
        ring-response/response))))
```

Once those changes are made, you can delete both of the hand-crafted JSON middleware functions and re-run the tests. The functionality hasn't changed in any particularly significant way, so they all pass.

JSON endpoints need not be especially daunting, provided you're smart about the abstractions that are available. Use middleware for parsing and encoding, but be very careful about applying it only where necessary and always think twice about the order in which middleware is applied. Avoid writing your own middleware if there's already a good open source solution for it. Although this section focused on JSON, you can easily apply the exact same principles to any other form of serialization.

EXAMPLE SERVICE

In this section, you'll be writing a link shortening service. In the process, you'll see how a CRUD (Create Read Update Destroy) app can work in Clojure. Your service will support the following endpoints:

- ➤ POST /links—Submit a URL and receive a shortened URL.
- ➤ GET /links/:id—Redirect to the URL associated with the ID.
- ➤ PUT /links/:id—Update the URL associated with the ID.
- ➤ DELETE /links/:id—Delete the shortened link.
- ➤ GET /links—Retrieve a listing of all IDs and their associated URLs in JSON format.

This project is a great way to illustrate main elements of every Clojure web service, including storage and testing. By the end of this chapter, you'll also have a great starting point for experimenting with more advanced features like authentication and database integration.

Create the Project

If you were following along with the earlier sections, that's great! We're still starting over, though. Set that project aside and start a new one with this familiar command:

```
lein new compojure ch3shortener
```

Have a look around in the project to familiarize yourself with what's available. There is only one namespace right now, and that's `ch3shortener.handler`. The next section lays out the project deliberately to make the namespaces clean and focused.

Additional Namespaces

The overview section used a single-namespace approach, because you were just trying a few things out and getting familiar with the concepts involved in Clojure web services. But it's time to start taking things more seriously, and that means separating our project into well-defined namespaces.

There are two main concerns when you're planning namespace layout: separation and dependencies. Separation is about keeping namespaces focused and keeping functions and data where you expect to find them. It doesn't sound complicated, but it often requires a lot of thought.

But you can't always just separate namespaces based on what they do. The layout has to also reflect the relationships between different pieces of code. Whenever one namespace `requires`, uses, or `imports` another, it creates a dependency relationship. Let's look at the namespace declaration for `ch3shortener.handler`:

```
(ns ch3shortener.handler
  (:require [compojure.core :refer :all]
            [compojure.route :as route]
            [ring.middleware.defaults :refer [wrap-defaults site-defaults]]))
```

This namespace depends on three others: `compojure.core`, `compojure.route`, and `ring.middleware.defaults`. We know that none of those namespaces depend on this one, but what if one of them did? Well, Clojure doesn't allow that sort of thing. If namespace A requires namespace B, then B can't also require A. That type of situation is called a cyclic dependency, and avoiding it is one of the main reasons to break namespaces up.

You've already seen how a web service is generally composed of handlers, routes, and middleware. The three concerns are pretty conceptually distinct, so that alone already suggests that they should be in different namespaces.

What clinches it, though, is the fact that they don't have any mutual dependencies. Think about it this way:

➤ Middleware shouldn't depend on handlers or routes.

➤ Handlers depend on middleware, but not routes.

➤ Routes depend on handlers, and maybe middleware.

So you're unlikely to get in a situation where your handlers namespace requires the middleware namespace *and vice versa*. Since the three roles are well defined and don't have cyclic dependencies, you should almost certainly maintain them in separate namespaces.

You're also going to create an `application` namespace to serve as the new entry point for our service. This namespace will be responsible for handling configuration, initializing resources, and returning a master handler that contains all of the routes you want to serve.

Middleware

You're undoubtedly going to need some middleware for this project, so let's create a new file at `src/ch3shortener/middleware.clj` with these contents:

```
(ns ch3shortener.middleware)
```

It's not much to look at for now, but it's a start. You should also be prepared to write middleware tests, so create another file at `test/ch3shortener/middleware_test.clj` with these contents:

```
(ns ch3shortener.middleware-test
  (:require [ch3shortener.middleware :refer :all]
            [clojure.test :refer :all]))
```

Even though you haven't done it yet, you can test middleware independently. Doing so helps you figure out whether a given bug is caused by the middleware itself, middleware ordering, or the handler. You'll have a look at that strategy later on when there is some middleware to test.

Routes

The `routes` namespace should look like a high-level overview of the endpoints your service makes available. It's important to have a good place to start when you're looking to add or update an existing route. Let's create the `routes` namespace at `src/ch3shortener/routes.clj` and copy over the `routes` themselves from `handler.clj`:

```
(ns ch3shortener.routes
  (:require [ch3shortener.handler :as handler]
            [ch3shortener.middleware :as mw]))

(defroutes app-routes
  (GET "/" [] "Hello World")
  (route/not-found "Not Found"))
```

You won't have independent tests for routes, so this is all you need for now.

Application

The application namespace is about to unseat `ch3shortener.handler` as the main point of entry for our service. Create the file `src/ch3shortener/application.clj` with the following contents:

```
(ns ch3shortener.application
  (:require [ring.middleware.defaults :refer [wrap-defaults site-defaults]]
            [ch3shortener.routes :as routes]))

(def app
  (wrap-defaults routes/app-routes site-defaults))
```

This should look familiar, since it's basically just the rest of the `ch3shortener.handler` namespace with the added dependency on `ch3shortener.routes`. Similarly, let's create `test/ch3shortener/application_test.clj` and move the existing handler tests there:

```
(ns ch3shortener.application-test
  (:require [ch3shortener.application :refer :all]
            [clojure.test :refer :all]
            [ring.mock.request :as mock]))

(deftest test-app
  (testing "main route"
    (let [response (app (mock/request :get "/"))]
      (is (= (:status response) 200))
      (is (= (:body response) "Hello World"))))

  (testing "not-found route"
    (let [response (app (mock/request :get "/invalid"))]
      (is (= (:status response) 404)))))
```

The last thing you need to do to make `ch3shortener.application/app` the main handler for your service is to update the `:ring` section in `project.clj`:

```
:ring {:handler ch3shortener.application/app}
```

This configuration option tells Ring which handler to use when starting a server with `lein ring server`. Once you update the setting, try that command out and verify that everything still works. You should see exactly the same behavior as before, only with better namespaces!

Handlers

Well, you should have just about gutted `ch3shortener.handler` by now. If you've copied out (but not deleted) app-routes and app, it's time to get rid of them. Here's what `handler.clj` looks like now.

```
(ns ch3shortener.handler
  (:require [ring.util.request :as req]
            [ring.util.response :as res]))
```

You need to be prepared to deal with requests and responses, but there is nothing to do just yet. That's fine, since there will be plenty to do here later. Let's also make sure that `handler_test.clj` is similarly empty:

```
(ns ch3shortener.handler-test
  (:require [clojure.test :refer :all]
            [ring.mock.request :as mock]
            [ch3shortener.handler :refer :all]))
```

Default Middleware

Let's take a look at the definition of app in `ch3shortener.application`:

```
(def app
  (wrap-defaults routes/app-routes site-defaults))
```

Ring comes with `ring.middleware.defaults/wrap-defaults`, which is some general-purpose middleware that sets your service up to behave pretty reasonably out of the box. The second argument there, `site-defaults`, is a configuration map that tells `wrap-defaults` that you're creating a website, and turns on the following options (among others):

➤ Anti-forgery tokens

➤ Session support

➤ Cross-site scripting protection

➤ Static resource serving

These are meant to represent the best practices for browser-based sites, but they don't apply to the service you're writing now. You don't want to have to worry about anti-forgery tokens and you won't have any static assets to serve.

Luckily, you can just swap in a set of options that better suits your own needs. Just change `site-defaults` to `api-defaults` in both places as it appears:

```
(ns ch3shortener.application
  (:require [ring.middleware.defaults :refer [wrap-defaults api-defaults]]
            [ch3shortener.routes :as routes]))

(def app
  (wrap-defaults routes/app-routes api-defaults))
```

Using the `api-defaults` saves a bit of work here and there by automatically setting the content type and charset, without getting bogged down in the extra stuff you don't need from `site-defaults`. It's a good balance, but you can upgrade to `secure-api-defaults` if you want to use SSL.

Configuring Ring's default middleware is one of the first really important decisions you can make in your application, and it's worth taking some time to get it right. The built-in configurations cover several common use cases, but don't be afraid to modify them yourself—they're just Clojure maps.

The Storage Protocol

It's time to introduce state. The service is going to need to store and retrieve data, specifically to associate IDs with full URLs. This section contains the creation, implementation, and testing of a fairly typical storage protocol.

Why a Protocol?

Clojure's protocol system is based on, but not identical with, Java's interfaces. Protocols define a set of *methods* that can have different implementations for different types of data. Since one type can implement any number of different protocols, it also serves as a form of multiple inheritance.

The key feature in this context is the ability to abstract away the exact storage implementation. During early development, it's very convenient to keep your application state in memory—this makes it easy to iterate on schemas and storage methods, simplifies testing, and generally speeds things along.

When you're running into production, however, using in-memory storage is suddenly a huge hindrance. You don't really have data persistence, access can be inefficient, and you don't have all of the features of a proper database.

Using a storage protocol provides the best of both worlds, albeit at a cost. Once you define what it means to be an instance of application storage, you can have a quick and easy implementation that uses a Clojure atom to use during development, then later on when you have a better understanding about the storage contract and requirements, you can write a second implementation using the database of our choice and seamlessly substitute it in. If you're smart about testing, you can even demonstrate that both implementations are functionally interchangeable.

On the other hand, using a storage protocol rather than specific storage functions adds complexity to the sample application, because there is an extra layer of indirection between the application code and the storage code. This makes it impossible for your editor or IDE to jump directly to the implementation of a storage method, since it won't be resolved until runtime. It also introduces the possibility for divergence between implementations, which is a very pernicious form of technical debt.

These drawbacks apply to protocols in general, and we urge you to think pretty hard about whether a protocol is really necessary for any given task. That said, it's almost always a good idea to use a protocol for storage in a stateful web service like this one, unless you're absolutely sure you'll only ever need one storage implementation.

Creating the Storage Protocol

Our storage protocol is not a handler, a route, or an application, so you need a new namespace. Let's create `src/ch3shortener/storage.clj`:

```
(ns ch3shortener.storage)

(defprotocol Storage
  )
```

Pause for a moment to think about what you need from storage:

➤ Create a link with the supplied ID and URL.

➤ Retrieve a link, given its ID.

➤ Update a link, given its ID and URL.

➤ Delete a link, given its ID.

➤ List all known links.

Translate them into five storage methods:

```
(defprotocol Storage
  (create-link [this id url]
    "Store the url under the id. Returns the id if successful, nil if the id is
      already in use.")
```

```
(get-link [this id]
  "Given an ID, returns the associated URL. Returns nil if there is no associated
    URL.")

(update-link [this id new-url]
  "Updates id to point to new-url. Returns the id if successful, nil if the id
    has not yet been created.")

(delete-link [this id]
  "Removes a link with the given ID from storage, if it exists.")

(list-links [this]
  "Returns a map of all known IDs to URLs."))
```

Testing Protocol Implementations

Even though you can't really test a protocol without an implementation, it's not too early to start writing tests. You know it's important to use tests to show the equivalence of different protocol implementations, and writing these tests ahead of time will help guide the development of your in-memory storage implementation.

The point of using a protocol is to avoid worrying too much about individual implementations, and testing should reflect that. The same exact tests should pass, regardless of the underlying implementation, or else there's probably something wrong. The key here is to write a testing *function*, rather than a normal test expression. Let's create test/ch3shortener/storage_test.clj:

```
(ns ch3shortener.storage-test
  (:require [ch3shortener.storage :refer :all]
            [clojure.test :refer :all]))

(defn is-valid-storage ;; note, not deftest
  "Given an implementation of the Storage protocol, assert that it fulfills the
  contract."
  [stg]
  (let [url "http://example.com/clojurebook"
        id "book"]
    (testing "can store and retrieve a link"
      (testing "create-link returns the id"
        (is (= id (create-link stg id url)))

        (testing "and it won't overwrite an existing id"
          (is (nil? (create-link stg id "bogus")))
          (is (= url (get-link stg id))))))

    (testing "can update a link"
      (let [new-url "http://example.com/nevermind"]
        (update-link stg id new-url)
        (is (= new-url (get-link stg id)))))

    (testing "can delete a link"
      (delete-link stg id)
```

```
    (is (nil? (get-link stg id)))))

(testing "can list all links"
  (let [id-urls {"a" "http://example.com/a"
                 "b" "http://example.com/b"
                 "c" "http://example.com/c"}
        ids (doseq [[id url] id-urls]
              (create-link stg id url))
        links (list-links stg)]

    (testing "in a map"
      (is (map? links))

    (testing "equal to the links we created"
      (is (= id-urls links))))))))
```

It may seem strange that the function's name starts with `is`, but it's helpful for functions that contain `is` assertions to be marked this way. You can choose to define a valid-storage predicate that returns `true` or `false`, but then you lose granularity that comes from having separate assertions for each of the expected behaviors.

The `is-valid-storage` function won't do anything until you call it, so the tests will continue to pass for now. But once you do have a concrete storage implementation, you will need to call this function in a `deftest` form and then know if it passes. For now, keep this around and you can use it for reference while writing the in-memory implementation.

In-Memory Storage

It's time to write a storage implementation. You can put this in the existing storage namespace, but it's a good idea to keep each implementation separate. Let's create `src/ch3shortener/storage/in_memory.clj`:

```
(ns ch3shortener.storage.in-memory
  (:require [ch3shortener.storage :refer :all]))
```

You can implement each storage method inline in one big `reify` expression, but that would be pretty hard to read. Instead, let's write functions for each storage method one at a time, using the `method*` naming convention so you don't clash with the storage methods themselves. Each of the functions takes a storage atom (`!stg`) as a parameter, and most also take a `url` and/or `id`.

First, let's handle `create-link`:

```
(defn create-link*
  [!stg id url]
  (when-not (contains? @!stg id)
    (swap! !stg assoc id url)
    id))
```

Remember to check first to see whether the id is already in storage, and if not then `nil` will be returned. The `when-not` macro is a big help here, and it also tells later developers that the function could return `nil`.

Let's move on to get-link, which is almost embarrassingly simple:

```
(defn get-link*
  [!stg id]
  (get @!stg id))
```

The storage contract specifies that get-link can return nil, so use get without the optional not-found argument. The update-link implementation is a nice mirror image of create-link:

```
(defn update-link*
  [!stg id url]
  (when (contains? @!stg id)
    (swap! !stg assoc id url)
    id))
```

This changes when-not to when, since the methods have opposite requirements. Let's move on to delete-link:

```
(defn delete-link*
  [!stg id]
  (swap! !stg dissoc id)
  nil)
```

There's no need to check whether the link actually exists, just simply ensure that it doesn't. Returning nil at the end isn't strictly required, but otherwise swap! will return the entire link map, which is not helpful.

Our last storage method to implement is also the simplest:

```
(defn list-links*
  [!stg]
  @!stg)
```

You can do something even shorter, like (def list-links* deref), but this definition is clearer.

Finally, it's time to write a constructor for the storage implementation. The plan here is to construct a blank storage atom and close over it with reify:

```
(defn in-memory-storage
  []
  (let [!stg (atom {})]
    (reify Storage
      (create-link [_ id url] (create-link* !stg id url))
      (get-link [_ id] (get-link* !stg id))
      (update-link [_ id url] (update-link* !stg id url))
      (delete-link [_ id] (delete-link* !stg id))
      (list-links [_] (list-links* !stg)))))
```

The reify function takes a protocol and some number of method definitions and returns an object with those defined methods. Since the !stg atom is in scope when reify is called, each of those methods will keep a reference to it for the lifetime of the storage object.

The constructor takes no options, but that's just because it's the simplest possible working storage implementation. A more realistic option for production use involves a database, and the constructor needs to take parameters for at least the database host and credentials. In a typical application, those credentials would come from environment variables and read at runtime using a library like `environ`.

Now you can test this using the `is-valid-storage` function defined earlier. Add the following to the end of `test/ch3shortener/storage_test.clj`:

```
(deftest in-memory-storage-test
  (let [stg (in-memory/in-memory-storage)]
    (is-valid-storage stg)))
```

Three leisurely lines is all it takes now to test a new storage implementation! It's unlikely that this form will change; instead, new tests should go in the `is-valid-storage` function to enforce consistency across implementations.

Separating storage into its own protocol is great for flexibility and it enforces a strict separation of concerns. The rest of the sample application can only use storage methods that are defined (and hopefully tested) ahead of time. Testing storage implementations with a single function provides assurance of consistency while minimizing code duplication.

Handlers

With the storage backend for your service in place, you can write handlers that rely on it. Thanks to the storage protocol, these handlers don't worry about whether the data's stored in an atom, a database, or a message board—they just call the protocol methods on whatever storage object gets passed in.

Let's now take a look at `handler.clj` and `handler_test.clj`.

get-link

The `get-link` handler should take an id and return one of two possible responses:

➤   If the link is found in storage, return a 302 redirect to the URL.

➤   If the link is not found, return a 404 response.

First, let's require the storage namespace in order to use storage methods:

```
(ns ch3shortener.handler
  (:require [ring.util.request :as req]
            [ring.util.response :as res]
            [ch3shortener.storage :as st]))
```

Now implement `get-link`, using `ring.util.response` helpers to do most of the work:

```
(defn get-link
  [stg id]
  (if-let [url (st/get-link stg id)]
    (res/redirect url)
    (res/not-found "Sorry, that link doesn't exist.")))
```

You may notice that this is more of a "handler" than a handler. That is to say, it doesn't take a full request object, just a link ID. That's okay; you just need to make sure to call it the right way when you add a route for it later on.

Let's add a test to `handler_test.clj` to make sure that this does what it should. For this test you need a storage object, so you'll also need to require the `in-memory-storage` function and the `storage` namespace:

```
(ns ch3shortener.handler-test
  (:require [clojure.test :refer :all]
            [ring.mock.request :as mock]
            [ch3shortener.handler :refer :all]
            ;; add the following two requirements
            [ch3shortener.storage.in-memory :refer [in-memory-storage]]
            [ch3shortener.storage :as st]))

(deftest get-link-test
  (let [stg (in-memory-storage)
        id "test"
        url "http://test.gov"]
    ;; store a link directly for the test
    (st/create-link stg id url)

    (testing "when the ID exists"
      (let [response (get-link stg id)]
        (testing "the result is a 302"
          (is (= 302 (:status response))))
        (testing "with the expected URL in the Location header"
          (is (= url (get-in response [:headers "Location"]))))))

    (testing "when the ID does not exist"
      (let [response (get-link stg "bogus")]
        (testing "the result is a 404"
          (is (= 404 (:status response))))))))
```

The tests pass, so you are on the right track. Let's move on to the next handler, `create-link`.

create-link

This handler takes a response with a POST body and returns one of two responses:

➤ If the ID isn't taken, return a 200 response with the short URL.

➤ If the ID is taken, return a 422 (unprocessable) response.

```
(defn create-link
  [stg id {url :body}]
  (if (st/create-link stg id url)
    (res/response (str "/links/" id))
    (-> (format "The id %s is already in use." id)
      res/response
      (res/status 422))))
```

Testing this can be awkward because it reads the body as if it's a string, but there is no middleware in place yet to make that happen. For the purposes of testing the handler, let's stringify the body by adding this test to `handler_test.clj`:

```
(deftest create-link-test
  (let [stg (in-memory-storage)
```

```
            url "http://example.com"
            request (-> (mock/request :post "/links/test" url)
                        ;; since we haven't added middleware yet
                        (update :body slurp))]
    (testing "when the ID does not exist"
      (let [response (create-link stg "test" request)]
        (testing "the result is a 200"
          (is (= 200 (:status response)))

          (testing "with the expected body"
            (is (= "/links/test" (:body response)))))

          (testing "and the link is actually created"
            (is (= url (st/get-link stg "test")))))))))

    (testing "when the ID does exist"
      (let [response (create-link stg "test" request)]
        (testing "the result is a 422"
          (is (= 422 (:status response)))))))))
```

With these tests passing, it's one more handler down, and three to go.

update-link

The update-link handler should have a very similar form to create-link. It should take an ID and a body containing a URL, then:

➤ If the ID exists in storage, return a 200 with the shortened URL.

➤ If the ID doesn't exist in storage, return a 404 response.

```
(defn update-link
  [stg id {url :body}]
  (if (st/update-link stg id url)
    (res/response (str "/links/" id))
    (-> (format "There is no link with the id %s." id)
      res/not-found)))
```

As promised, this is extremely similar to the create-link handler. The tests will also be pretty similar, including the :body workaround:

```
(deftest update-link-test
  (let [stg (in-memory-storage)
        url "http://example.com"
        request (-> (mock/request :put "/links/test" url)
                    ;; since we haven't added middleware yet
                    (update :body slurp))]
    (testing "when the ID does not exist"
      (let [response (update-link stg "test" request)]
        (testing "the result is a 404"
          (is (= 404 (:status response))))))

    (testing "when the ID does exist"
      (st/create-link stg "test" url)
      (let [new-url "http://example.gov"
```

```
                  request (assoc request :body new-url)
                  response (update-link stg "test" request)]
      (testing "the result is a 200"
        (is (= 200 (:status response)))

      (testing "with the expected body"
        (is (= "/links/test" (:body response))))

      (testing "and the link is actually updated"
        (is (= new-url (st/get-link stg "test")))))))))))
```

Testing the handlers directly can really pay off later. If you run into a problem while testing the full application, the status of the handler tests will tell you a lot about what might be causing the failures.

delete-link

This is another pseudo-handler, since it only needs the storage object and link ID. It also can't really fail, so don't worry about an error response. Since you won't have any useful information to report back to the caller, just return a 204 (no content) response. Here's a nice, quick implementation:

```
(defn delete-link
  [stg id]
  (st/delete-link stg id)
  (-> (res/response "")
    (res/status 204)))
```

Note, the empty string is returned, rather than omitting the body entirely. This is standard practice for responses that don't have a body. The tests are just a little bit more involved:

```
(deftest delete-link-test
  (let [stg (in-memory-storage)
        id "test"
        url "http://example.com/foo"]
    (testing "when the link exists"
      (st/create-link stg id url)
      (let [response (delete-link stg id)]
        (testing "the response is a 204"
          (is (= 204 (:status response))))

        (testing "the link is deleted"
          (is (nil? (st/get-link stg id))))))

    (testing "when the link does not exist"
      (let [response (delete-link stg "bogus")]
        (testing "the response is still 204"
          (is (= 204 (:status response)))))))))
```

You're almost done writing the handlers, but there is still one more to go.

list-links

This handler is going to return a JSON response, so it's time to add a couple of new dependencies to project.clj:

```
:dependencies [[org.clojure/clojure "1.7.0"]
               [compojure "1.4.0"]
               [ring/ring-defaults "0.1.5"]
               ;; add these two:
               [ring/ring-json "0.4.0"]
               [cheshire "5.5.0"]]
```

Both of these libraries were mentioned before, but to review: The ring/ring-json library contains middleware that you can use to help return a JSON response, while cheshire is a more general-purpose JSON library that you'll be using in tests.

Let's require wrap-json-response in the handler namespace first:

```
(ns ch3shortener.handler
  (:require [ring.util.request :as req]
            [ring.util.response :as res]
            [ring.middleware.json :refer [wrap-json-response]] ;; new line
            [ch3shortener.storage :as st]))
```

Since there is a plan to have one JSON route, you might as well wrap the handler directly, so let's write the final handler:

```
(defn list-links
  "Returns a handler! Call the handler if you want a response."
  [stg]
  (wrap-json-response
   (fn [_] ;; we don't need the request at this point
     (res/response (st/list-links stg)))))
```

This function is definitely a little odd, since it closes over the storage object and returns a handler, so calling the handler is going to take some extra parentheses. The advantage to doing it this way is that you can wrap the inner handler with wrap-json-response directly, avoiding any need to manually encode the body or set the content type. All you have to do is put the map into the response body and you're done.

Let's have a look at the tests. First, add one more dependency to the handler-test namespace:

```
(ns ch3shortener.handler-test
  (:require [clojure.test :refer :all]
            [ring.mock.request :as mock]
            [ch3shortener.handler :refer :all]
            [ch3shortener.storage.in-memory :refer [in-memory-storage]]
            [ch3shortener.storage :as st]
            [cheshire.core :as json])) ;; add this
```

Use `cheshire` to decode the response from the new handler. After that, add the `list-links-test` to the end of the namespace:

```
(deftest list-links-test
  (let [stg (in-memory-storage)
        id-urls {"a" "http://link.to/a"
                 "b" "http://link.to/b"
                 "c" "http://link.to/c"}]
    (doseq [[id url] id-urls]
      (st/create-link stg id url))

    (let [handler (list-links stg)
          response (handler (mock/request :get "/links"))
          parsed-links (json/decode (:body response))]
      (testing "the response is a 200"
        (is (= 200 (:status response))))

      (testing "with a body that decodes to the original map"
        (is (= id-urls parsed-links))))))
```

Note how we're calling `(list-links stg)` to get the handler, not a response. Proceed to call the handler with the kind of request expected (even though it doesn't use the request), and then parse the response as JSON.

The first, last, and most important thing to remember about handlers is that they are ordinary Clojure functions that take and return maps. The Clojure standard library comes with dozens of functions that work on maps, and those functions can help you write handlers. Additionally, Ring itself comes with a wealth of useful handler-specific functions, found in `ring.util.request` and `ring.util.response`.

Middleware

We have middleware to handle the JSON responses, but you need to bring back `wrap-slurp-body`. Let's add it to `src/ch3shortener/middleware.clj`:

```
(ns ch3shortener.middleware
  (:import [java.io InputStream]))

(defn wrap-slurp-body
  [handler]
  (fn [request]
    (if (instance? InputStream (:body request))
      (let [prepared-request (update request :body slurp)]
        (handler prepared-request))
      (handler request))))
```

There were no specific tests for this middleware before, but you can add some by switching over to `test/ch3shortener/middleware_test.clj`:

```
(ns ch3shortener.middleware-test
  (:require [ch3shortener.middleware :refer :all]
            [ring.mock.request :as mock]
            [clojure.test :refer :all]))
```

```
(deftest wrap-slurp-body-test
  (let [body "This is a body."
        request (mock/request :post "/foo" body)
        expected-request (assoc request :body body)
        identity-handler (wrap-slurp-body identity)]

    (testing "when given a request with a ByteArrayInputStream body"
      (let [prepared-request (identity-handler request)]
        (testing "the body is turned into a string"
          (is (= body (:body prepared-request)))

          (testing "and the rest of the request is unchanged"
            (is (= expected-request prepared-request))))))

    (testing "when given a request that has no body"
      (let [no-body (mock/request :get "/")]
        (testing "there's no effect"
          (is (= no-body (identity-handler no-body))))))

    (testing "applying the middleware a second time has no effect"
      (let [request (mock/request :post "/foo" body)]
        (is (= expected-request
               (-> request
                 identity-handler
                 identity-handler)))))))
```

Rather than testing the middleware with a real handler, use the middleware to wrap Clojure's `identity` function. All `identity` does is return its argument, so when the wrapped "handler" is passed a request, you get the prepared request back. It's a neat trick that works well as long as your middleware doesn't ever expect a Ring response.

The tests should demonstrate that the middleware ignores requests with missing bodies and requests where the body isn't an `InputStream`, but otherwise converts the body into the right string. With that out of the way, let's move onto routes.

Routes

The handlers are tested and ready, but we haven't served anything over HTTP! That's because you still need to set up some routes. This is the last step before you can run the server locally, and it is time to do it.

These routes have something that was missing from the earlier examples—a data dependency. Much like the `in-memory-storage` constructor, you're going to write a function that closes over a dependency and returns the thing you actually want, which is a Compojure handler.

Here's an empty version, just to have something to start with. Go ahead and add this to the bottom of `src/ch3shortener/routes.clj`:

```
(defn shortener-routes
  [stg]
  (routes
   (route/not-found "Not Found")))
```

It's important to have this function defined early, though, because the tests going forward will happen at the application-level from now on.

Let's move over to `src/ch3shortener/application.clj`, where two changes must be made. First, construct a storage object to pass into the handler; then use that to get the Compojure routes:

```
(ns ch3shortener.application
  (:require [ring.middleware.defaults :refer [wrap-defaults api-defaults]]
            [ch3shortener.storage.in-memory :refer [in-memory-storage]]
            [ch3shortener.routes :as routes]))

(def app
  (let [stg (in-memory-storage)
        app-routes (routes/shortener-routes stg)]
    (wrap-defaults app-routes api-defaults)))
```

This temporarily breaks almost every application test we have, so let's clear out `test/ch3shortener/application_test.clj` a little bit:

```
(deftest test-app
  (testing "not-found route"
    (let [response (app (mock/request :get "/invalid"))]
      (is (= (:status response) 404)))))
```

Once that's done, we'll have a storage-backed 404 service that you can run with `lein ring server`. As we add routes over the course of the rest of the section, they'll also become active as soon as you re-run `lein ring server`, so feel free to try them out.

POST /links/:id

Let's start with the C in CRUD, POST `/links/:id`. The handler written for this endpoint takes an ID and the request body, but the body has to be turned into a string first. Let's add the route and the middleware to `shortener-routes`:

```
(defn shortener-routes
  [stg]
  (-> (routes
        (POST "/links/:id" [id :as request] (handler/create-link stg id request))
        (route/not-found "Not Found"))
    (wrap-routes mw/wrap-slurp-body)))
```

The `create-link` handler takes both the id and the full request map, so grab the former by matching on its name in the binding vector and the latter using `:as` destructuring.

Notice that you're indiscriminately wrapping everything with `wrap-slurp-body` for now, and that you're using `wrap-routes` to do it. With these tests it's safe to use `wrap-slurp-body`, but you need to use `wrap-routes` to make sure the middleware only gets called when a route matches. Otherwise, you're risking destroying the contents of a request body.

In terms of tests, make sure that the route is matching and behaving somewhat expectedly. Let's add a simple example to the `ch3shortener.application-test` namespace:

```
(deftest test-app
  (let [url "http://example.com/post"
```

```
        id "test"
        path (str "/links/" id)]
    (testing "creating a link"
      (let [response (app (mock/request :post path url))]
        (is (= 200 (:status response)))
        (is (= path (:body response))))))

  (testing "not-found route"
    (let [response (app (mock/request :get "/invalid"))]
      (is (= (:status response) 404)))))
```

You don't have a way to test whether creating the link is effective yet, but you will soon. Until then, the fact that the handler and the storage layer are both tested should give you some confidence that things are going well.

GET /links/:id

Now that you can create short links, it's time to actually use them. Let's add a route that will redirect you to the URL you want when you give it a short link ID. Add this to shortener-routes:

```
(defn shortener-routes
  [stg]
  (-> (routes
        (POST "/links/:id" [id :as request] (handler/create-link stg id request))
        (GET "/links/:id" [id] (handler/get-link stg id))
        (route/not-found "Not Found"))
    (wrap routes mw/wrap-slurp-body)))
```

Augment the tests to verify that both link creation and retrieval work:

```
(deftest test-app
  (let [url "http://example.com/post"
        id "test"
        path (str "/links/" id)]
    (testing "creating a link"
      (let [response (app (mock/request :post path url))]
        (is (= 200 (:status response)))
        (is (= path (:body response)))))

    (testing "visiting a link"
      (testing "when the link exists"
        (let [response (app (mock/request :get path))]
          (testing "returns a 302"
            (is (= 302 (:status response)))

            (testing "with the correct location"
              (is (= url (get-in response [:headers "Location"]))))))

      (testing "when the link does not exist"
        (let [response (app (mock/request :get "/links/nothing"))]
          (testing "returns a 404"
            (is (= 404 (:status response))))))))

    (testing "not-found route"
      (let [response (app (mock/request :get "/invalid"))]
        (is (= (:status response) 404)))))
```

This is called an MVP (Minimum Viable Product). You can now shorten a link and redirect to it when asked to do so. You still need to implement updating, deleting, and listing.

PUT /links/:id

It's time to implement the `mirror-universe` version of link creation: link updating. This should be easy since it's so similar to POST `/links/:id`. Just add this line to `shortener-routes`:

```
(defn shortener-routes
  [stg]
  (-> (routes
        (POST "/links/:id" [id :as request] (handler/create-link stg id request))
        (PUT "/links/:id" [id :as request] (handler/update-link stg id request))
          ;; new
        (GET "/links/:id" [id] (handler/get-link stg id))
        (route/not-found "Not Found"))
     (wrap-routes mw/wrap-slurp-body)))
```

Add this new `deftest` form to the end of `ch3shortener.application-test`:

```
(deftest link-updating
  (let [id "put"
        url "http://example.com/putTest"
        path (str "/links/" id)]

    (testing "when the link does not exist"
      (let [response (app (mock/request :put path url))]
        (testing "the response is a 404"
          (is (= 404 (:status response))))))

    (testing "when the link does exist"
      (app (mock/request :post path "http://example.post"))
      (let [response (app (mock/request :put path url))]
        (testing "the response is a 200"
          (is (= 200 (:status response))))))))
```

You are now up to CRU on the CRUD scale, so just a little further to go.

DELETE /links/:id

This should be getting routine by now. Add a single line to `shortener-routes`:

```
(DELETE "/links/:id" [id] (handler/delete-link stg id))
```

And a quick test to make sure it works:

```
(deftest delete-link
  (let [id "thing"
        url "http://example.com/thing"
        path (str "/links/" id)]

    (testing "when the link doesn't exist"
      (let [response (app (mock/request :delete path))]
        (testing "the result is a 204"
          (is (= 204 (:status response))))))))
```

```
(testing "when the link does exist"
  (app (mock/request :post path url))
  (let [response (app (mock/request :delete path))]
    (testing "the response is still a 204"
      (is (= 204 (:status response)))

      (testing "and the link is now a 404"
        (is (= 404 (:status (app (mock/request :get path)))))))))))))
```

GET /links

All right, it's time for the final endpoint in the example service. You may remember that this handler is a little different, because you need to call the function to construct it. Well, thankfully Compojure handles that perfectly well without you having to do anything particularly unusual. Go ahead and add this line somewhere inside shortener-routes:

```
(GET "/links" [] (handler/list-links stg))
```

When Compojure matches this route, it evaluates the form on the right and checks the type of the return value. If it's a function, it assumes that it's a handler and passes it the request map. In this case, the form does evaluate to a handler, so everything's fine.

In order to test this, you'll need cheshire again, so add this line to the application-test namespace declaration:

```
(ns ch3shortener.application-test
  (:require [ch3shortener.application :refer :all]
            [clojure.test :refer :all]
            [ring.mock.request :as mock]
            [cheshire.core :as json] ;; add this
            [clojure.string :as str]))
```

Then add this somewhere else in the file:

```
(deftest list-links
  ;; first make sure there are some links to list
  (let [id-urls {"a" "http://example.com/a"
                 "b" "http://example.com/b"
                 "c" "http://example.com/c"}]
    (doseq [[id url] id-urls]
      (app (mock/request :post (str "/links/" id) url)))

    (let [response (app (mock/request :get "/links"))
          parsed-body (json/decode (:body response))]
      (testing "the response is a 200"
        (is (= 200 (:status response)))

        (testing "and the decoded body contains all of the links we added"
          (is (= id-urls
                 (select-keys parsed-body ["a" "b" "c"]))))))))
```

That concludes the implementation of the link-shortener, from start to finish. It may be simple, but it has a solid foundation and a well-defined structure that make it a good codebase to iterate on and expand. The minimal storage implementation is ready to be swapped out for something more robust if and when that becomes necessary. The majority of the functions are short and focused, taking ordinary Clojure data as arguments and returning ordinary Clojure data structures, which helps to make it accessible to developers without much specialized experience.

Finally, tests at multiple levels of composition (handlers, middleware, routes) give you confidence that the application works as designed—and they'll help narrow down the root cause if something does show unexpected behavior. If you add other storage implementations, you can test that they truly are interchangeable with just a few lines of code.

If you're feeling up to the challenge, now would be a great time to experiment with adding authentication, writing a new storage implementation, or adding a front end for the service in Clojurescript! There's no substitute for creative tinkering, and now that you understand the fundamentals, you'll be able to take this project in any direction that interests you.

DEPLOYMENT

So far, you've mainly interacted with the shortener service by calling the handler in tests with `ring-mock` in this chapter. You may also have used `lein ring server` and experimented a bit, but you don't want to be one of the people who use that command for a production web service.

In this section, let's examine a few other options for running a Clojure web service, either in development, a production server of your own, or a cloud hosting service like Heroku.

Using Leiningen

You've already seen `lein ring server` (or `lein ring server-headless`), but it's worth pointing out that this option is actually pretty flexible. First, all of the `lein ring` functionality is provided by the creatively-named `lein-ring` plugin. The options we're about to cover here are actually handled by that plugin rather than by Ring directly, so keep that in mind.

You saw earlier that you can set the default Ring handler in `project.clj` with this line:

```
:ring {:handler example-project.handler/app}
```

But that's just the start. A more complete set of lein-ring options looks more like this:

```
:ring {:init example-project.app/init ;; called when the handler starts
       :destroy example-project.app/destroy ;; called when the handler exits
       :adapter example-projects.app/adapter-opts ;; passed to the ring adapter
       :handler example-project.handler/app}
```

The `:init` and `:destroy` keys should both point to functions that can be called with no arguments to initialize and dispose of any resources your handlers might need at runtime. In general, you probably won't see these used very frequently. It's usually a better idea to handle your application setup and teardown yourself, preferably using something like Stuart Sierra's component or Puppet Labs' trapperkeeper, both of which are designed to manage the lifecycles of long-running services.

The :adapter key, if present, should point to a map of options that will be passed to the Ring adapter. The term "adapter" in Ring parlance is essentially the HTTP server itself. Ring uses Jetty by default, and it's quite good for most purposes, but it is swappable. Whether you choose to substitute the adapter or not, you may want to further configure the adapter to listen on a different port, tune the number of threads available for requests, or encrypt traffic using specific SSL certificates. Note that this will have no effect if you compile your project into a WAR file.

The lein ring server process listens on the first open port it finds, starting at 3000 and counting up. If you would prefer for it to listen to a different port, you can either add the port as a command-line argument (e.g., lein ring server 8080), or change it in the configuration map like this:

```
:ring {:handler example-project.handler/app
       :port 8080}
```

It's not a good idea to try to use this to run on port 80, or any other privileged port. Doing so would require you to run lein as root, which is actively discouraged by Leiningen. If you do want to run on a port below 1024, you're much better off building an uberjar and running that.

Using the lein-ring plugin is very convenient during development, but it has some clear disadvantages. Running anything in Leiningen has a performance cost, since it uses JVM options that prioritize startup time over general speed. The restriction against running on a privileged port, though not insurmountable, makes things at least unpleasant. In general, lein ring server is not suitable for use in production.

Compiling an Uberjar or Uberwar

The preferred way to deploy a dedicated Clojure web service is as an uberjar. An uberjar is a JAR (Java Archive) file that contains not only your project, but every single dependency, including all of the Clojure compiler and standard library.

In most Clojure projects, you create an uberjar using the lein uberjar command. Ring projects are slightly different, since they need to include a main function to start a server and register the application handler, but creating them is almost as easy when you're using lein-ring. Instead of lein uberjar, just run lein ring uberjar. Once you have the uberjar, you can run it with java -jar project-name.jar. Take the shortener service developed earlier as an example:

```
~/src/ch3shortener$ lein ring uberjar
Compiling ch3shortener.application.main
Created target/ch3shortener-0.1.0-SNAPSHOT.jar
Created target/ch3shortener-0.1.0-SNAPSHOT-standalone.jar
~/src/ch3shortener$ java -jar target/ch3shortener-0.1.0-SNAPSHOT-standalone.jar
2016-02-03 01:51:11.225:INFO:oejs.Server:jetty-7.x.y-SNAPSHOT
2016-02-03 01:51:11.287:INFO:oejs.AbstractConnector:Started
  SelectChannelConnector@0.0.0.0:3000
Started server on port 3000
```

The port here is determined either by the :port setting in the :ring map or the :adapter settings, if any. In this case it's using the default of 3000 (or the next available).

Uberjars are great because they're portable to any system with Java installed; you don't necessarily need to worry about whether or how another web server is installed and configured, nor any other dependencies. Even though it's common to use another web server like Nginx or Apache to proxy to your Clojure service, it's not always necessary.

In some organizations, there may already be infrastructure in place to run Java WAR (Web Archive) files. In that case, there's a WAR counterpart to the uberjar called an uberwar. Creating it is, as you'd expect, as simple as `lein ring uberwar`. Running the uberwar is considerably more complicated, and is almost entirely dependent on the application server running the WAR file.

Hosting

If you have access to a shell on your target host, your deployment options are limitless. In the simplest case, you can get away with simply configuring your service to run on the appropriate port and running the uberjar directly.

But you can't always rely on that level of access to the host, and you may not want to. If you want to run your application on AWS (Amazon Web Services) Elastic Beanstalk or Heroku, you'll have to jump through another hoop or two initially, but ultimately you'll spend far less time managing the configuration of your server.

Heroku

Heroku is a PaaS (Platform as a Service) solution for serving web applications written in almost any language, including Clojure. It's a favorite of hobbyists because it offers a free tier that's suitable for personal or demonstration use, but also easily scales up for more serious projects.

Heroku has excellent support for deploying Ring-based Clojure applications like the link shortener from earlier in this chapter. The exact steps for deploying are subject to change at any time, so it's best to follow Heroku's official documentation for Clojure services.

Amazon Elastic Beanstalk

Amazon Elastic Beanstalk is a PaaS offered by Amazon as part of the AWS (Amazon Web Services) collection of products. It doesn't have the same kind of official support for Clojure that Heroku does, but that hasn't stopped the Clojure community from adopting it as a platform.

There are two main approaches to deploying to Elastic Beanstalk. The first takes advantage of Java interoperability to use Amazon's own Java API. The most convenient way to do this is with the `lein-beanstalk` plugin, which adds new Leiningen tasks for deploying to AWS. Once you add the plugin to your project and provide your AWS credentials, it's as simple as `lein beanstalk deploy {environment}`.

The second method relies on Docker, a lightweight virtualization technology that relies on the Linux kernel for process isolation rather than running a full virtual machine. Elastic Beanstalk supports running software from Docker containers, so once you containerize your Clojure service you can run it on AWS or several other cloud providers.

SUMMARY

Writing web services in Clojure the right way is a real joy, in no small part because of the simple, powerfully composable abstractions that Clojure service developers work with. Once you understand request and response maps, you can understand handlers. And once you understand handlers, you can understand middleware. Combine those with routes and you're unstoppable!

The libraries we've covered here are popular, but they're far from the only ones you'll see in the Clojure ecosystem. Although frameworks are not especially popular, there are certainly some commonly-used libraries that veer into that territory. Take Liberator, for instance. Liberator is a Clojure library that takes a much more active role in the definition of your API by encouraging you to adhere to the HTTP specifications in a very defined way. Liberator *resources* (a form of specialized handler) resemble a map of functions marked by keywords like `:handle-ok`, `:malformed?`, and `:delete`. Liberator will pass a request through these functions is a painstakingly documented order to determine what type of response to return.

For example, instead of choosing to return a 400 error, as was done in the shortener earlier, it will return a 400 response if and only if it has defined a `:malformed?` predicate that returns true. If the predicate returns false, Liberator will then call the `:authorized?` function (if defined), followed by `:allowed?`. The flow is complicated enough that developers on projects that use Liberator have invariably bookmarked the Liberator decision graph, of which this is just a small portion (see Figure 3-2):

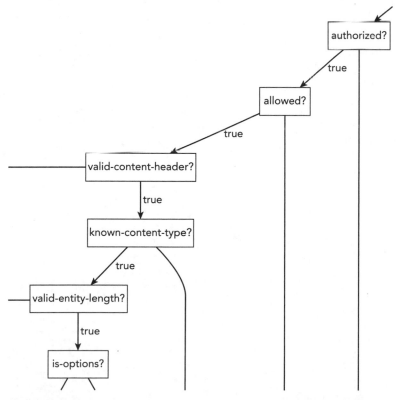

FIGURE 3-2

Although it removes a lot of flexibility from a project, Liberator has its uses and it can make a complicated API much easier to maintain. It's based on Ring, so it's fully compatible with any Ring middleware, and it works well with Compojure or other Ring-based routing libraries.

Luminus, a "micro-framework" for Clojure, has also garnered some attention. It's based mainly on the same libraries covered in this chapter—Ring and Compojure—while packaging a few others, and imposing a specific project structure and layout. It also provides great out-of-the-box support for deployment. Luminus seeks to walk the line between convenience and flexibility, and many developers really like it.

Once you understand the fundamental abstractions of Clojure web services, you'll find that it's much easier to choose the libraries that help you the most without getting in your way. There's no one approach that works for every project, and being able to mix and match libraries to suit your needs is one of the great advantages that Clojure offers that other languages can't match.

4

Testing

WHAT'S IN THIS CHAPTER?

➤ Introducing the basics of testing in Clojure

➤ Understanding common testing strategies

➤ Leveraging code quality tools to improve your code

There are few topics in the software development world more polarizing than testing. Almost everybody agrees that testing software is a necessary activity, and to develop software professionally without testing would be irresponsible. In some communities such as the Ruby on Rails community, they advocate test driven development, or TDD, and due to their heavy focus on testing they have pioneered and inspired many testing frameworks and techniques.

Some people may get the impression that many in the Clojure community are not serious about testing, or even flat out anti-testing; however, nothing could be further from the truth. Many of the maintainers and developers in the community are very much in favor of testing, and they feel it would be irresponsible to deliver software without quality tests proving that your software does as it intends.

No amount of testing can make up for not being able to reason about your code. Having tests alone doesn't mean that you are safe from defects and able to confidently make changes to your code. You must first have a deep understanding of what constitutes a good test for your particular problem.

This chapter covers the basics of testing Clojure code using the clojure.test framework. The chapter also details examples that are more difficult and investigates some common testing strategies, such as how to handle external dependencies and things outside of your control to make your tests more deterministic.

The chapter then moves on to the topic of how to measure code quality and identify areas of concern, so that you can help reduce technical debt. You will also measure your test coverage using the `clover-age` plugin, run static analysis against your code using the `kibit` plugin, and identify low hanging fruit using the `bikeshed` plugin. You will also learn how to keep a close eye on the dependencies of your project and make sure they're up to date using `lein-deps` and `lein-ancient`.

Finally, because we realize that there are other alternatives out there besides `clojure.test`, this chapter takes a quick survey of other testing tools available for Clojure. You'll also examine frameworks such as `expectations`, frameworks that are inspired by the popular testing frameworks from the Ruby world such as `speclj`, and frameworks such as `cucumber` that have been ported to the JVM and have excellent Clojure support.

TESTING BASICS WITH CLOJURE.TEST

When it comes to testing in Clojure there are many choices you can make, but the de facto standard seems to be the `clojure.test` library, and for good reasons. It is the testing library that is included with the Clojure runtime itself, meaning that you need to just have Clojure installed in order to make use of it. It's also simple in its API, meaning that you can learn what you need to know very quickly. Don't let its simplicity fool you though; there is a lot of depth to this library, which supports various styles of testing.

At the heart of the library you'll find the `is` macro. This seemingly simple construct is what allows you to make assertions about any expression you would like. Just keep in mind that the expression itself is evaluated according to Clojure's rules for determining truthiness that was discussed earlier in Chapter 1. An example of how to use this macro is shown here:

```
user> (require '[clojure.test :refer :all])
nil
user> (is (= 4 (+ 2 2)))
true
user> (is (= 4 (+ 2 2 3)))

FAIL in clojure.lang.PersistentList$EmptyList@1 (form-init2032220466808583016.
clj:1)
expected: (= 4 (+ 2 2 3))
  actual: (not (= 4 7))
false
user>
```

You may also specify an optional second argument to the `is` macro providing a documentation string like the following:

```
(is (= 3 (+ 1 1)) "Only for large values of 1")
```

This will include the message in the test output report if this test fails.

There are basically two ways to write tests using the `clojure.test` library. The first is to use the `with-test` macro and the second, more common way, is to use the `deftest` macro.

with-test

The `with-test` macro is a way to package up your tests as metadata with your function:

```
(with-test
  (defn my-add [x y]
    (+ x y))
  (is (= 4 (my-add 2 2)))
  (is (= 7 (my-add 3 4))))
```

In this example, we've defined a function that will be available to call as if you didn't wrap it using the `with-test` macro. Evaluating the expression above will not actually run the tests. In order to run the tests, you must use the function `run-tests` as shown here:

```
user> (run-tests)

Testing user

FAIL in (my-add) (test.clj:7)
expected: (= 7 (my-add 3 5))
  actual: (not (= 7 8))

Ran 1 tests containing 2 assertions.
1 failures, 0 errors.
{:test 1, :pass 1, :fail 1, :error 0, :type :summary}
```

While it is nice to have the ability to keep the tests close to the code, you are having to pollute your namespace by requiring `clojure.test` inside of your production code.

deftest

A better way to write tests is to use the `deftest` macro. The main benefit to using `deftest` over `with-test` is that it allows you to define your tests in a separate namespace from the function you are trying to test, which will feel more familiar to people experience with testing frameworks like JUnit or RSpec. The other benefit is that when you go to package up your application and distribute it, you're not also packaging up all of your tests to distribute along with it. You can see a rewritten example of the `my-add` function using `deftest`:

```
(ns ch4.core-test
  (:require [clojure.test :refer :all]))

(defn my-add [x y]
  (+ x y))

(deftest addition
  (testing
    (is (= 4 (my-add 2 2)))
    (is (= 7 (my-add 3 4)))))

ch4.core-test> (run-tests)
```

```
Testing ch4.core-test

Ran 1 tests containing 2 assertions.
0 failures, 0 errors.
{:test 1, :pass 2, :fail 0, :error 0, :type :summary}
```

You can also nest the testing macro arbitrarily deep to create multiple contexts similar to a style made popular by RSpec:

```
(deftest addition
  (testing "using let to bind x to 2"
    (let [x 2]
      (is (= 4 (my-add x 2)))
      (is (= 7 (my-add x 5)))
      (testing "and y to 3"
        (let [y 3]
          (is (= 5 (my-add x y)))))))
  (testing "adding negative numbers"
    (is (= -3 (my-add -10 7)))
    (is (= 5 (my-add 10 -5)))))
```

If you were to change the test for (is (= 5 (my-add x y))) to be incorrect, such as (is (= 6 (my-add x y))), then the test runner will simply append the strings following the testing macro to give you a context where the test is failing.

```
Testing ch4.core-test

FAIL in (addition) (core_test.clj:15)
using let to bind x to 2 and y to 3
expected: (= 6 (my-add x y))
  actual: (not (= 6 5))

Ran 1 tests containing 5 assertions.
1 failures, 0 errors.
{:test 1, :pass 4, :fail 1, :error 0, :type :summary}
```

As you can see in the output, the error occurs inside of the addition test, but more specifically: using let to bind x to 2 and y to 3.

are

If typing is over and over in the same testing block feels like you're violating DRY (Don't Repeat Yourself) principles, then you're in luck. There is also a macro called are, which allows you to define a template and provide concrete examples:

```
(deftest addition
  (testing
    (are [expected actual] (= expected actual)
        7 (my-add 2 5)
        4 (my-add 2 2)))
  (testing "adding negative numbers"
    (are [expected actual] (= expected actual)
      5 (my-add 10 -5)
      -3 (my-add -10 7))))
```

As you can see—because the test in the `is` macro follows a similar pattern—you can clean it up a bit and provide a more concise definition to the test. If you later discover another example you want to test for one of these functions, you can simply add the two parameters to your list of examples, instead of having to duplicate an entire `is` macro.

Using Fixtures

If you're at all familiar with other testing frameworks, you may be asking yourself right now, "How do I execute setup and teardown code in my tests?" If you need to set up some sort of state before running tests, such as inserting data into a database, you need to leverage fixtures to do so. The way to define fixtures in `clojure.test` is to define a normal function, which takes a single argument, or a function. The body of the fixture function then performs any setup tasks that need to occur before executing the function passed to the fixture, before performing any cleanup after calling the `passed` function. To tell `clojure.test` to execute these functions around your tests, just hook them into the testing lifecycle by using the use-fixtures form as shown here:

```
(ns ch4.core-test
  (:require [clojure.test :refer :all]
            [ch4.core :refer :all]))

(defn my-add [x y]
  (+ x y))

(defn my-sub [x y]
  (- x y))

(deftest addition
  (is (= 4 (my-add 2 2))))

(deftest subtraction
  (is (= 3 (my-sub 7 4))))

(defn once-fixture [f]
  (println "setup once")
  (f)
  (println "teardown once"))

(defn each-fixture [f]
  (println "setup each")
  (f)
  (println "teardown each"))

(use-fixtures :each each-fixture)
(use-fixtures :once once-fixture)
```

Fixtures that are specified with the `:each` keyword are run around every `deftest` macro defined, and fixtures configured with the `:once` keyword are executed only once for all tests defined. You can see the output below after running `lein test`.

```
Testing ch4.core-test
setup once
setup each
```

```
        teardown each
        setup each
        teardown each
        teardown once

        Ran 2 tests containing 2 assertions.
        0 failures, 0 errors.
        {:test 2, :pass 2, :fail 0, :error 0, :type :summary}
```

Notice that you only see `setup once` being output at the very beginning of the test execution, then `teardown once` being executed at the very end.

TESTING STRATEGIES

In some ways, testing in Clojure is much easier than testing in any imperative language. Because of Clojure's focus on values and immutability, many classes of tests simply fade away into obscurity. For example, in many other languages, because there are methods that are executed solely for their side effects, you have to rely on a testing construct called a spy to verify that some interaction between the objects under test happened. In Clojure, you should be concerned with the values that are returned from the functions, so you don't generally need to concern yourself with such tests.

Let's examine some of the likely scenarios that you'll encounter when testing your Clojure applications. You will use the sample code that can be found at `https://github.com/backstopmedia/ clojurebook`. This sample application is a simple ROI (Return On Investment) calculator that interacts with the Yahoo Financial APIs in order to retrieve historical stock pricing information. It's simple enough so you don't get bogged down in too many details; however, it illustrates most of the testing and design concepts covered in the rest of this chapter. Hopefully, you'll see how much simpler testing in Clojure seems when compared to other testing ecosystems.

In an ideal world, all tests would be simple and isolated, but in the real world, you're often required to interact with some sort of external service in order to get things done. Whether you're running queries against a database, fetching some data from the file system, or calling a web service, your tests should be repeatable and not dependent on the availability of these services. In the next few sections we'll discuss strategies to help in mitigating this non-deterministic behavior.

Tests Against DB

When it comes to testing against a database, there are usually two schools of thought. The first is to start with a pristine database, then set up whatever data you'll need for the test, and once the test is done, do it all over again. One problem with this approach is that as your application gets larger, it will cause your tests to run slower and slower. The other issue is that sometimes you don't have the luxury of starting with a clean database. Finally, you may require entirely too much data to exist in the database in order to run meaningful tests, so it would be cumbersome to try and manage that.

The other option is to have each of your tests run inside a transaction, and then have that transaction automatically rolled back at the end of your test run. To illustrate, let's create a simple database and table to hold a list of stock symbols you may want to use with the sample application.

Let's begin by opening up the REPL by typing `lein repl` in the root of your project. First, create a variable to hold the database connection information:

```
user=> (def db "postgresql://localhost:5432/fincalc")
#'user/db
```

Now you can go ahead and create the table using the following command.

```
user=> (sql/db-do-commands db (sql/create-table-ddl :stocks [:symbol "varchar(10)"]
))
(0)
```

This will create a table with a single column named `symbol` and mark it as being the primary key for the table. Once that is created, go ahead and populate it with some data using the following command.

```
(sql/insert! db :stocks {:symbol "AAPL"}
                        {:symbol "MSFT"}
                        {:symbol "YHOO"}
                        {:symbol "AMZN"}
                        {:symbol "GOOGL"}
                        {:symbol "FB"})
```

Here are two simple database functions that you want to test:

```
(ns fincalc.db
  (:require [clojure.java.jdbc :as sql]))

(defn get-symbols [db-spec]
  (map :symbol (sql/query db-spec ["select * from stocks"])))

(defn add-symbol [db-spec sym]
  (sql/insert! db-spec :stocks {:symbol sym}))
```

Now let's take a look at the code for the test.

```
(ns fincalc.db-test
  (:require [clojure.test :refer :all]
            [clojure.java.jdbc :as sql]
            [fincalc.db :refer :all]))

(declare ^:dynamic *txn*)

(def db "postgresql://localhost:5432/fincalc")

(use-fixtures :each
  (fn [f]
    (sql/with-db-transaction
      [transaction db]
      (sql/db-set-rollback-only! transaction)
      (binding [*txn* transaction] (f)))))

(deftest retrieve-all-stocks
  (testing
    (is (some #{"AAPL"} (get-symbols *txn*)))
    (is (some #{"YHOO"} (get-symbols *txn*)))))
```

```
(deftest insert-new-symbol
  (testing
    (add-symbol *txn* "NOK")
    (is (some #{"NOK"} (get-symbols *txn*)))))

(deftest inserted-symbol-rolled-back
  (testing
    (is (not (some #{"NOK"} (get-symbols *txn*))))))
```

In this example, you can see that you can leverage the `use-fixtures` functionality provided by `clojure.test`. This fixture is initiating a transaction, then immediately marking it as `db-set-rollback-only!`. This ensures that the transaction is rolled back regardless of what happens in the test function. This will help ensure that the tests are good citizens, and that you don't leave the database in an inconsistent state. As you can see in the `insert-new-symbol` test, the new stock symbol "NOK" is added to the database, so when calling `get-symbols` you can see that it exists in the list of stocks. In the very next test, however, you'll check to see if it exists in the table to make sure the previous insert has indeed been rolled back.

Testing Ring Handlers

When developing web apps in Clojure using Ring, your handlers are simple functions. This means that you can test them as you would any other function. For example, if you want to test the /api/ stocks endpoint in the sample application that returns a list of stock symbols stored in the database as a JSON array, you can write a test like the one here, which you can find in the `test/fincalc/api_test.clj` file:

```
(ns fincalc.api-test
  (:require [fincalc.api :refer :all]
            [cheshire.core :as json]
            [clojure.test :refer :all]))

(deftest get-all-stocks
  (testing
    (is (some #{"AAPL"} (json/parse-string (all-stocks))))))
```

As you can see, you can test the all-stocks function as if it were any normal function, which it really is. Testing your Ring handlers as simple functions will only get you so far. This does nothing to ensure that your URL mappings and request parameter bindings are behaving as expected. It also does not allow you to test other things such as HTTP response code, headers, or other things about the actual response. To better enable this level of testing you can leverage the `ring-mock` library. Rewrite the above test to be a bit better:

```
(ns fincalc.api-test
  (:require [fincalc.handler :refer [app]]
            [fincalc.api :refer :all]
            [cheshire.core :as json]
            [clojure.test :refer :all]
            [ring.mock.request :as mock]))
```

```
(deftest get-all-stocks
  (testing
      (is (some #{"AAPL"} (json/parse-string (all-stocks))))))

(deftest get-all-stocks-ring-mock
  (let [response (app (mock/request :get "/api/stocks"))]
    (is (= (:status response) 200))
    (is (some #{"AAPL"} (json/parse-string (:body response))))))
```

The `ring-mock` library allows you to construct mock HTTP requests to pass to your application object you've defined in the `src/fincalc/handler.clj` file, as if the servlet container were making a real request. While the `ring-mock` library is nice, it does have its limitations. If you need to test complex interactions, or things that rely on some session state, you'll have a hard time using the `ring-mock` library alone. To allow this level of testing, there is another library you can use called the `peridot` (`https://github.com/xeqi/peridot`) library. Peridot is a testing library that is based on the `Rack::Test` suite from Ruby.

Not only does Peridot allow you to test your handlers by calling their endpoints, it also allows you to test complex interactions across multiple requests, because it maintains cookies and sessions for you across requests. It manages to do this by use of the threading macro ->, which it's designed around. This means that you can do things like authenticate in one request, then call a secured endpoint without having to mock or do devious things to simulate an authenticated state.

To illustrate how to use the Peridot library, let's create a simple example. Here is a sample definition of a simple Ring handler:

```
(ns simple-api.handler
  (:require [compojure.core :refer :all]
            [compojure.route :as route]
            [ring.middleware.session :as session]
            [ring.middleware.defaults :refer [wrap-defaults site-defaults]]))

(defn login [req]
  (let [user (get-in req [:params :user])
        session (get-in req [:session])]
    {:body "Success"
     :session (assoc session :user user)}))

(defn say-hello [{session :session}]
  (if (:user session)
    {:body (str "Hello, " (:user session))}
    {:body "Hello World"}))

(defroutes app-routes
  (GET "/" req say-hello)
  (POST "/login" req login)
  (route/not-found "Not Found"))

(def app
  (-> app-routes session/wrap-session))
```

Here are two very simple endpoints. The first is the /login endpoint, which is simply going to store a user in the session. The second endpoint is the /, which will return a generic Hello World if no user is stored in the session, and a more personalized one if there is. Here is the test code showing how to leverage Peridot:

```
(ns simple-api.handler-test
  (:require [clojure.test :refer :all]
            [peridot.core :refer :all]
            [simple-api.handler :refer :all]))

(deftest test-app
  (testing "main route logged in user"
    (let [response (:response (-> (session app)
                                  (request "/login"
                                           :request-method :post
                                           :params {:user "Jeremy"})
                                  (request "/")))]
      (is (= (:status response) 200))
      (is (= (:body response) "Hello World"))))

  (testing "main route"
    (let [response (:response (-> (session app)
                                  (request "/")))]
      (is (= (:status response) 200))
      (is (= (:body response) "Hello World")))))
```

As you can see, you can exercise a test that spans multiple requests.

Mocking/Stubbing Using with-redefs

Sometimes, though, you don't want your tests to interact with external services. In those instances, you need to leverage some sort of mocking/stubbing technique. In Clojure you have that ability built right into the language itself with two functions called with-redefs and with-redefs-fn. To illustrate, let's take a look at the src/fincalc/core.clj file:

```
(ns fincalc.core
  (:require [clj-time.core :as t]
            [clj-time.format :as f]
            [cemerick.url :refer (url)]
            [cheshire.core :as json]
            [clj-http.client :as client]))

(defn today []
  (t/today))

(defn one-year-ago
  ([] (one-year-ago (today)))
  ([date] (t/minus date (t/years 1))))

(defn yesterday []
  (t/minus (today) (t/days 1)))
  ...
```

You can see the two methods here that are very dependent on the current date. You can test these:

```
(ns fincalc.core-test
  (:require [clojure.test :refer :all]
            [clj-time.core :as t]
            [fincalc.core :refer :all]))

(deftest date-calculations
  (testing "1 year ago"
    (is (= (t/minus (t/today) (t/years 1)) (one-year-ago)))))
```

If you look at this test above, it exhibits a distinct code smell known as The Ugly Mirror (http://jasonrudolph.com/blog/2008/07/30/testing-anti-patterns-the-ugly-mirror/). If the test itself mirrors the exact implementation as the actual code, then it's not a very useful test. So how do you rewrite this test to more accurately express the intent of the test without having to resort to mirroring the implementation? You can leverage Clojure's built in ability to mock functions using with-redefs as shown here:

```
(ns fincalc.core-test
  (:require [clojure.test :refer :all]
            [clj-time.core :as t]
            [fincalc.core :refer :all]))

(deftest date-calculations
  (testing "1 year ago"
    (is (= (t/minus (t/today) (t/years 1)) (one-year-ago)))))

(deftest date-calculations-with-redefs
  (with-redefs [t/today (fn [] (t/local-date 2016 1 10))]
    (testing "1 year  ago"
      (are [exp actual] (= exp actual)
        (t/local-date 2015 1 10) (one-year-ago)
        (t/local-date 2015 1 1) (one-year-ago (t/local-date 2016 1 1))))
    (testing "yesterday"
      (is (= (t/local-date 2016 1 9) (yesterday))))))
```

As you can see, the date calculations have been rewritten to test using with-redefs. You make use of it in the same way that you use let and let* to define local variables. Using with-redefs creates a local binding that will call your mock implementation of a function within the form; then when execution leaves the form, the local binding goes out of scope and Clojure rebinds the original function as it was before.

You must take great care when using with-redefs, because running tests concurrently could permanently change the binding if you aren't careful. This occurs when the execution of your code is complete and it tries to rebind the function or variable back to its original value. If there are many threads executing at once, the function or variable may have already had its binding changed, so when with-redefs gets executed again, it will store off what it thinks is the original implementation of the function. Then when it is finished executing, it will rebind the bogus implementation as illustrated here from the ClojureDocs for with-redefs:

```
user> (defn ten [] 10)
#'user/ten
```

```
user> (doall (pmap #(with-redefs [ten (fn [] %)] (ten)) (range 20 100)))
...
user> (ten)
79
```

This is more of an issue if your actual code, not your tests, uses `with-redefs`. However, this may be what you're experiencing, if you are seeing inconsistent behavior in your tests that are making heavy use of `with-redefs`.

Redefining Dynamic Vars

Another technique for mocking out your dependencies involves using dynamic vars and changing the binding during the execution of your tests. This provides the thread safety that is missing when using `with-redefs`; however, you must now define your functions that you may want to mock out as being dynamic. You can rewrite the date functions from earlier to show this technique:

```
(ns fincalc.core
  (:require [clj-time.core :as t]
            [clj-time.format :as f]
            [cemerick.url :refer (url)]
            [cheshire.core :as json]
            [clj-http.client :as client]))

(defn ^:dynamic today []
  (t/today))

(defn one-year-ago
  ([] (one-year-ago (today)))
  ([date] (t/minus date (t/years 1))))

(defn yesterday []
  (t/minus (today) (t/days 1)))
```

Notice the only thing that had to change in the source was to add the `^:dynamic` decoration to the `today` function? Now you can update your tests:

```
(ns fincalc.core-test
  (:require [clojure.test :refer :all]
            [clj-time.core :as t]
            [fincalc.core :refer :all]))

(deftest date-calculations
  (testing "1 year ago"
    (is (= (t/minus (t/today) (t/years 1)) (one-year-ago)))))

(deftest date-calculations-with-redefs
  (binding [today (fn [] (t/local-date 2016 1 10))]
    (testing "1 year  ago"
      (are [exp actual] (= exp actual)
        (t/local-date 2015 1 10) (one-year-ago)
        (t/local-date 2015 1 1) (one-year-ago (t/local-date 2016 1 1))))
    (testing "yesterday"
      (is (= (t/local-date 2016 1 9) (yesterday))))))
```

> **NOTE** *Again, you didn't have to make drastic changes to the test code, since you just replaced* with-redefs *with* binding *so everything behaves as it did earlier.*

Record/Replay with VCR

If your application makes use of external APIs that return a significant amount of data, sometimes mocking is not a feasible solution. The sheer amount of setup code that would be required is time consuming not only to create, but to maintain if you need to change it later on. As an example, let's create a function that will call the Yahoo Finance APIs to fetch data about stocks, and return the closing price for a given stock on a given day. Knowing that this data changes quite frequently, how in the world can you test that your function returns the correct data? Mocking and stubbing would work; however, the tests would be littered with all kinds of noise for setting up the mock data to be returned from the service.

Instead, you can use a library called vcr-clj (https://github.com/gfredericks/vcr-clj) to record and play back calls to this external service. Here is the src/fincalc/core.clj file that contains the test functions:

```clojure
(ns fincalc.core
  (:require [clj-time.core :as t]
            [clj-time.format :as f]
            [cemerick.url :refer (url)]
            [cheshire.core :as json]
            [clj-http.client :as client]))

(defn ^:dynamic today []
  (t/today))

(defn one-year-ago
  ([] (one-year-ago (today)))
  ([date] (t/minus date (t/years 1))))

(defn yesterday []
  (t/minus (today) (t/days 1)))

(defn build-yql [sym date]
  (let [formatted-date (f/unparse-local-date (f/formatters :year-month-day) date)]
    (str "select * from yahoo.finance.historicaldata where symbol = \"" sym  "\"
         and startDate = \"" formatted-date "\" and endDate = \""
         formatted-date "\"")))

(defn build-get-url [sym date]
  (-> (url "https://query.yahooapis.com/v1/public/yql")
      (assoc :query {:q (build-yql sym date)
                     :format "json"
                     :env "store://datatables.org/alltableswithkeys"})
      str))
```

```clojure
(defn get-close-for-symbol [sym date]
  (loop [close-date date retries 5]
    (let [result (get-in
                   (json/parse-string
                     (:body (client/get (build-get-url sym close-date))))
                   ["query" "results" "quote" "Adj_Close"])]
      (if (and (nil? result) (> retries 0))
        (recur (t/minus close-date (t/days 1)) (dec retries))
        (read-string result)))))

(defn roi [initial earnings]
  (double (* 100 (/ (- earnings initial) initial))))
```

As you can see, you're making a call to the Yahoo API by issuing a GET request in the `get-close-for-symbol` function. In order to test this and have repeatable results, you can record and replay the results from this HTTP request by wrapping the test using the `with-cassette` macro:

```clojure
(ns fincalc.core-test
  (:require [clojure.test :refer :all]
            [clj-time.core :as t]
            [vcr-clj.clj-http :refer [with-cassette]]
            [fincalc.core :refer :all]))

...

(deftest vcr-tests
  (with-cassette :stocks
    (is (= 97.129997 (get-close-for-symbol "AAPL" (t/local-date 2016 1 17))))
    (is (= 29.139999 (get-close-for-symbol "YHOO" (t/local-date 2016 1 17))))))
```

Each time you run these tests, `vcr-clj` will check to see if there is a cassette in the /cassettes directory of the project, and if that cassette contains a recorded request that matches the HTTP request being called. If it does exist, it will simply return the previously recorded results. That way you can be sure that every time you call `fetch-stock-price`, it will return the same stock data as before. You could even disconnect from the network altogether and your tests will still run and pass.

If for some reason you wish to record new results, you simply delete the file in the /cassettes directory with the corresponding filename of the cassette you wish to re-record.

MEASURING CODE QUALITY

Having a comprehensive suite of quality tests is certainly a good thing to have when developing software, but how can you be certain that it's enough? Sometimes just measuring test coverage is not enough, and sometimes you need to analyze your code to identify potential bugs and improvements that can be made to the overall quality of your code. In this next section you'll get to peek at a few useful tools to help you with that.

Code Coverage with Cloverage

Code coverage, while being a useful metric, is not a golden hammer (http://c2.com/cgi/wiki?GoldenHammer). Unfortunately, it is a metric that is often misused and misrepresented.

It will not guarantee that your code is free of defects if you somehow achieve 100 percent code coverage.

When used properly though, it is a very useful metric to help identify what areas of your code you may have overlooked when testing, especially if those areas that are lacking coverage are of high risk.

In order to measure code coverage in your Clojure projects, you need to leverage a tool called cloverage (https://github.com/lshift/cloverage). As of this writing, cloverage only supports measuring code coverage with the clojure.test library. In order to use the plugin, you can add [lein-cloverage "1.0.6"] to the :plugins section of your ~/.lein/profiles.clj file. Once you have added that you will be able to run lein cloverage in your project directory. After it's done running your tests, you'll see a nice summary printed out to the console:

```
Loading namespaces:  (fincalc.views.contents fincalc.api fincalc.db fincalc.core
fincalc.handler fincalc.views.layout)
Test namespaces:  (fincalc.api-test fincalc.core-test fincalc.db-test
fincalc.handler-test fincalc.views.contents-test)
Loaded  fincalc.core  .
Loaded  fincalc.db  .
Loaded  fincalc.api  .
Loaded  fincalc.views.layout  .
Loaded  fincalc.views.contents  .
Loaded  fincalc.handler  .
Instrumented namespaces.

Testing fincalc.api-test

Testing fincalc.core-test

Testing fincalc.db-test

Testing fincalc.handler-test

Testing fincalc.views.contents-test

Ran 10 tests containing 18 assertions.
0 failures, 0 errors.
Ran tests.
Produced output in /Users/jeremy/Projects/clojure/fincalc/target/coverage  .
HTML: file:///Users/jeremy/Projects/clojure/fincalc/target/coverage/index.html
```

:name	:forms_percent	:lines_percent
fincalc.api	29.41 %	55.56 %
fincalc.core	59.78 %	71.43 %
fincalc.handler	51.13 %	68.42 %
fincalc.views.contents	55.04 %	50.00 %
fincalc.views.layout	53.26 %	100.00 %

```
Files with 100% coverage: 1

Forms covered: 54.39 %
Lines covered: 68.06 %
```

Cloverage will also output an HTML report that you can drill down into and see exactly what lines of code have been covered by tests and which haven't. Figure 4-1 shows the HTML summary page, which can be found in the `target/coverage` folder of your project.

Namespace	Forms		Forms %	Lines		Lines %	Total	Blank	Instrumented
fincalc.api	10	24	29.41 %	5	4	55.56 %	14	2	9
fincalc.core	92		100.00 %	21		100.00 %	37	7	21
fincalc.db	20		100.00 %	6		100.00 %	10	3	6
fincalc.handler	68	65	51.13 %	10	3 6	68.42 %	31	5	19
fincalc.views.contents	71	58	55.04 %	7	7	50.00 %	33	3	14
fincalc.views.layout	98	86	53.26 %	2	1	100.00 %	17	2	3
Totals:			60.64 %			76.39 %			

FIGURE 4-1

Then if you click on the hyperlink for an individual namespace, it will drill down into the coverage report and show you the actual line-by-line coverage as shown in Figure 4-2.

```
001  (ns fincalc.api
002    (:require [fincalc.core :refer :all]
003              [fincalc.db :refer :all]
004              [cheshire.core :as json]))
005
006  (defn all-stocks []
007    (let [stocks (get-symbols db-spec)]
008      (json/generate-string stocks)))
009
010  (defn calculate [sym]
011    (let* [final (get-close-for-symbol sym (yesterday))
012           initial (get-close-for-symbol sym (one-year-ago))
013           result (roi initial final)]
014      (json/generate-string {:initial initial :final final :roi result})))
```

FIGURE 4-2

In Figure 4-2 you can see that we've managed to test the `all-stocks` function sufficiently, but have not tested the body of the `calculate` function. The cloverage plugin provides many options for how it measures coverage, as well as what format to output your report in to support various continuous integration servers. All of these options can be found in the `parse-args` function in the `cloverage.clj` source file within the project (https://github.com/lshift/cloverage/blob/master/cloverage/src/cloverage/coverage.clj#L78). Unfortunately, the project doesn't provide much in the way of documenting them elsewhere.

Static Analysis with kibit and bikeshed

A couple of very useful libraries that fall under the same category as cloverage, but should not be considered competing libraries, are `kibit` and `bikeshed`. Both provide static analysis of your code to help identify potential problems and make suggestions about your coding style to ensure it adheres to Clojure's best practices; they will, however, report different things about your code.

The first plugin to look at is `lein-kibit` (https://github.com/jonase/kibit), and to use this plugin you can add `[lein-kibit "0.1.2"]` to the `:plugins` section of your `~/.lein/profiles .clj` file. You can then run the analysis against your project by running `lein kibit` in your project directory. The output shown in the following snippet is a result of running `lein kibit` against the `ring-core` project:

```
At /Users/jeremy/Projects/clojure/ring/ring-core/src/ring/middleware/session.clj:61
:
Consider using:
  (update-in response [:cookies] merge cookie)
instead of:
  (assoc response :cookies (merge (response :cookies) cookie))

At /Users/jeremy/Projects/clojure/ring/ring-core/src/ring/middleware/session.clj:
102:
Consider using:
  (session-response (handler new-request) new-request options)
instead of:
  (-> (handler new-request) (session-response new-request options))

At /Users/jeremy/Projects/clojure/ring/ring-core/src/ring/util/request.clj:58:
Consider using:
  (clojure.string/join (:body request))
instead of:
  (apply str (:body request))
```

You can see that `kibit` is primarily concerned with code style. It makes helpful suggestions about how you can improve your Clojure code to follow a style more in line with the community. There are some limitations, though, and you're likely to get some false positives returned in the analysis.

The second plugin to look at is the `bikeshed` plugin (https://github.com/dakrone/lein-bikeshed). This plugin is installed like other plugins discussed in this section. Simply add `[lein-bikeshed "0.2.0"]` to the `:plugins` section of your `~/.lein/profiles.clj` file. Then you can run `lein bikeshed` in your project directory. Once again we'll look as some output from running `lein bikeshed` against the `ring-core` library:

```
Checking for lines longer than 80 characters.
Badly formatted files:
/Users/jeremy/Projects/clojure/ring/ring-core/src/ring/middleware/cookies.clj:23:
:doc "Attributes defined by RFC6265 that apply to the Set-Cookie header."}
/Users/jeremy/Projects/clojure/ring/ring-core/src/ring/middleware/cookies.clj:81:
(instance? DateTime value) (str ";" attr-name "=" (unparse rfc822-formatter value))
/Users/jeremy/Projects/clojure/ring/ring-core/src/ring/middleware/file.clj:25:
(let [opts (merge {:root (str root-path), :index-files? true, :allow-symlinks?
false} opts)]
...

Checking for lines with trailing whitespace.
Badly formatted files:
/Users/jeremy/Projects/clojure/ring/ring-core/src/ring/middleware/params.clj:56:
Accepts the following options:
/Users/jeremy/Projects/clojure/ring/ring-core/src/ring/util/response.clj:20:
```

```
"Returns a Ring response for an HTTP 302 redirect. Status may be
...

Checking for files ending in blank lines.
No files found.

Checking for redefined var roots in source directories.
No with-redefs found.

Checking whether you keep up with your docstrings.
120/159 [75.47%] functions have docstrings.
Use -v to list functions without docstrings

Checking for arguments colliding with clojure.core functions.
#'ring.middleware.cookies/write-value: 'key' is colliding with a core function
#'ring.middleware.multipart-params.temp-file/do-every: 'delay' is colliding
with a core function
...
```

The `bikeshed` plugin runs several different inspections. The first few inspections deal with the formatting of your source files, whether you have lines containing more than 80 characters long, trailing whitespace, or files ending with blank lines. These are of course simple housekeeping tasks. The next inspection checks to see if you are potentially introducing bugs into your code by using `with-redefs`. Then `bikeshed` checks to see if you're a good citizen with your code and ensures that you define docstrings on all of your functions. This last check is probably the most important, because it points out areas in your code where you are facing potential namespace collisions and may need to adjust your `:requires` statements in your files to exclude certain functions in namespaces you're requiring, or rename functions you are defining. You should take each and every one of these warnings seriously, and determine whether or not they need to be addressed.

Keeping Dependencies Under Control

Sometimes you run across strange bugs due to mismatched versions of dependencies. Even if you only directly depend on a small handful of libraries, the transient dependency graph can quickly become unwieldy. Leiningen provides you with the tools to help keep tabs on all of this. In order to retrieve a graph of all of the libraries your project depends on, you simply type `lein deps :tree` in your project directory. Leiningen will then gladly provide you with a multitude of information. The following snippet is from the output of running `lein deps :tree` on the sample project:

```
Possibly confusing dependencies found:
[lein-ring "0.9.7"] -> [org.clojure/data.xml "0.0.8"] -> [org.clojure/clojure
"1.4.0"]
 overrides
[lein-kibit "0.1.2"] -> [jonase/kibit "0.1.2"] -> [org.clojure/core.logic
"0.8.10"] -> [org.clojure/clojure "1.6.0"]
 and
[lein-ancient "0.6.8"] -> [jansi-clj "0.1.0"] -> [org.clojure/clojure "1.5.1"]
 and
[lein-ancient "0.6.8"] -> [version-clj "0.1.2"] -> [org.clojure/clojure "1.6.0"]
 and
[lein-ancient "0.6.8"] -> [rewrite-clj "0.4.12"] -> [org.clojure/clojure "1.6.0"
:exclusions [org.clojure/clojure]]
 and
```

```
[lein-ancient "0.6.8"] -> [ancient-clj "0.3.11" :exclusions [com.amazonaws/aws-
java-sdk-s3]] -> [org.clojure/clojure "1.7.0" :exclusions [joda-time
org.clojure/clojure]]
 and
[lein-kibit "0.1.2"] -> [jonase/kibit "0.1.2"] -> [org.clojure/clojure "1.6.0"]

Consider using these exclusions:
[lein-kibit "0.1.2" :exclusions [org.clojure/clojure]]
[lein-ancient "0.6.8" :exclusions [org.clojure/clojure]]
[lein-ancient "0.6.8" :exclusions [org.clojure/clojure]]
[lein-ancient "0.6.8" :exclusions [org.clojure/clojure]]
[lein-ancient "0.6.8" :exclusions [org.clojure/clojure]]
[lein-kibit "0.1.2" :exclusions [org.clojure/clojure]]
```

As you can see, this shows you the few libraries that can potentially cause issues. It is telling you that several of the libraries included in your project depend on conflicting versions of `org.clojure/clojure`, and it gives you a helpful suggestion to mitigate this potential issue. The rest of the output is shown here:

```
[cheshire "5.5.0"]
  [com.fasterxml.jackson.core/jackson-core "2.5.3"]
  [com.fasterxml.jackson.dataformat/jackson-dataformat-cbor "2.5.3"]
  [com.fasterxml.jackson.dataformat/jackson-dataformat-smile "2.5.3"]
  [tigris "0.1.1"]
[cider/cider-nrepl "0.10.0-20151127.123841-44"]
  [org.tcrawley/dynapath "0.2.3" :exclusions [[org.clojure/clojure]]]
[clj-http "2.0.0"]
  [commons-codec "1.10" :exclusions [[org.clojure/clojure]]]
  [commons-io "2.4" :exclusions [[org.clojure/clojure]]]
  [org.apache.httpcomponents/httpclient "4.5" :exclusions [[org.clojure/clojure]]]
    [commons-logging "1.2"]
  [org.apache.httpcomponents/httpcore "4.4.1" :exclusions [[org.clojure/clojure]]]
  [org.apache.httpcomponents/httpmime "4.5" :exclusions [[org.clojure/clojure]]]
  [potemkin "0.4.1" :exclusions [[org.clojure/clojure]]]
    [clj-tuple "0.2.2"]
    [riddley "0.1.10"]
  [slingshot "0.12.2" :exclusions [[org.clojure/clojure]]]
[clj-time "0.11.0"]
  [joda-time "2.8.2"]
[clojure-complete "0.2.3" :exclusions [[org.clojure/clojure]]]
[com.cemerick/url "0.1.1"]
  [pathetic "0.5.0"]
    [com.cemerick/clojurescript.test "0.0.4"]
      [org.clojure/clojurescript "0.0-1586"]
        [com.google.javascript/closure-compiler "r2180"]
          [args4j "2.0.16"]
          [com.google.code.findbugs/jsr305 "1.3.9"]
          [com.google.guava/guava "13.0.1"]
          [com.google.protobuf/protobuf-java "2.4.1"]
          [com.googlecode.jarjar/jarjar "1.1"]
          [org.apache.ant/ant "1.8.2"]
            [org.apache.ant/ant-launcher "1.8.2"]
          [org.json/json "20090211"]
        [org.clojure/google-closure-library "0.0-2029-2"]
          [org.clojure/google-closure-library-third-party "0.0-2029-2"]
        [org.mozilla/rhino "1.7R4"]
```

```
[com.gfredericks/vcr-clj "0.4.6" :scope "test"]
  [fs "1.3.3" :scope "test"]
    [org.apache.commons/commons-compress "1.3" :scope "test"]
  [org.clojure/data.codec "0.1.0" :scope "test"]
[compojure "1.4.0"]
  [clout "2.1.2"]
    [instaparse "1.4.0" :exclusions [[org.clojure/clojure]]]
  [medley "0.6.0"]
  [org.clojure/tools.macro "0.1.5"]
  [ring/ring-codec "1.0.0"]
  [ring/ring-core "1.4.0"]
    [commons-fileupload "1.3.1"]
    [crypto-equality "1.0.0"]
    [crypto-random "1.2.0"]
    [org.clojure/tools.reader "0.9.1"]
[hiccup "1.0.5"]
[javax.servlet/servlet-api "2.5" :scope "test"]
[org.clojure/clojure "1.7.0"]
[org.clojure/java.jdbc "0.4.1"]
[org.clojure/tools.nrepl "0.2.12"]
[org.postgresql/postgresql "9.4-1201-jdbc41"]
[ring/ring-defaults "0.1.5"]
  [ring/ring-anti-forgery "1.0.0"]
  [ring/ring-headers "0.1.3"]
  [ring/ring-ssl "0.2.1"]
[ring/ring-jetty-adapter "1.2.1"]
  [org.eclipse.jetty/jetty-server "7.6.8.v20121106"]
    [org.eclipse.jetty.orbit/javax.servlet "2.5.0.v201103041518"]
    [org.eclipse.jetty/jetty-continuation "7.6.8.v20121106"]
    [org.eclipse.jetty/jetty-http "7.6.8.v20121106"]
      [org.eclipse.jetty/jetty-io "7.6.8.v20121106"]
        [org.eclipse.jetty/jetty-util "7.6.8.v20121106"]
  [ring/ring-servlet "1.2.1"]
[ring/ring-mock "0.3.0" :scope "test"]
```

In the ever-changing world of software development, it's difficult to keep up with every version of every dependency of your project or library. Thankfully, someone has gone to the trouble to create a very useful plugin named `lein-ancient` that will look through each of the dependencies listed in your `project.clj` and determine whether or not there are newer versions available. In order to leverage this plugin just add `[lein-ancient "0.6.8"]` to the `:plugins` section in your `~/.lein/profiles.clj`. Once you have added this, you can run the `lein-ancient` command in your project directory. If there are any dependencies out of date in your project, you'll see them listed similar to the output shown here:

```
WARNING: update already refers to: #'clojure.core/update in namespace:
clj-http.client, being replaced by: #'clj-http.client/update
[ring/ring-jetty-adapter "1.4.0"] is available but we use "1.2.1"
[org.clojure/java.jdbc "0.4.2"] is available but we use "0.4.1"
[org.postgresql/postgresql "9.4.1207"] is available but we use "9.4-1201-jdbc41"
```

Empowered with this knowledge, you can decide whether or not you want to update your dependencies.

TESTING FRAMEWORK ALTERNATIVES

Testing frameworks and styles of testing are very much a personal preference. Fortunately, there are a number of different testing frameworks available to you. In this last section, let's examine a few of these frameworks briefly, comparing and contrasting them to what was discussed earlier in this chapter.

Expectations

Expectations (http://jayfields.com/expectations/) is probably one of the simplest testing frameworks available. It is based on clojure.test, but it's stripped down to the very basics of testing and rooted in the belief that each test should test one and only one thing. To use expectations in your project, you can add [expectations "2.0.9"] to the :dependencies section in your project.clj and [lein-expectations "0.0.7"] to the :plugins section. Then you can write your tests as shown here:

```
(ns sample.test.core
  (:use [expectations]))

(expect 2 (+ 1 1))
(expect [1 2] (conj [] 1 2))
(expect #{1 2} (conj #{} 1 2))
(expect {1 2} (assoc {} 1 2))
```

As you can see, the entirety of the framework revolves around a single construct, expect. This single macro is extremely flexible and powerful, but don't let its simplicity fool you. As you may have guessed by now, you can run these tests by executing lein expectations in the root of your project.

Speclj

Speclj (https://github.com/slagyr/speclj), pronounced speckle, is a testing framework that seems to be a favorite of converted Rubyists, probably because it's heavily inspired by the RSpec framework. Similar to RSpec, your tests are referred to as "specs" and should follow the naming convention of being postfixed with _spec.clj. It will follow the same convention for directories and namespaces as before, only in a directory named spec instead of test. Here is an example directory structure for a project that uses speclj for testing:

```
├── README.md
├── project.clj
├── spec
│   └── speclj_project
│       └── core_spec.clj
└── src
    └── speclj_project
        └── core.clj
```

In order to use speclj in your project, you'll need to add the following configuration to your project.clj file:

```
:profiles {:dev {:dependencies [[speclj "3.3.1"]]}}
:plugins [[speclj "3.3.1"]]
:test-paths ["spec"])
```

Once you have that configured, you can rewrite simple tests from earlier in the chapter for `my-add` and `my-sub` as specs:

```
(ns speclj-project.core-spec
  (:require [speclj.core :refer :all]
            [speclj-project.core :refer :all]))

(describe "addition"
          (it "can add two numbers correctly"
            (should (= 4 (my-add 2 2)))))

(describe "subtraction"
          (it "can subtract two numbers"
            (should (= 3 (my-sub 7 4)))))
```

Let's take a look at the pieces that make up the simple spec. The `describe` macro is the topmost construct in your specification, and is typically used to describe the context of your test. The `describe` form will contain any number of specifications denoted by the `it` macro. Then within the `it` form, you can make any number of assertions using `should`, `should-not`, or any of the other variants of `should`. To run your specs, you simply run the command `lein spec` in your project directory.

Cucumber

Cucumber (`http://cukes.info`) is a framework for running automated acceptance tests, designed to support a behavior driven development style. It gained popularity in the Ruby community as a part of the RSpec framework, but it soon forked off into its own project. Shortly after that, it was ported to run on other platforms such as the JVM, and now runs on a number of different platforms. Cucumber is designed to enable and encourage discussion between the developer and the customer to create a sort of executable documentation using a generic language known as Gherkin. Here is the example that is shown on the homepage of the Cucumber project:

```
Feature: Addition
  In order to avoid silly mistakes
  As a math idiot
  I want to be told the sum of two numbers

  Scenario: Add two numbers
    Given I have entered "50" into the calculator
    And I have entered "70" into the calculator
    When I press "add"
    Then the result should be "120" on the screen
```

As you can see, the language used to write these specifications is very much written in plain English, and with a little training and practice it can be collaborated on, or possibly even written, by your business users. Notice that they are written at a very high level, and should only exercise the external most layer of your applications such as a REST API or by interacting with the browser using Selenium.

Cucumber executes code based on these feature files by trying to match a step from your feature file to a matching step definition in one of your step definition files. An example step definition for the feature file above looks like the following:

```
(Given #"^I have entered \"(.*?)\" into the calculator$" [arg1]
  (do-something-cool-here))
```

The steps definition consists of a macro, in this case called Given, which contains a regular expression, with optional capture groups defined. These capture groups then get bound to the parameter list immediately following the regular expression. The rest of the macro consists of what you need to implement the step, whether that be to set up some state, click a link on the page, or assert some values.

Let's start off simply by defining a Cucumber feature to define the acceptance criteria for some REST APIs. Below is the feature file defined for interacting with the `/api/stocks` endpoints that can be found at `/features/stocks_api.feature`.

```
Feature: Stocks REST API
  As an admin
  I want to be view and modify the stocks table
  So that I can manage it appropriately

  Scenario: Get All Stocks
    When I send a GET request to "/api/stocks"
    Then the response status should be "200"
    And I should see the following JSON in the body:
    """
    ["AAPL"]
    """

  Scenario: Add New Stock
    When I send a POST request to "/api/stocks" with the following params:
    | param | value |
    | sym   | NOK   |
    Then the response status should be "201"
    And the response body should be empty
    And a stock with symbol "NOK" exists in the database

  Scenario: Remove Stock
    Given a stock with symbol "NOK" exists in the database
    When I send a DELETE request to "/api/stocks/NOK"
    Then the response status should be "204"
    And a stock with symbol "NOK" does not exist in the database
```

The first time you run `lein cucumber` in your project you will be presented with the following output:

```
Running cucumber...
Looking for features in:  [/Users/jeremy/Projects/clojure/fincalc/features]
Looking for glue in:  [/Users/jeremy/Projects/clojure/fincalc/features/
step_definitions]
UUUUUUUUUUU

3 Scenarios (3 undefined)
11 Steps (11 undefined)
0m0.000s


You can implement missing steps with the snippets below:

(When #"^I send a GET request to \"(.*?)\"$" [arg1]
  (comment  Write code here that turns the phrase above into concrete actions  )
  (throw (cucumber.api.PendingException.)))
```

```
(Then #"^the response status should be \"(.*?)\"$" [arg1]
  (comment  Write code here that turns the phrase above into concrete actions  )
  (throw (cucumber.api.PendingException.)))

(Then #"^I should see the following JSON in the body:$" [arg1]
  (comment  Write code here that turns the phrase above into concrete actions  )
  (throw (cucumber.api.PendingException.)))

(When #"^I send a POST request to \"(.*?)\" with the following:$"
  [arg1 arg2]
  (comment  Write code here that turns the phrase above into concrete actions  )
  (throw (cucumber.api.PendingException.)))

(Then #"^the response body should be empty$" []
  (comment  Write code here that turns the phrase above into concrete actions  )
  (throw (cucumber.api.PendingException.)))

(Then #"^a stock with symbol \"(.*?)\" exists in the database$" [arg1]
  (comment  Write code here that turns the phrase above into concrete actions  )
  (throw (cucumber.api.PendingException.)))

(Given #"^a stock with symbol \"(.*?)\" exists in the database$" [arg1]
  (comment  Write code here that turns the phrase above into concrete actions  )
  (throw (cucumber.api.PendingException.)))

(When #"^I send a DELETE request to \"(.*?)\"$" [arg1]
  (comment  Write code here that turns the phrase above into concrete actions  )
  (throw (cucumber.api.PendingException.)))

(Then #"^a stock with symbol \"(.*?)\" does not exist in the database$" [arg1]
  (comment  Write code here that turns the phrase above into concrete actions  )
  (throw (cucumber.api.PendingException.)))
```

This is exceptionally useful because it gives you the templates for implementing the step definitions without having to remember how to write the regular expressions. You can then go ahead and copy/paste this output directly into your steps definition file. The completed steps definition file for the stocks API can be found at /features/step-definitions/stock_api_steps.clj:

```
(require '[clojure.test :refer :all]
         '[clj-http.client :as client]
         '[cheshire.core :as json]
         '[fincalc.db :as db])

(def response (atom nil))
(def base-url "http://localhost:3000")

(When #"^I send a GET request to \"(.*?)\"$" [path]
      (let [endpoint (str base-url path)]
        (reset! response (client/get endpoint))))

(When #"^I send a POST request to \"(.*?)\" with the following params:$"
  [path req-params]
      (let [endpoint (str base-url path)
            form-params (kv-table->map req-params)]
        (reset! response (client/post endpoint {:form-params form-params}))))
```

```
(When #"^I send a DELETE request to \"(.*?)\"$" [path]
    (let [endpoint (str base-url path)]
      (reset! response (client/delete endpoint)))))

(Then #"^the response status should be \"(.*?)\"$" [status-code]
    (assert (= (str status-code) (str (:status @response))))))

(Then #"^I should see the following JSON in the body:$" [expected-body]
    (assert (= (json/parse-string expected-body)
               (json/parse-string (:body @response))))))

(Then #"^the response body should be empty$" []
    (assert (empty? (:body @response)))))

(Given #"^a stock with symbol \"(.*?)\" exists in the database$" [sym]
    (assert (not (empty? (db/get-symbol db/db-spec sym))))))

(Then #"^a stock with symbol \"(.*?)\" does not exist in the database$" [sym]
    (assert (empty? (db/get-symbol db/db-spec sym)))))
```

Notice how at the beginning of the steps definition style, we set up some global state to store our HTTP response. Without this, since each step is defined as a separate function, you don't have the ability to query your response after making the request. In addition, notice that you're using `assert` instead of `is` in tests for testing correctness. This is due to the way that Cucumber works under the covers and expects to see a `java.lang.AssertionError` in order to determine whether or not a step has passed or failed. Next, define a value to store the base URL for all of the HTTP requests. The next thing to take note of is how to handle the data table in the POST step. Use the `kv-table->map` function to convert the data table into a map so you can pass it as `:form-params` in the POST request.

Now that you have the step definitions implemented, you can run the Cucumber tests by using `lein cucumber` in the project directory. Since Cucumber executes against an actual running application, you have to ensure that your app is running by typing `lein ring server-headless` in another terminal window; otherwise your Cucumber tests will all fail.

One other thing to watch out for is that given how the Cucumber tests run against a live running system, there's no good way to wrap the tests in a transaction to have them roll back as earlier in the DB tests. Therefore, you'll need to be mindful to clean up after yourself somehow using either the `Before` and `After` step definitions, or somehow within the tests themselves.

Now that you can see how to leverage Cucumber to test your REST APIs, let's leverage it to test your application from end-to-end by using Selenium's webdriver API to remotely control a web browser such as Firefox. Start by taking a look at the feature file, which can be found at `features/roi_calc.feature`.

```
@ui
Feature: ROI Calculator
  As a budding investor
  I want to be able to check the ROI on various stocks
  So that I can determine whether or not to purchase a stock

  Scenario: Link in navbar takes me to homepage
    Given I am at the "homepage"
    When I click the title bar
    Then I should be at the "homepage"
```

```
Scenario: Submit a symbol for calculation
  Given I am at the "homepage"
  When I calculate the ROI for the symbol "AAPL"
  Then I should see an initial value
  And I should see a final value
  And I should see an ROI

Scenario: Page not found
  Given I am at an invalid page
  Then I should see a message stating "Page Not Found"
  When I click on the "Home" button
  Then I should be at the "homepage"
```

Notice the level of abstraction used to define these feature file steps. You don't define the feature as fine-grained steps of "click this field," "type this string," "click that button," etc. Instead, keep it at a high enough level that your customer would leave some of the implementation details out of the feature. Therefore, if you have to move things around or implement them in a different way, you don't have to rewrite the feature file.

Before you can implement the steps definition, you need to create a helper to manage the connection to the browser. This file can be found at `test/fincalc/browser.clj` and is shown here:

```
(ns fincalc.browser
  (:require [clj-webdriver.taxi :refer :all]))

(def ^:private browser-count (atom 0))

(defn browser-up
  "Start up a browser if it's not already started."
  []
  (when (= 1 (swap! browser-count inc))
    (set-driver! {:browser :firefox})
    (implicit-wait 60000)))

(defn browser-down
  "If this is the last request, shut the browser down."
  [& {:keys [force] :or {force false}}]
  (when (zero? (swap! browser-count (if force (constantly 0) dec)))
    (quit)))
```

For this example you're using the Firefox browser, but you can also configure it to use Chromium or even the headless PhantomJS browser if you wish. If you decide to use something other than Firefox, all you need to do is change the `:browser` symbol in `set-driver!`. Next, let's take a look at our step definitions for the feature:

```
(require '[clj-webdriver.taxi :as taxi]
         '[fincalc.browser :refer [browser-up browser-down]]
         '[clojure.test :refer :all])

(Before ["@ui"]
        (browser-up))
```

```
(After ["@ui"]
       (browser-down))

(Given #"^I am at the \"homepage\"$" []
       (taxi/to "http://localhost:3000/"))

(Given #"^I am at an invalid page$" []
       (taxi/to "http://localhost:3000/invalid"))

(When #"^I click the title bar$" []
      (taxi/click "a#brand-link"))

(Then #"^I should be at the \"homepage\"$" []
      (assert (= (taxi/title) "Home")))

(When #"^I calculate the ROI for the symbol \"(.*?)\"$" [sym]
      (taxi/input-text "input[name=\"sym\"]" sym)
      (taxi/click "button[type=\"submit\"]"))

(Then #"^I should see an initial value$" []
      (taxi/wait-until #(= (taxi/title) "Results"))
      (assert (re-find #"Stock price one year ago:" (taxi/text "#initial"))))

(Then #"^I should see a final value$" []
      (assert (re-find #"The latest close was" (taxi/text "#final"))))

(Then #"^I should see an ROI$" []
      (assert (re-find #"Calculated ROI" (taxi/text "#roi"))))

(Then #"^I should see a message stating \"(.*?)\"$" [arg1]
      (assert (= "Page Not Found" (taxi/text "h1.info-warning"))))

(When #"^I click on the \"Home\" button$" []
      (taxi/click "#go-home"))
```

This steps file looks similar to what you saw earlier for the REST API, with a few differences. The first one to take note of is the usage of the Before and After macros to start and kill the browser at the beginning and end of every Scenario. The parameter being passed to these macros, "@ui" indicates that you only want to run these on Scenarios that have been tagged with the "@ui" tag in the feature file, as was done above. Next, see how you can leverage the clj.webdriver.taxi library to interact with the browser. The documentation for this API can be found at https://github.com/semperos/clj-webdriver/wiki/Taxi-API-Documentation.

Finally, there are several different ways to output the results from the execution of lein cucumber, and a common one is the HTML report. By default, it will simply produce output using the progress plugin, but you can specify that it should also use the HTML plugin by typing lein cucumber --plugin html:target/cucumber --plugin progress. If you then open the HTML report in a browser, you should see a report like what is shown in Figure 4-3.

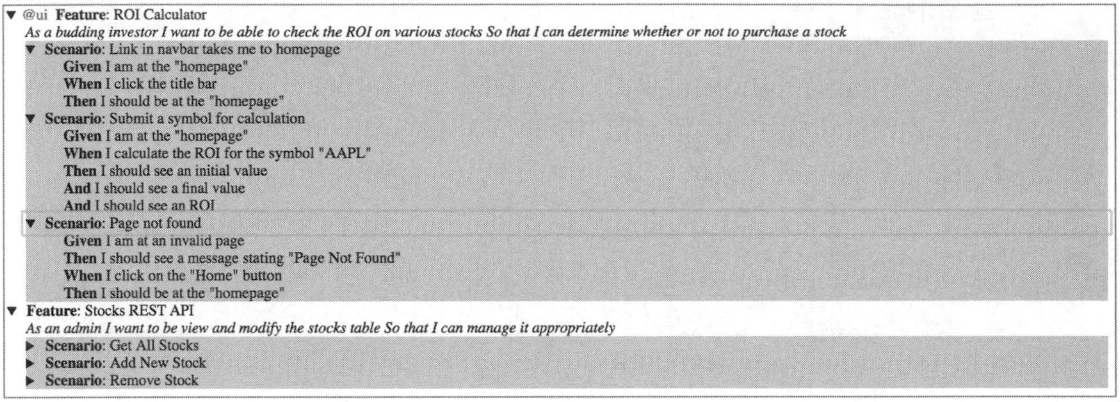

FIGURE 4-3

This output can then also serve as documentation that lives on with your project and hopefully never becomes out of date, because it is generated every time you execute your Cucumber tests.

These two simple examples should give you a good taste of what you can do with Cucumber. Unfortunately, we can't cover every use case or bit of the API, yet there are entire books dealing with this subject that do an outstanding job. Most of them are written to the Ruby or Java versions of Cucumber, but with a little effort you can translate the information to Clojure.

Kerodon

One last framework to look at is the Kerodon (`https://github.com/xeqi/kerodon`) framework. It's similar to Cucumber, in that it allows you to do acceptance level testing through the browser, but this time using Capybara instead of Selenium. Where they differ is that Kerodon is designed with the developer in mind, and Cucumber is designed with the product owner or business analyst in mind. If you don't have a product owner, business analyst, or similar type of person to collaborate on acceptance tests with, the overhead of writing Cucumber features may not make sense.

If you were to write a test to exercise the ROI calculator page similar to what we did in Cucumber, you would end up with something similar to the following:

```
(ns fincalc.integration.roi-calc-test
  (:require [clojure.test :refer :all]
            [kerodon.core :refer :all]
            [kerodon.test :refer :all]
            [fincalc.handler :refer [app]]))

(deftest user-can-calculate-roi-on-stock
  (-> (session app)
      (visit "/")
      (has (status? 200) "page exists")
      (within [:h2]
              (has (text? "Enter a Stock Symbol to calculate ROI on...")
                   "Header is there"))
      (fill-in :input.form-control "AAPL")
      (press :button)
```

```
(within [:h2]
        (has (text? "Results") "made it to results page"))
(within [:#initial]
        (has (some-text? "Stock price one year ago:")))
(within [:#final]
        (has (some-text? "The latest close was:")))
(within [:#roi]
        (has (some-text? "Calculated ROI"))))))
```

As you can see, the tests themselves are very fine grained and can get a bit verbose. So, consider abstracting some of the behaviors out to helper functions.

One thing to keep in mind when testing with Kerodon verse using Cucumber is how you don't need your application running when using Kerodon, because it doesn't run through an HTTP server. This allows you to use things like database transactions around your tests by leveraging fixtures. This will also make for faster execution times compared to using Cucumber, allowing them to run as part of your automated continuous integration suite. However, since it's not running through an actual browser against a running application, it may not detect and report errors stemming from issues specific to a web browser.

SUMMARY

We've covered a lot of information in this chapter, empowering you to more confidently test and improve your code. You were introduced to some common situations you'll encounter when trying to test your application code, from simple isolated unit tests, all the way to full end-to-end tests using both Kerodon and Cucumber.

The intent of this chapter was not to convince you to adopt any one testing methodology—whether it be test first, test last, or test during—but to instead show you how you can test your code more effectively. Testing, just like development itself, requires mindful practice to become comfortable and efficient, but keep at it and it will become like second nature.

5

Reactive Web Pages in ClojureScript

WHAT'S IN THIS CHAPTER?

➤ The value proposition of ClojureScript

➤ Defining reactive view components

➤ Modeling state and changes to state

➤ Styling, routing, and server communication

➤ Using workflow tools for accelerated development

➤ Leveraging mature libraries in your application

If you aren't using ClojureScript to make web pages, you are missing out. This style of programming is fast, fun, simple, and rewarding. And when I say fast, I mean really fast. It is a quantum leap from any other style of programming. You really have to experience it to appreciate it.

In this chapter you create a project, build a page, and deploy it. You build a project management tracking web page where users can create stories, change status, and track progress of their project. Then the chapter covers the common libraries used to leverage ClojureScript as a platform for developing useful solutions.

First take a broader look at what ClojureScript has to offer.

CLOJURESCRIPT IS A BIG DEAL

Interest in ClojureScript among web developers is growing strong. The two most watched presentations from the 2015 Conj conference are about ClojureScript. There is good reason for this attention: ClojureScript is eclipsing the current alternatives for building web applications.

> **NOTE** *At the time of writing, "Om Next" by David Nolen had 8,429 views and "ClojureScript for Skeptics" by Derek Slager had 7,705 views on the ClojureTV YouTube channel.*

ClojureScript is a perfect fit for building reactive web pages. The language idioms are aligned with the philosophy of the successful React framework from Facebook, which is proving to be a winning approach to building rich and robust interfaces. The React philosophy is that there should be a central app-state, functions that render from that state to HTML elements, and a process that automatically propagates change to the browser. Change propagation occurs by calculating the difference between the results of rendering with what is currently on the page. React determines the minimal set of updates required to transition to the new view state and applies those updates. Reactive web pages provide view model separation without the complexity of having to enumerate transitional behaviors. The web pages are fast to build and avoid common errors associated with state management and callback dependencies.

Reactive pages are unlike JQuery style pages. JQuery style pages update elements directly in response to events. You can write ClojureScript in JQuery style, but you will not be getting nearly as much leverage. Having the leverage of a reactive view/model relationship opens new opportunities for creating interactive experiences for your users. When you embrace the React paradigm you get the most out of your code. In the arena of single-page applications, ClojureScript React style dominates Angular, Ember, Backbone, and React because of the expressive power gained by combining Clojure with HTML.

The interactive development story with ClojureScript is especially compelling. Code is reloaded into the browser as soon as you save the file you are working on. This is better than refreshing the browser. Instead of your application being completely reset, you maintain state throughout the development session. This allows better focus on the part that you are currently working on. You no longer need to click through the application to check the change you just made. Even better, you can set up a test page that displays your components bound to many different states, which is perfect for verifying your interface without needing to click around. The combination of fast feedback and multistate testing facilitates an interactive path for development.

ClojureScript has a simple, stable syntax consisting of only data literals, function application, destructuring, special forms, and macros. Expressions are concise, abstractions are functional, and values are immutable.

ClojureScript compiles to JavaScript, has convenient interop capabilities, and you can use existing JavaScript libraries with little ceremony. You have the full reach of JavaScript and can draw upon its vast and rich ecosystem.

The ClojureScript compiler leverages the Google Closure Compiler and Library, which provides convenient access to a high-quality, full-featured, and well-maintained platform. Google Closure handles many recurring concerns well, and it does so in a cross-browser-compatible way. You rarely need to concern yourself about cross-browser behavior when writing ClojureScript, which is fantastic.

When you're developing, source maps link from the minified JavaScript back to the ClojureScript source code. Modern browsers support source maps, so debugging is obvious. From reading the developer console you can see where the error is in the original ClojureScript source code rather than in the compiled JavaScript.

In addition to having access to JavaScript libraries, you also gain access to many Clojure libraries. ClojureScript is not compatible with Clojure at the platform level, but it is compatible at the language level. Hence, many libraries are available in both Clojure and ClojureScript as the same code base, with any platform-specific differences handled by reader conditionals. For example, you can use Instaparse from both Clojure and ClojureScript.

Clojure and ClojureScript have a strong community and ecosystem. There are many simple and powerful libraries to choose from, many tools to help your workflow, and plenty of blogs with helpful tips. StackOverflow answers are quickly answered. The IRC and Slack channels are well populated with helpful and friendly denizens. Furthermore, an increasing number of employers are adopting Clojure/ClojureScript stacks.

One particularly intriguing capability inherited from the Clojure world is the ability to represent communicating sequential processes using the core.async library. Wherever you have a callback, you can put the result on a channel and write your logic as a sequential process consuming from the channel. This style for coordinating asynchronous actions was popularized by the Go language, and it's now possible in the browser.

Defining modules is easily achieved by specifying a namespace to target to an output file. The ClojureScript compiler automatically moves remaining code to a shared module. The Google Closure Compiler ensures the modules get only the code they need. Thus, for very large projects you are able to break up the artifacts as you see fit to provide the best load times for your users.

A typical ClojureScript application is smaller than a typical JavaScript application because of the code shrinking done by advanced compilation. Dead code is removed; live code is minified. Performance is great. The result is efficient code. In JavaScript you have to deal with a quagmire of build tools such as grunt, gulp, node package manager, yeoman, babel, bower, and brunch. The good news is that you need only one easily installed build tool for ClojureScript: Leiningen. You need to install Java, but you never have to directly interact with Java.

ClojureScript has been evolving rapidly over the past several years. Now the core tooling has stabilized to provide a production-ready platform for developing reactive web pages. Meanwhile new libraries continue to push the boundaries of what is possible. This is a great time to be adopting ClojureScript. The JavaScript equivalents require learning and being locked into complex frameworks, whereas ClojureScript libraries are small, simple, and unentangled. ClojureScript is a better way to make interactive interfaces. The idioms, libraries, and tooling are robust.

You are one command line away from a fast and fun coding experience!

A FIRST BRUSH WITH CLOJURESCRIPT

It's time to dive in and build a reactive website. The goal is to write a solution for tracking the status of tasks and assigning people to work on them. You need Java, Leiningen, and your favorite text editor. (We used Java 1.8.0_25 and Leinigen 2.5.3.) If you are new to ClojureScript, stick with your existing code editor. It likely has syntax highlighting, which is all you really need. Don't get hung up on editor integrations or learning a new IDE and key combinations; stick with an editor that is comfortable and familiar. You don't need a REPL or anything fancy. Fast feedback comes directly from the browser itself.

Starting a New ClojureScript Project

Open a terminal and type `lein new figwheel whip --` `--reagent`. Go into the whip project directory `cd whip` and examine the files created with the tree shown in Figure 5-1.

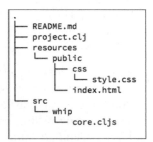

You see a readme file, a project file, a style sheet, index.html, and core.cljs source file. Type `lein figwheel` to start the process that builds and notifies the browser of file changes. Position your browser on the left and navigate to `http://localhost:3449`. Wait until you see the Successfully Compiled message in the terminal and then reload the browser. You see the Hello World! page shown in Figure 5-2, which indicates that everything is working so far.

FIGURE 5-1

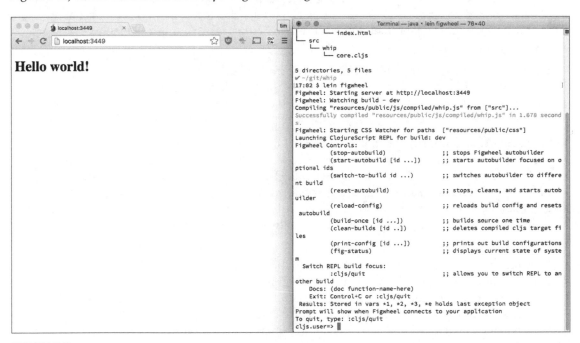

FIGURE 5-2

Getting Fast Feedback with Figwheel

Open the dev console in your browser. Open the `core.cljs` file from the source directory under `whip`. Position your text editor on the right so you can see the code and your page side by side. Edit the print string on line 6 of the source code to write a new message. The browser console logs the output immediately (see Figure 5-3).

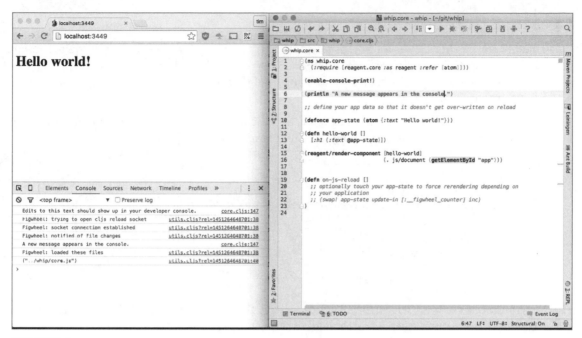

FIGURE 5-3

The current state of your application is kept inside a ratom called `app-state`. This is a Reagent atom, which causes your web page to be re-rendered whenever the app-state changes.

Note that defonce does nothing when evaluated if the var is already defined. So app-state is not re-created on reload. It can only be updated by either code execution or refreshing the browser. Refreshing the browser clears everything.

The `on-js-reload` function is called whenever new code is loaded from any namespace. You can remove it. Instead, annotate `whip.core` with `^:figwheel-always`, which causes this namespace to be reloaded when any change is detected, not necessarily in this file. Forcing the main namespace to reload on any change effectively re-renders the interface.

```
(ns ^:figwheel-always whip.core
  (:require [reagent.core :as reagent :refer [atom]]))
```

When we created the project with the `lein` command, we used the figwheel template. All it did was include the figwheel plug-in in our project definition and enable figwheel in the default build. Figwheel works by establishing a websocket from your page to the build process. When any source or resource files change, the build process detects them. If they are source changes, recompilation occurs, and the new JavaScript code is loaded. If they are resource changes such as CSS, they are also reloaded. One of the great things about figwheel is that you really don't need to know very much about it at all! So long as it is configured in your project, your code and resources load in the browser as you change them.

Creating Components

Reagent components are functions that return HTML in hiccup form. Hiccup looks quite similar to HTML, but it's more compact. Hiccup forms are vectors where the first element is the tag, which may be followed by an optional map of attributes and then any children, which may be hiccup forms or values.

Our generated `core.clj` contains an example because `hello-world` is a function that returns a vector representing an `<h1>` tag containing some text taken from the app-state:

```
(defn hello-world []
  [:h1 (:text @app-state)])
```

Edit the example to a complete example of what hiccup can look like:

```
[:h1
  {:id "stories"
   :class "stories main"
   :style {:font-family "cursive"}}
  "Whip project management tool"]
```

Here you can see several attributes have been set: the ID, class, and style. As these are common attributes, there is a shorthand way for adding them that expands to the same HTML elements.

```
[:h1#stories.stories.main
  {:style {:font-family "cursive"}}
  "Whip project management tool"]
```

You see that the tag can be suffixed with an optional single ID preceded by a hash and any number of classes preceded by periods. If an ID is specified it must come as the first suffix. Unlike jQuery where IDs are commonly used to find and modify elements, React style components rarely need an ID because they are functions of state. Note that styles expand according to CSS syntax. So the example expands to

```
<h1 id="stories" class="stories main" style="font-family:cursive">
  Whip project management tool
</h1>
```

In your browser, right-click the text and select Inspect Element. The code has produced DOM elements, just like normal HTML.

> There are several other approaches to a component definition, and the most widespread is Om. The concepts and syntax are very similar and straightforward, so it will be easy to understand both.

EXERCISE

Add an SVG element to your page containing a circle of radius 20 and color green at location 40,40.

HINT

The HTML elements to create are

```
<svg><circle r=20 cx=40 cy=40 fill="green"></circle></svg>
```

Can you express the hiccup syntax equivalent to draw the circle on your page? `https://developer.mozilla.org/en-US/docs/Web/SVG/Element` has a reference of shapes you might like to use. Making games and visualizations is very convenient because you can build up SVG elements with conditional code.

Modeling the Data

Now you have the basics in place to render your page. How are you going to model the project management tracking solution? Before you worry too much about how to organize the code for the project, instead focus on what data your application will be dealing with. A project will consist of stories. Stories have a status, which will be visualized as a lane. Users can be assigned to stories. Stories can be moved between lanes to indicate status changes (see Figure 5-4).

Project title description team	**Story** title description status owners tags	**Person** title email

FIGURE 5-4

You need to be able to add stories to your app-state. It's useful to have some example data to work with, so create some data. There are many options available for modeling data. We suggest that you work with nested maps where possible.

```clojure
(defonce app-state
  (reagent/atom
    {:projects
     {"aaa"
      {:title "Build Whip"
       :stories
       {1 {:title "Design a data model for projects and stories"
           :status "done"
           :order 1}
```

```
         2 {:title "Create a story title entry form"
            :order 2}
         3 {:title "Implement a way to finish stories"
            :order 3}}}}}))
```

You need to reload the browser for this change to take effect because of the defonce. Take some time to think about why this is the case. It is important to be mindful of how code reloading interacts with existing data. The code reloading model is more powerful than simply refreshing the page. Code reloading causes execution without re-creating the entire app-state. When you want to re-create the entire app-state, reloading the page is the way to do it.

With this data in place you can spend some time drawing a basic list of the stories that are in the project. Create a project-board component that can be an unordered list of stories:

```
(defn project-board [app-state project-id]
  (into [:ul]
    (for [[id {:keys [title]}] (get-in @app-state [:projects project-id :stories])]
      [:li title])]))
```

This for expression calculates a sequence of list item elements, which are then put into the parent unordered list vector.

Inside the whip-main component, nest the project-board component. To nest a component, place it in a vector as though it was a regular function call surrounded by square brackets instead of parenthesis:

```
(defn whip-main [app-state]
  [:div
    [:h1 "Whip project management tool"]
    [whip-content app-state]])
```

Great! Now you can see your stories in your example project.

Responding to Events and Handling State Change

It's time to make the user interface more interactive. You want to be able to complete these stories, so add a button to do that. You attach an event handler function to the on-click attribute. In the project-board function, in the list item form, append the hiccup to create a button:

```
[:button
  {:on-click
    (fn done-click [e]
      (println "You clicked me!"))}
  "done"]
```

> Note that on-click (kebab-case) is translated as the HTML attribute onClick (camelCase). Attributes are mapped according to a defined list of React attributes (https://facebook.github.io/react/docs/tags-and-attributes.html), so where you might expect to be able to use :autofocus, instead :auto-focus is the right keyword to use. React looks for the camelCase attribute autoFocus.

It is helpful to start with the handler function printing to the console so you can confirm events are occurring as you expect. Click the Done button and check the console for the expected message. Now that you know your clicks are registered, update the app-state instead of printing to the console.

```
(swap! app-state assoc-in [:projects "aaa" :stories id :status] "done")
```

Now conditionally render the list item based upon its status. If the status is done, show the title in a `<del>` tag, which is HTML for strikethrough. Otherwise, show the title and the button to complete the task. The list item contains quite a lot of code now, so pull it out into a component called story-card.

```
(defn story-card [app-state story-id {:keys [title status]}]
  [:li.card
    (if (= status "done")
      [:del title]
      [:span
       title
       " "
       [:button
        {:on-click
         (fn done-click [e]
           (swap! app-state assoc-in [:projects "aaa" :stories id :status]
                  "done"))}
        "done"]])])
```

Notice that you don't update the DOM directly. Instead you are updating the app-state, and the interface changes flow out from your functional definitions of how to render app-state. This feels a lot like templating, but without moustaches {{}} and with a more Clojure-like syntax. The components are mostly data with some code for conditionals and transformations. Why not use a templating approach based upon HTML instead of hiccup? There are options to do that, but we urge you to persist with hiccup because it provides an excellent way to mix code and data. Hiccup forms as data are much more amenable to data transformations (see Figure 5-5).

FIGURE 5-5

Understanding Errors and Warnings

ClojureScript has useful error and warning messages. As a general approach to locating the source of errors you will be well served by following a scientific approach. You can make a hypothesis, do an experiment, refine to a more precise experiment by removing possible causes, and iterate until you find the actual cause, or move on to a new hypothesis when all possibilities are exhausted. This section covers how to get notified of problems, and how to read common notifications.

Let's step through some common debugging scenarios. At the top of core.cljs, add an obvious error `(+ "hello" 1)` and save the file. You will immediately see in the browser a yellow popup showing the warning. figwheel declines to load code that has warnings; it just displays what went wrong (see Figure 5-6).

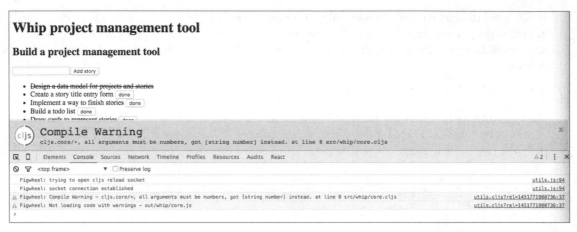

FIGURE 5-6

The source code file and line number are displayed in an overlay, and you can see the warning in the console as well. Usually the warning message, filename, and line number are enough to identify the problem. In this case it is clear that you should be passing numerical arguments to the addition function.

Let's try something a little more egregious, `(defn (inc 1))`. This gives you a popup indicating the problem (see Figure 5-7). The code cannot be compiled, so is treated as an error.

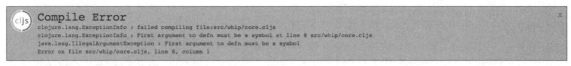

FIGURE 5-7

If you like to see warnings and errors in your editor, CursiveClojure provides inline error/warning detection and highlighting.

Now let's look at an error that is not detected at compile time.

```
(rand-nth (range 0))
```

Here you can choose a random element from an empty sequence. The code compiles just fine because there is no non-empty type to enforce that the sequence argument to `rand-nth` contains a value. So figwheel will load the code, but when it is running you get a runtime error because there are no items to choose from. Expand the stacktrace by clicking the triangle at the start of the error message (see Figure 5-8).

```
⊗ ▼ Uncaught Error: Index out of bounds                              core.cljs:8501
     cljs.core.Range.cljs$core$IIndexed$_nth$arity$2 @ core.cljs:8501
     cljs.core.nth.cljs$core$IFn$_invoke$arity$2      @ core.cljs:1646
     cljs$core$rand_nth                               @ core.cljs:9413
     (anonymous function)                             @ core.cljs:8
```

FIGURE 5-8

The important thing to note about the stacktrace is that again you have the filename and line number to guide you, but you have to do a little more work to identify the root cause. One confusing element is that there are four lines that occur in core.cljs; however, these are actually different files. The first three lines are in ClojureScript itself, and only the last line is from the source file. You can mouse over the filenames to see the full path. We recommend keeping very little code in your core .cljs namespace, so that you can mentally ignore most lines that contain core.cljs. In this case those lines do provide valuable hints; that the error occurred while calling `rand-nth`, trying to get an element from range.

We highly recommend renaming core.cljs to main.cljs. You will save yourself a world of confusion when looking at stacktraces, and it really is the main entry point for the browser.

Because of JavaScript restrictions, the compiled code namespaces contain $ and _ where you might expect . or / and -, but the names make it fairly obvious what is going on. However, the fourth line containing the problem in the code is quite opaque. Say instead that you put the code in a function (see Figure 5-9).

```
(defn choose []
  (rand-nth (range 0)))
(choose)
```

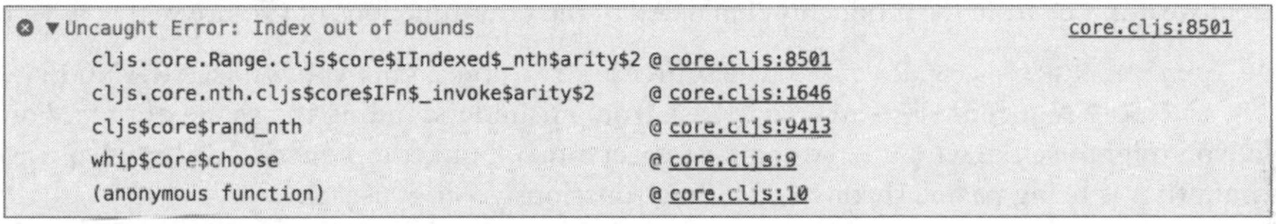

```
⊗ ▼Uncaught Error: Index out of bounds                                          core.cljs:8501
    cljs.core.Range.cljs$core$IIndexed$_nth$arity$2 @ core.cljs:8501
    cljs.core.nth.cljs$core$IFn$_invoke$arity$2      @ core.cljs:1646
    cljs$core$rand_nth                               @ core.cljs:9413
    whip$core$choose                                 @ core.cljs:9
    (anonymous function)                             @ core.cljs:10
```

FIGURE 5-9

Now you can see that the problem is in the `whip.core/choose` function. The function names are quite useful when debugging, so you should always give functions names, even when they don't require them. For example, when creating event handlers on a component, instead of coding them as `(fn [e] ...)`, write `(fn click-ok [e] ...)` and then if an error is thrown you will have a far more readable stacktrace.

The details on where the error occurs are only meaningful if you are building source maps. In the current project.clj cljsbuild configuration, the "dev" build creates a source map, because it is not an optimized build. But the "min" build is set to `:optimizations :advanced`, so no source map is created. This is a sensible default, avoiding any source level identifiers being revealed in production releases. You can enable source maps for advanced compilation as well. Indeed it is sometimes necessary to create a source map enabled minified build, since it is pretty much the only way to pinpoint a missing extern, thus causing the advanced mode build to throw an error.

To enable source maps for the "min" build, add the configuration `:source-map` "resources/public/js/compiled/whip.js.map" `:output-dir` "resources/public/js/compiled/min."

To run the minified build, go to the terminal and cancel the current build process, then run **lein do clean, cljsbuild once** to run the advanced mode compilation. Then you need to open resources/public/index.html (see Figure 5-10).

```
⊗ ▼Uncaught Error: No item 0 in vector of length 0                    core.cljs:4662
    oh                      @ core.cljs:4662
    qh                      @ core.cljs:4686
    h.aa                    @ core.cljs:4895
    Ue                      @ core.cljs:3962
    (anonymous function) @ view.cljs:2336
    (anonymous function) @ core.cljs:14
```

FIGURE 5-10

The minified build is much slower than the dev build, so cancel the minified build and return to using `lein figwheel`.

There is plenty of feedback about what went wrong, but how do you fix it? Print debugging is very convenient when you have code reloading on your side. As soon as you save code to print a value, you will see it in the console. Your code needs to explicitly enable printing to the console by calling `(enable-console-print!)`, which we already do in core.cljs. However, let's move that code to a-init.cljs and require it from core.cljs. So long as it is the first require, other namespaces will be able to print as well. This is convenient because you may want to drop print statements around while debugging. A-init should stay at the top, even after alphabetically sorting. You can also set up the build to later remove a-init.clj from the production build. All of the print functions of Clojure will now work.

Let's add `(prn "RANGE:" (range 0))` to the source code. Upon saving you will see RANGE: (), indicating an empty sequence. Typical errors arise from misunderstanding the shape of data. For example, you might use the wrong keyword, or expect a map but get a sequence. So simply printing out the data that is being passed through to failing functions is often useful.

Keep in mind that `(doto x (prn "*****"))` is a handy way to spy on expressions. It will return the value of x after printing it with some stars to draw your attention. You can wrap `(doto ... (prn ...))` around existing expressions to see them as the code executes, and remove the doto later by raising the expression using structural editing in Cursive or paredit in Emacs.

If you are working with JavaScript objects, it can be convenient to use JavaScript's built in `(js/console.log x)` function because it will render a nice object explorer in the console. If you are working with large nested maps, use `(cljs.pprint/pprint m)` to see a nicely formatted output on the console.

The ClojureScript compiler's designation of what is a warning and what is an error is somewhat arbitrary, and has a permissive nature inherited from JavaScript. As such, it is important to be attentive to warnings, which will be your main source of clues as to what is going wrong when debugging is required. We encourage you to treat warnings as errors, because in ClojureScript, warnings are almost always errors.

To treat warnings as errors in the build, you need the build process to return an error code when there are warnings. To do this you can add a custom warning-handler to the project.cljs file under the `:cljsbuild` section. Now the build system will be able to recognize and stop problems before they make it into releasable artifacts.

```
:warning-handlers
[(fn treat-warnings-as errors [warning-type env extra]
```

```
(when-let [s (cljs.analyzer/error-message warning-type extra)]
  (binding [*out* *err*]
    (println "WARNING:" (cljs.analyzer/message env s)))
(System/exit 1)))]
```

Namespace Layout

ClojureScript and libraries like Reagent do not prescribe any particular namespace layout for your code. However, some structure is useful for navigating your source code and isolating areas of responsibility.

Conceptually you have a global app-state, view components, and state transition functions. Let's put the component rendering code in a "view" folder. You'll have separate namespaces for the navbar, project, projects list, and story views. The app-state and state transition functions go in the model namespace, and be sure to leave the route dispatching in main.

A reagent component is a function that returns a hiccup vector. So let's make a separate function for each of those three components. Reagent components are nested in vectors. So instead of calling the components directly by placing them inside parentheses, place them inside square brackets.

All of the namespaces are a nice comprehensible size; around 50 lines of code. It is obvious where the rendering code is, and how it relates to the user interface. And the state manipulation is isolated away from the rendering. Main contains the bare bones required for stitching together the views, model, and routing.

Styling

To style markup you can use CSS or inline styles. Inline styles are standard attributes of HTML.

Where you might write an inline style in HTML as:

```
<span style="font-family:fantasy"> Whip</span>
```

You express this in hiccup as:

```
[:span {:style {:font-family "fantasy"}} " Whip"]
```

Let's create a navbar and apply some styling.

```
(defn navbar [app-state]
  [:nav
   [:ul.nav-list
    [:li
     [:a
      {:href "#/"}
      [:img
       {:src "img/logo.png"}]
      [:span
       {:style {:font-family "fantasy"}}
       " Whip"]]]
    [:ul.nav-list
     {:style {:float "right"}}
```

```
[:li
 [:a {:href "#/"} "About"]]
[:li
 (if-let [username (:username @app-state)]
   [:a {:href "#/settings"} username]
   [:a {:href "#/login"} "Login"])]]]])
```

Here you see a mix of both HTML and hiccup. The ul elements have a nav-list class on them that comes from style.css, which is included from index.html.

```
.nav-list {
    list-style-type: none;
    margin: 0;
    padding: 0;
    overflow: hidden;
    background-color: #383838;
}
```

In contrast, the span containing the application named "Whip" has an inline style specifying a font-family "fantasy." It is up to you how much you want to rely on classes or inline styles. A good rule of thumb is to build up with inline styles and convert them to classes as you discover good abstractions for what they are trying to accomplish. It is rare that you know what the nesting and abstractions will be in advance. You can choose to use an established set of CSS classes. For instance you might include bootstrap and leverage their many styles (see Figure 5-11).

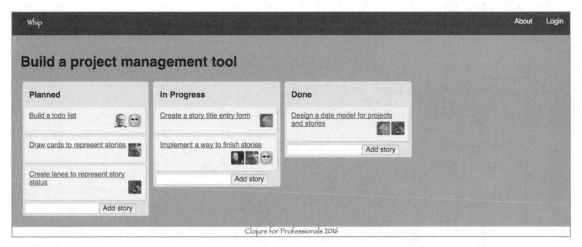

FIGURE 5-11

Form Inputs and Form Handling

Forms and inputs are represented in hiccup in the same way as static HTML elements. The difference is that you can use the values that the user provides to the input elements. There are two approaches to getting the values of input elements:

1.   Listen to the form submit event. The event target is the form itself, which contains the input elements and their current values.

2. Listen to an element's on-change event. The event target contains the element, which has the new value of the input.

Before examining the approaches in detail, let's think about state management. For the Whip tool, you want the capability to add stories. You will have a form that allows users to edit the title, description, and add members. You should use the first approach and simply act on the data when the user submits their changes. There is no use for the intermediary values as they are typed, so you should leave their state management entirely to the input elements themselves. The sample application code will not track the form state at all. The global state will be updated once when the submit event is processed.

Now, consider adding a search filter. In this case you want to provide immediate feedback to the user as they type their search query. So you should use the second approach and listen for changes to the search box input, instead of waiting for a submit event. The global state will be kept in sync with whatever the user types in the search box. We describe this state as global, because the filtering will be done above the search box's scope. The code that renders the stories we are filtering must know the current search term.

Finally, let's think about form validation. Say you want to enforce some constraints such as "two stories cannot have the same title." And you also want to highlight in red the title when it breaks this rule, even before the submit button is pressed. This rule can be contained inside the scope of the form as local state. You don't need this information in other parts of the application. In Reagent, a common way to handle local state is to close over a ratom (see the second form in the Reagent section of this chapter). Track the current rule state for every rule, and highlight elements that have broken rules. The submit button can be activated if there are no broken rules. To achieve this you need to listen to the on-change events to apply the rules, and to the submit event to update the application with the story. Keep in mind that HTML has input attributes to restrict user input, which for basic use cases are often preferable to custom rules.

Let's build an add story form. You need an event handler that can gather the current values in all the input elements in the form when a user clicks "submit." Attach to the form on-submit event, rather than a button on-click event, because the on-submit event target is the entire form, whereas the button's on-click event target is just the button itself.

```
[:form {:on-submit (fn [e])}
  [:input {:type "submit"}]]
```

You will want to prevent the form from performing a POST directly to the server. If you allow the normal submit process to POST, the form to the server will cause the result page to be loaded. Instead, let's control the view. To prevent a form POST, call `preventDefault` on the event when handling it in the on-submit handler.

```
(defn add-story-form [app-state project-id status]
  [:form
   {:on-submit
    (fn add-story-submit [e]
      (.preventDefault e)
      (model/add-story!
        app-state
        project-id
        (forms/getValueByName (.-target e) "story-title")
```

```
        status))}
    [:input
     {:type "text"
      :name "story-title"}]
    [:input
     {:type "submit"
      :value "Add story"}]]])
```

To get the current values from the inputs, use the `getValueByName` helper method from `goog.dom.forms` in the Closure Library. There is also a `toMap` function, which is convenient if you have a large form that you would like to interpret as data. The target of the event is the form itself, so you don't need any other external references to the form or its elements to look up their values. Setting the name attribute on inputs allows you to access their values. You can get values by the id or the name, but bear in mind that ids need to be unique to the entire page, whereas names only need to be unique within the form. Using names is usually the right choice.

When the user is typing changes to a title, do you want the new title to be instantly reflected in the global app-state? No, you want to follow the idiom of current edits being transitory until such time as they are submitted. So there is no need to listen to change events, and you can focus on just the form submit event.

What about if you want to edit an existing story instead? You would want to pre-populate the form with the current values. It may seem tempting to provide the values when rendering:

```
[:input {:type "text" :name "title" :value "Some story title"}]
```

But this has a severe limitation; the user can't change the text in the input anymore! The user is typing, but as soon as the text changes, the difference is detected, and the DOM gets reset back to the value specified by the render function. You can close over a local atom to store the transient title. The atom can be updated by the on-change event, and thus rendered with the new value, which matches the current input. This works, but is completely unnecessary. Instead, you should use the `defaultValue` attribute.

```
[:input {:default-value "Some story title"}]
```

This is a standard HTML input attribute that provides the initial value for an input. It will populate the value of the element when it is mounted into the DOM. Be sure to only render the input when you know what the default value should be. You want to avoid rendering an element with a blank `defaultValue`, then updating it, because this will have no effect. For checkboxes use `defaultChecked`. For options within a select element, use `defaultSelected`.

Now let's look at the case where you do want to modify global `app-state` as the user types. Let's implement a search box. The main difference is that you don't need a submit button or a form at all, you just need an input. Bear in mind that HTML is very permissive, so while your page will work without a form, strictly valid inputs should occur inside a form. Feel free to wrap this input in an empty form, but if you do, you will still need to handle and suppress the submit event as the user can press enter to submit a form without a submit button.

```
[:input {:type "text" :on-change (fn [e] (prn (.. e -target -value)))}]
```

When you type in the search input box, the console prints out the value of the input element, which is the target of the event. You can see the search term printed as soon as you type it. Instead of printing it, let's update app-state instead:

```
(swap! app-state assoc :search-term (.. e -target -value))
```

Now when you render the stories, you can filter by the search term:

```
(defn filter-stories [stories search-term project-id status]
  (filter
    (fn filter-match [[id story]]
      (and (= (:project-id story) project-id)
           (= (:status story) status)
           (story-search-match search-term story)))
    stories))
```

State management is not limited to forms, but it is something you do need to think about carefully when working with user inputs. How you manage state can greatly affect the user's experience. Losing state unnecessarily, or not following the edit/apply paradigm, can be very frustrating to users.

The definitions of global and local state are ambiguous, but the terms come up often when discussing how and where components get and store data. Data can be held in HTML elements, in React properties, passed in to the render function, and closed over or read from a global def. That is a lot of places! The distinctions about how you access them are subtle, so it is helpful to be able to relate state management concepts to the concrete examples presented. Understanding them enables you to reason about when to use which approach, and the behavior it will produce in your user interaction. As much as possible, leave state in the HTML elements and rely on data passed in to the render function.

Avoid making assumptions about global state in your components; instead contain interactions with global state in model centric namespace. This is the flexible and isolated approach. It is simple in that components do not directly interact with each other, but can still effect coordinated state change. Keeping global state interaction out of the components allows you to replace your data representation without rewiring all your components. It may initially seem like a bit of a chore to write a model function that just does a swap!, but as your data model matures and changes you will find having all data shape related code co-located makes understanding your application much easier.

Navigation and Routes

The sample Whip application has three main views: the list of projects, a project's stories, and a story details view. In order to render different pages dependent on the state, you need to update the whip-content function to conditionally render the relevant view. You can choose to set a view value in the app-state and have a case statement to choose which component to render. Setting the view value will cause a different view to show.

Browser navigation is based around URLs and back/forward. In order for users to be able to have a comfortable navigation experience, you need to hook into the browser's navigation mechanism. Fortunately this is easily accomplished, thanks to the Closure library.

```
(doto (History.)
  (events/listen EventType/NAVIGATE model/navigation)
  (.setEnabled true))
```

The goog.History class allows you to listen to navigation events.

```
(defn navigation [event]
  (swap! app-state assoc :route (.-token event)))
```

The listener needs to record the token of the event. The token is the text after the # anchor in a URL, which can be used for linking.

You can dispatch to the appropriate component directly based upon the string. This indeed works fine for basic routes, but you can access some very useful features by using a routing library to parse an anchor # tag appended to the site URL. For example, let's consider the story-details view. We want to pass a story-id to determine which story to show. You can write some parsing code to figure out the values that you need from the URL string, but it would be better to leverage a library that provides a well thought out abstraction for routes.

There are many good libraries to help route a string, but let's use Bidi. Bidi defines routes as data, works in both Clojure and ClojureScript, and is bidirectional (you can build routes as well as parse them). The important thing to keep in mind is that this type of routing is exactly the same sort of string pattern matching that occurs when you write a server side route, but the big difference is that we will be dispatching on the string after the # anchor.

There is nothing magical about the # in a URL, which is a standard HTML mechanism for linking to an element inside a page. It is called the fragment identifier and tells a browser to open a page, but moves the view to the element with the id specified after the # symbol. This is how you link to a specific paragraph on a web page. However it is a common technique in single page applications to use the fragment identifier for routing instead of providing an element with the id. It is convenient because you can use it to link to a different state of the same page. Page fragment identifiers are never passed to the server on page requests; they exist only in the browser. So the server will always serve the same page, regardless of what follows the # symbol.

Bidi routes are expressed as nested vectors. You can use maps instead, but we encourage you to use the vector notation. The map version does not guarantee the order in which the rules will be applied. The syntax is [pattern matched], where matched can be a result, or recur into another vector.

```
(def routes
  ["/"
   [["projects" projects/projects-list]
    [["project/" :project-id] project/project-board]
    [["story/" :story-id] story/story-details]]])
```

The routing root context is /. You will match against "projects" and return the projects-list component. You will next match against "project/project-id" and return the project-board component. Finally, you can match against "story/story-id" and return the story-detail component. To use these routes call (bidi/match-route routes route), where route is the string you are matching, and `routes` is the data defined above. The result of `match-route` is a map containing a handler and `route-params`. The handler will be the last value in the route vectors, which is a component function. The `route-params` are the captured key value pairs containing `project-id` or `story-id`.

```
(defn whip-content [app-state]
  (let [route (:route @app-state)
        {:keys [handler route-params]} (bidi/match-route routes route)]
    [(or handler projects/projects-list) app-state route-params]))
```

We match against the routes, and then render whichever component matches. You can have a default in case the user types an unknown URL. The routed components get passed the `route-params` as a map containing the additional `id` they need to render a specific story or project. As you can see there is a regular structure here that extends nicely to handling multiple arguments and optional arguments as well.

Routing is very powerful and concise, so it warrants contemplation. But the principles are very simple:

1. Hook up a function to the browser navigate event.

2. Record the token (string after the # fragment identifier) of the URL.

3. Dispatch to the appropriate component function on the token.

4. Use a routing library to succinctly define string patterns to match to component functions.

HTTP Calls: Talking to a Server

The goal is for teams of people to interact with the sample project tracking system and see each other's changes. In order to accomplish this you need central storage of the data. Thus, you need a web app to communicate with a backend server. This can be done with HTTP requests or WebSockets.

An important restriction on HTTP requests made from JavaScript in a browser is that the browser can only communicate with the same host that served the page. This is called the same-origin policy. A resource may only be accessed by the same scheme (http or https), from the same hostname (domain where the page is hosted) on the same port. Your page can only make requests to the server hosting it, so you can proxy your page requests. When your page requests resources from your host, they can be forwarded to the third party.

There is a standard way to allow access called Cross-Origin Resource Sharing (CORS), where the server adds a header explicitly allowing an origin access. This means you can allow access from JavaScript on a page that you host from one server to another service running on a different port or host that you control. But you can't grant your JavaScript access to third party hosts. It is possible to provide a wildcard to allow everyone access to your service, but popular service providers rarely do. In practical terms, this means that calling the Twitter API directly from JavaScript hosted on the Whip website is not possible.

It is a common mistake to build a ClojureScript project and host it on localhost:3449 by running figwheel, and then run a Ring service in a separate project hosted on localhost:8080 and try to make calls to this service. This will not work, because of the same-origin policy. So the easiest approach when starting out is to host the service code in the same project. This is easily achieved by supplying a ring handler to the figwheel configuration, so that the page, the JavaScript, and the services are all hosted from the same port.

To integrate with third party APIs, you can proxy a call to the server to the third party server. In such a scenario, the browser loads a page from the Whip website, which runs JavaScript that sends requests to the Whip host, which then makes a request to the third party server, and passes the result back to the browser when it arrives.

Another approach to getting around the same-origin policy is JSONP, which is a common way to include a script from a third party site, which will deliver a JSON object. This relies on the third party exposing this method. For example, the Gravatar API allows JSONP requests, so you can make them from ClojureScript using `goog.net.Jsonp` from the Closure Library.

```
(defn member-details [email]
  (doto (Jsonp. (str "//www.gravatar.com/" (md5-hash email) ".json"))
    (.send
      nil
      (fn profile-success [result]
        (model/set-member! model/app-state email
          (with-out-str (pprint/pprint ((js->clj result) "entry")))))
      (fn profile-error [error]
        (model/set-member! model/app-state email "No profile")))))
```

The Gravatar API allows you to look up profile information of users by making a request to `https://www.gravatar.com/HASH.json`, where HASH is calculated by taking an email address, trimming surrounding whitespace, forcing it to lower-case, and taking the md5 hash. You can use the result in the "title" of the member component to make a tooltip that shows more information about the user (see Figure 5-12).

For now, you can call a static endpoint served from a file to avoid the need to create and host a server process. Create a file data.edn under resources/public and put some data in it:

```
{:foo "bar"}
```

Check that the file is being served by navigating to `http://localhost:3449/data.edn`. Let's add some code to make the request. Add `[goog.net.XhrIo :as xhr]` to the namespace `:require` form, then use xhr/send to make the request.

```
(xhr/send "data.edn"
  (fn [e]
    (prn (.. e -target getResponseText))))
```

FIGURE 5-12

The most common way to make requests is cljs-http. Add `[cljs-http "0.1.39"]` to the dependencies in project.clj and restart the figwheel process in the terminal to pick up the new dependency.

```
(:require
   [cljs.core.async :refer [<!]]
   [cljs-http.client :as http])
 (:require-macros
   [cljs.core.async.macros :refer [go]])

(go (let [response (<! (http/get "data.edn"))]
      (prn (:status response))
      (prn (:body response))))
```

Cljs-http is a nice way to manage HTTP requests. It uses core.async channels to deliver its results. For now, all you need to focus on is that http/get and http/post calls should occur inside a go form, and the result is a channel that can have its result read with <!.

> **EXERCISE**
>
> Call some service endpoints from this ClojureScript application.
>
> **HINT**
>
> Add {:ring-handler server/handler} to the figwheel configuration in project. clj, and co-locate the code from both projects.

When it comes to WebSockets, Scntc is a fantastic library to establish a persistent bi-directional link between the client and server. An example is beyond the scope of this book, but we highly recommend using it when you need to stream information. The abstraction fits very well with reactive web pages. It is very convenient to be able to push patches of a data model over the wire and apply it at the other end.

Drag and Drop

You can attach drag and drop handlers by adding attributes to the story card.

```
{:draggable "true"
 :on-drag-start
 (fn card-drag-start [e]
   (.setData (.-dataTransfer e) "text/plain" story-id)
   (set! (.. e -dataTransfer -dropEffect) "move"))}
```

And attributes to the columns.

```
{:on-drop
 (fn drop-on-column [e]
   (.preventDefault e)
   (let [story-id (.getData (.-dataTransfer e) "text")]
     (model/set-story-status! app-state story-id status)))
 :on-drag-over
 (fn drag-over-column [e]
   (.preventDefault e)
   (set! (.. e -dataTransfer -dropEffect) "move"))}
```

Publishing

It is time to publish the web page. Github Pages is an easy way to get code online. Create a new Github repository, "git init" for the project, and commit and push all of the files. To publish the built version you need to create a branch called gh-pages. Anything in this branch will be hosted at `<username>.github.io/<project>`, so it should contain an index.html and the compiled JavaScript.

This script creates a clean minified build, and then makes a fresh gh-pages branch containing only the files in resources/public, where the index.html and compiled code are. Replace `<username>` and `<project>` with your Github username and project name. Put these steps into a deploy.sh, and use this script to deploy.

```
#!/bin/bash
set -e
lein do clean, cljsbuild once min
cd resources/public
git init
git add .
git commit -m "Deploy to GitHub Pages"
git push --force --quiet "git@github.com:<username>/<project>.git" master:gh-pages
rm -fr resources/public/.git
```

Navigate to `<username>.github.io/<project>` to see your page. The deployed version from the book is located at `http://timothypratley.github.io/whip`.

There are many good hosting options besides Github, and the steps to deploy are always straightforward. Push the resource/public directory containing the HTML, styles, images, and compiled JavaScript to the hosting platform.

When deploying with a backend you may choose to structure your project such that the backend and frontend code live in the same project. For example, you might have the Clojure Ring server code side-by-side with ClojureScript user interface code. This can be quite convenient for development. For deployment, the resources get can be wrapped up in the same WAR file with the service code. There is one easy step to push the war to a Tomcat container or something similar.

For large applications consider separating the ClojureScript project from the backend service. The advantages of having separate projects are subtle but substantial. Dependency conflicts are avoided. Building the browser artifacts separately opens up more options for server configuration. Testing is often easier to reason about where a clear division has been made between the client project and the service project.

One option to consider is presenting a consistent routing layer using Nginx to avoid the CORS situation, and a reverse proxy to underlying services running on different hosts and ports. In this way you present a single hosting entry point, but have control over how the services are configured internally. Only embark upon fine-grain routing if you truly need many services.

It is good to be aware of the ring-cors middleware library, which allows you to very easily wrap a handler with the necessary OPTIONS request handling to allow cross-origin requests. Using this library you can use multiple hosts without a routing layer, which can be handy for projects where co-hosting the service and HTML artifacts is not desirable due to hosting cost structures, or the desire to use a CDN for HTML artifacts.

Ultimately your project structure will be guided by your desired deployment architecture. Clojure and ClojureScript work very well with many popular hosting options and architecture configurations. There is plenty of flexibility in the deployment unit choice and how deployment units should communicate.

REAGENT IN DEPTH

At this point you have at your disposal all of the tools necessary to build and deploy a fully featured interactive webpage. It is time to expand your horizons and examine some more advanced abstractions that are available. Let's start with a deeper dive into Reagent's capabilities.

Break down exactly what is happening in a Reagent application:

1. Create global state as a ratom:

```
(def app-state (reagent/atom {:title "An example story title"}))
```

2. Create component functions:

```
(defn story-card [title]
  [:div "Story: " title])
```

3. Define a main component that uses global state and passes down values to children states:

```
(defn main-view []
  [story-card (:title @app-state)])
```

4. Hook into the React system to make changes to the UI:

```
(reagent/render-component [main-view] (dom/getElement "app"))
```

Reagent components are functions. You write functions to render a view from an app state. React renders to a virtual DOM, diffs with the existing DOM, and updates only what has changed into the live DOM. Components that deref a reagent atom (ratom) will be called when the ratom changes. The component functions produce new elements, which are compared with the existing DOM. A set of minimal changes will be calculated and applied to the live DOM to make it match exactly the result of component rendering.

Reagent components can be written in three forms: a function that returns a vector, a function that returns a component, or a function that returns a React class.

Form 1: A Function That Returns a Vector

The first element in the vector is either an HTML tag or a component. Components are followed by arguments to pass to the component when it is invoked. Refer to the "Creating Components" section for the full description of what Hiccup can represent.

```
(defn story-card [title]
  [:div "Story " title])

(defn main []
  [story-card "world"])
```

This first form is the most common way to define a component. It is concise and elegant, and the syntax is regular ClojureScript. We aren't using any libraries at all. Reagent can consume this data to create components and hook them into the React framework.

Hiccup is expressed as data, which introduces no new words to learn in order to create elements, call components, format strings, and so forth. Data has better editor support than string templating, making it easier to type and format. Also, it is impossible to miss a closing HTML tag in Hiccup.

The result vector must contain a first element that is either a tag or component. Beware that returning a vector of several divs is not a valid Reagent component.

```
(defn bad []
  [[:div] [:div]])
```

But nesting several divs inside a parent div is valid.

```
(defn good []
  [:div [:div] [:div]])
```

Why put components in vectors instead of calling them directly? In fact calling them by using parentheses instead of braces works just fine. The problem with direct function calls is that we don't want every view recalculated during the render phase, only views that depend on state that has changed. Reagent takes care of this. When you use a vector instead of a function call, it allows Reagent to only render sub components in response to changes in ratoms that they depend on, because immediate execution has not been forced.

Form 2: A Function That Returns a Component

Consider a situation where you need to perform some initialization on a component. Perhaps you want to be able to add stories directly from the project board view into any of the columns representing status. Having an add story form at the bottom of every column would be visually noisy. Instead, the add story form could be brought up by clicking a button (see Figure 5-13).

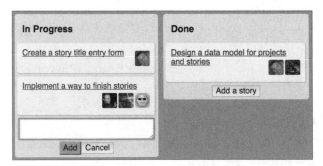

FIGURE 5-13

A component can be defined as a function that returns a function. Use this form to close over a ratom flag that indicates whether the user is adding a story or not. The flag will be initialized once. The component will re-render when the flag changes.

```
(defn maybe-add-story-form [app-state project-id status]
  (let [adding? (reagent/atom false)]
    (fn a-maybe-add-story-form [app-state project-id status]
      (if @adding?
        [add-story-form app-state project-id status adding?]
        [:button
         {:on-click
          (fn add-story-click [e]
            (swap! adding? not)
            nil)}
         "Add a story"]))))
```

The component here is returning a function, not a vector. The outer function is called once when the component is first created. The inner function is called whenever the arguments or a ratom that it depends on changes. The inner function returns a Hiccup vector.

Be extra careful to ensure that the inner function has exactly the same parameters as the outer function. It is easy to forget an argument or typo it, causing the outer functions argument to be used in the inner function. Such an error can be confusing, because the outer argument is never updated. Keep this in mind when refactoring.

Form 2 is useful when you need local state, because you can use the "let over lambda" style close over a local ratom instead of relying on global state. The beauty of a local ratom is that each component has its own state encapsulated. However, you can instead decide that you only want one add story form active at any one time. In that case you need a shared ratom that indicates which column the form is currently in. We might choose to put that state in the global app-state, or in the project-board component.

Making a strong distinction between local and global state is somewhat illusory. Don't fret too much about trying to localize state. But do be careful to separate display concerns from data model concerns such as transformation, as this has a direct impact on the flexibility of your code.

Form 3: A Function That Returns a Class

Reagent provides the `create-class` function to expose the underlying React lifecycle methods.

As a motivating example of how this can be useful, consider a case where you need to perform some task after the element is mounted. You want to make the project title editable, so you can use a similar approach to the add story form; however, there is a wrinkle. When you click to edit the project title, autofocus puts the cursor at the start of the input box. For editing we prefer the cursor to go to the end. In order to achieve this you need to call `setSelectionRange` after the input is mounted into the DOM.

```
(defn project-title-input [title]
  (reagent/create-class
    {:display-name "project-title"
     :component-did-mount
     (fn project-title-input-did-mount [this]
       (doto (.getDOMNode this)
         (.setSelectionRange 10000 10000)))
     :reagent-render
     (fn project-title-input-render [title]
       [:input
        {:default-value title
```

```
:required "required"
:auto-focus "autofocus"
:name "project-title"}])})))
```

Pass a map to `create-class` that contains the lifecycle methods you wish to specify. Now, when the component is mounted into the DOM, you call `setSelectionRange` on the DOM node. Note that you do not need to rely on an element `id` lookup, as the `component-did-mount` lifecycle method receives the component as the first argument.

The lifecycle methods are useful for interop with JavaScript libraries that need to interact with the element directly (threejs, google charts, select2). For example, you can subscribe to a window resize event in `componentDidMount` and unsubscribe in `componentWillUnmount`. The resize event handler can change the renderer for a threejs webgl scene to account for a new canvas size. You can read about other lifecycle methods in the React documentation; they are rarely useful for a Reagent application and should be avoided.

There is an alternate style of form 3, which is to attach the map of lifecycle methods as metadata to a function instead of calling `create-class`. Avoid the metadata style, as metadata provides no syntactic advantage. It is common to attach metadata to a var in Clojure, but Reagent looks for the metadata on the function itself. Avoid this confusing behavior. When you need to use a class, create it explicitly.

Sequences and Keys

Up to this point we have been creating sequences of elements by putting them into a parent vector. But this is not always the best approach. Consider a list of story cards.

```
(into
  [:ul]
  (for [[story-id story] stories]
    [story-card app-state story-id story]))
```

The DOM elements get created with four stories.

```
<ul>
  <li><a href="#/story/3">Implement a way to finish stories</a></li>
  <li><a href="#/story/4">Build a todo list</a></li>
  <li><a href="#/story/5">Draw cards to represent stories</a></li>
  <li><a href="#/story/6">Create lanes to represent story status</a></li>
</ul>
```

And then the `app-state` is updated such that the stories are reversed in order.

```
<ul>
  <li><a href="#/story/6">Create lanes to represent story status</a></li>
  <li><a href="#/story/5">Draw cards to represent stories</a></li>
  <li><a href="#/story/4">Build a todo list</a></li>
  <li><a href="#/story/3">Implement a way to finish stories</a></li>
</ul>
```

In the absence of any special information, the number of DOM updates required to transition between the forward list and reverse list is relatively large. Every `<li>` element would have its contents replaced. However it is obvious to us that nothing really changed except the order. The most efficient update is to re-order the elements, not to re-create their contents.

For React to be able to re-order elements instead of blindly updating them it needs some concept of identity. We assign a unique key to each `<li>` element, and React uses this to do re-ordering efficiently.

```
(doall
  (for [[story-id story] stories]
    ^{:key story-id}
    [story-card app-state story-id story]))
```

Now the `<li>` elements are re-ordered instead of being changed in place. The same end state is achieved with fewer updates to the DOM. Note that `doall` forces a lazy sequence evaluation. Lazy sequences that `deref` ratoms are not allowed.

If the list of stories is short and the story HTML is small, then the difference in performance will not be noticeable, as only a few DOM updates occur either way. But what if we encounter a very long list of stories, and each story has several detailed fields associated with it like the description, owner, and links to other parts of the system? Imagine an update that reverses this large list of detailed stories. In such a scenario, the performance difference will be significant.

> **EXERCISE**
>
> Create a function to generate a random story and call it to create 1000 stories, then change the sequence code and witness the noticeable difference in performance.

To encourage keying sequences React warns you in the console about unkeyed arrays of elements.

```
Unkeyed:     [:ul [[:li] [:li] [:li] [:li]]]
```

It is good practice to explicitly choose to represent a sequence either as children, or as an array of elements with an identifying key. The latter will be more efficient for reordering, so if you have uniquely identifiable elements in your sequence, you should go ahead and assign a key.

```
Children:    [:ul [:li] [:li] [:li] [:li]]
Keyed:       [:ul [^3[:li] ^4[:li] ^5[:li] ^6[:li]]]
```

You can represent sequences in three slightly different ways. The resulting DOM elements are indistinguishable. The difference is in how React will update the elements in response to changes.

Custom Markup

If you pass properties to native HTML elements that do not exist in the HTML specification, React will not render them. If you want to use a custom attribute, you need to prefix it with data.

```
[:span {:awesome "maximus"}]      ;; will not have the awesome attribute
[:span {:data-awesome "maximus"}]    ;; will have the data-awesome attribute
```

The support for standard tags and attributes is comprehensive, but there is also an escape hatch. If you need some custom markup that is not recognized by React as standard, you can dangerously set

HTML. As the name suggests, there is a danger involved with supplying HTML. The main problem to avoid is accidentally forgetting to close a tag, or in some way creating invalid HTML.

An example of where this can be useful is when dealing with SVG. Say you want to create a simple burn-down chart component for the projects. You can build an SVG image with lines representing the remaining tasks over time (see Figure 5-14).

```
(defn burndown-chart []
  (into
    [:svg
     {:width 300
      :height :200
      :style {:border "1px solid lightgrey"}}
     [:text {:x 200 :y 30} "Burn Down"]]
    (for [i (range 9)]
      [:line
       {:x1 (* (inc i) 30)
        :y1 180
        :x2 (* (inc i) 30)
        :y2 (+ (* 15 i) (rand-int 50))
        :stroke "green"
        :stroke-width 15}])))
```

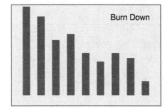

FIGURE 5-14

To add a logo image to the chart, try an SVG image tag.

```
[:image {:hlink:href "img/logo.png" :x 170 :y 15 :height 20 :width 20}]
```

But you now discover that there is no attribute mapping for the `xlink:href` attribute. The logo does not show up. Instead you can specify the markup as a string.

```
[:g {:dangerouslySetInnerHTML
     {:__html "<image xlink:href=img/logo.png x=170
              y=15 height=20 width=20 /> "}}]]
```

Be very careful to close your tags when using this escape hatch! An unclosed tag will result in strange behavior. Also note that the coverage of mapped tags and attributes is growing. When Reagent 6 is released, you will be able to use `:xlink-href`, because the underlying React 14 now supports this and many more SVG related attribute mappings.

Reactions

Reagent knows when to update React by observing ratoms. Ratoms behave similarly to atoms in that you can watch, deref, swap!, and reset! them. Additionally, ratoms trigger rendering when they change. If you use a regular atom instead of a ratom, your interface will still render initially, but rendering upon change will not be triggered. So be careful to always define state using the implementation of atom from reagent.core, not a regular atom.

To create a reaction, write an expression inside a (reaction ...) macro form. Reaction expressions are re-evaluated when any ratom or reaction it derefs change. Components containing derefed reactions will be re-rendered with the new result. In this way you can build up a signal graph where changes propagate in a controlled manner.

```
(ns whip.view.reactions
  (:require [reagent.core :as reagent]
            [devcards.core :refer-macros [defcard-rg deftest]])
  (:require-macros [reagent.ratom :refer [reaction]]))

(def a (reagent/atom {:x 100 :y 200}))
(def b (reaction (:x @a)))
(def c (reaction (+ @b 10)))

(defn view-c []
  (prn "Rendering view-c")
  [:div
   [:div @c]
   [:button {:on-click (fn [e] (swap! a update :x inc))} "inc x"]
   [:button {:on-click (fn [e] (swap! a update :y inc))} "inc y"]])

(defcard-rg reaction-example
  [view-c])
```

Reactions are a very concise way to express data flow. Here you start with a ratom containing x and y values. You then build a reaction b that only observes the x value. Next, introduce another reaction c that observes the sum of b and 10. Then create a component that renders c reactively. Observe that when you click the "inc x" button, the view is updated with the result of applying the expressions. When you click the "inc y" button, nothing happens. Check the console to confirm that the "Rendering view-c" message is only printed when clicking "inc x." This is a very good thing, because the view does not depend on y in any way. If you were to deref a instead of c in the view, it would be re-rendered even if y changed.

Reagent reacts to reactions and ratoms via requestAnimationFrame. So, changing many ratoms and reactions that depend on them only results in one render phase.

Currently, when you render a project-board, you render multiple columns. For every column you are filtering, all of the stories in app-state are sorted by order. Any time anything at all changes in app-state, everything is recalculated. If you want to isolate the effects of changing app-state, you can introduce some reactions.

When defining reactions, be careful to think about when they will really change. Reactions use identical? instead of = to test whether the computation should be re-evaluated. Identical means the same object.

For the view-c example identical? is perfect. But, in the case of filtering stories, the calculation produces results that are equal but not identical. You can introduce equality semantics by remembering the last calculated value in a plain atom a, and then only by returning newly calculated results when they are not equal to a.

```
(defn stories-by-project-status-reaction [app-state project-id status]
  (let [search-term (reaction (:search-term @app-state))
        all-stories (reaction (:stories @app-state))
        a (atom nil)
        filtered-stories
        (reaction
          (let [b (filter-stories @all-stories @search-term project-id status)]
            (if (= b @a)
              @a
              (reset! a b))))]
    (reaction (sort-by (comp :order second) @filtered-stories))))
```

Reactions provide efficient data views and change propagation, which are powerful features. But as the application grows you need to be careful to keep the data and data access organized. The Reframe library can help with this.

One final thing to think about is that if you had chosen a different model to store the stories, you could have avoided the need to calculate derivative values. Instead of storing all of the stories in one map by id that is filtered by project and column, you could have chosen to store the stories exactly how the view would consume them. You could have created something perfectly tailored to the view you are building.

```
{:projects {"project-id" {:status "in progress" [{:story :data}]}}}
```

If you chose to use a nested structure like this that has stories organized by project, then status, and already sorted in a vector, then you don't need to do any transformations at all. But you have given up the ability to find stories by their id. Clearly there are tradeoffs involved in choosing what data is appropriate to send to the client. Often there are multiple views that overlap in the data they consume. DataScript and Om are libraries that can help with this. DataScript is an in browser database, giving the ultimate of flexible data models. Om provides a component query and reconciler abstraction ideal for defining the shape of the data that the view needs from a server.

A Note on Style

Be sure you take new lines liberally.

```
[:button
  {:on-click
    (fn done-click [e]
      (task-done id))}
  "done"]
```

You could collapse this expression down to one line. However, there is a tendency for the attribute map to grow. Also, nested vectors lend themselves to "hangers." Git diffs are easier to understand when you take more vertical space. You'll find it easier to be consistent if you regularly take a new line for attribute maps and event functions.

Don't feel the need to push all of the style code into your styles.css file. Inline styles are convenient when you are building out a new interface. You already have view model separation by isolating your component functions in a view namespace away from your state modification code. So inline styling in the view code is not a bad thing. Create classes for common styles as you discover them and move them to your styles.css to avoid repeating the same styling throughout your code.

Give event handler functions a name. It communicates intent, and error stacktraces are clearer. When returning to the code, the name is very helpful as a summary of what the function is for.

TESTING COMPONENTS WITH DEVCARDS

Figwheel frees you from having to click through your application while you are working on a particular feature. But isn't it annoying now when you have to click through the application to see if everything else is still working? Tests and examples are a great way to drive development toward a goal and clarify design decisions. Testing user interfaces has traditionally been considered difficult. Automation is tedious and brittle, while unit tests rarely capture the look and behavior. Wouldn't it be great if you could see the entire application without having to step through every path? Devcards is a library for showcasing components in various states. You can display several states right next to each other. Devcards is perfect for examples and testing in a web application.

So, before proceeding on to more features for the whip project management tracker, let's add testing feedback to the workflow. Don't worry, this won't be the boring style of testing you may be expecting.

Edit the project.clj file. In the dependencies section add [`devcards` `"0.2.1"`]. In the cljsbuild builds section, copy the dev build to a devcards build. Specify `:devcards true` in the new devcards build's `:figwheel` section. Change `:compiler` `:output-dir` to "resources/public/js/compiled/ devcards," so that the intermediary compiled files do not collide with other builds. Change `:asset-path` to "js/compiled/devcards". Change `:compiler` `:output-to` to "resources/public/js/compiled/ devcards.js," so that the final artifact does not collide with other builds.

```
{:id "devcards"
 :source-paths ["src"]
 :figwheel {:devcards true}
 :compiler {:main whip.core
            :asset-path "js/compiled/devcards"
            :output-to "resources/public/js/compiled/devcards.js"
            :output-dir "resources/public/js/compiled/devcards"
            :source-map-timestamp true}}
```

You don't want to try and render the entire app when looking at the devcards, so modify core.cljs to only conditionally render the entire app:

```
(ns whip.main (:require [goog.dom :as dom]))
(when-let [app (dom/getElement "app")]
  (reagent/render-component [whip-main] app))
```

In the project's resources/public directory, copy the index.html file to devcards.html. Edit devcards.html. Remove the `<div id=app>...</div>` element. Replace whip.js with devcards.js in the `<script>` tag.

Start both the dev build and the new devcards build configured by running in the terminal: **lein figwheel devcards dev**. Check that the app still works at `http://localhost:3449` and then open a new tab and navigate to `http://localhost:3449/devcards.html`. Seeing this page in Figure 5-15 indicates that everything is working so far.

FIGURE 5-15

In the view.cljs source file, add devcards to the namespace require. Refer the defcard macro [`devcards.core :refer-macros [defcard-rg deftest]`]. Instead of defcard, use a more specific version, `defcard-rg`, which renders reagent components. You can define a card that shows the project-board.

```
(defcard-rg project-board-example
  [project-board model/app-state "aaa"])
```

Now you can isolate a single component to work on, instead of having to observe the entire application.

The big idea with Devcards is that because components are functions of state, you can view them in isolation. Imagine how you might approach this without any library support. You might create a page and mount your component with various states. In fact, that is pretty much how you develop any page, except that you throw away all of the intermediary code and only keep the final application. Devcards provides structure for this intuitive approach. The key concept is a macro to create a "card." Devcards collects cards by namespace into a navigable page showing all of the cards. Thanks to dead code removal, you can conveniently intermingle example cards with your application code without worrying about bloat. The cards will not be present in your production build.

Notice how we started with some example data that you were going to throw away? Now you have a way to preserve the hard work and get the benefit of being able to show and test the UI in the states you have designed it for (see Figure 5-16).

```
(defn projects-list [app-state]
  [:div "Project List"])
(defcard-rg projects-list-example
  [projects-list model/app-state])
```

EXERCISE

Write the projects-list function.

HINT

See online code if you get stuck.

A string can optionally be specified in a card as the first argument. The string is rendered as markdown, so you can have richly formatted text and even format code.

```
(defcard test-card
  "=Hello hello"
  [hello])
```

Refer deftest from devcards instead of test.

```
(ns example
  (:require [devcards :refer [deftest]]))
```

Write a test, and see how the test is rendered into the page. Failing tests are colored red. Add an on-jsload hook to report a test summary to the console while developing.

Notice that you are passing the app-state around everywhere. You can instead rely on a global app-state; but we recommend against it. Passing dependencies tends to make code more testable, in the same way that backend functions might pass a database parameter down instead of relying on a global variable. Depending on what you are testing, it might be convenient to share a single state for your cards, or completely isolate them with their own state. For example, say you want to have an example of a story card that does not change the state of the other cards. In that case, you might do something like so:

```
(defn story-card-example-component []
  (let [app-state (reagent/atom example-projects)]
    (fn a-story-card-example-component []
      [story-card app-state "aaa" 2
                  (get-in @app-state [:projects "aaa" :stories 2])])))

(defcard-rg story-card-example
  [story-card-example-component])
```

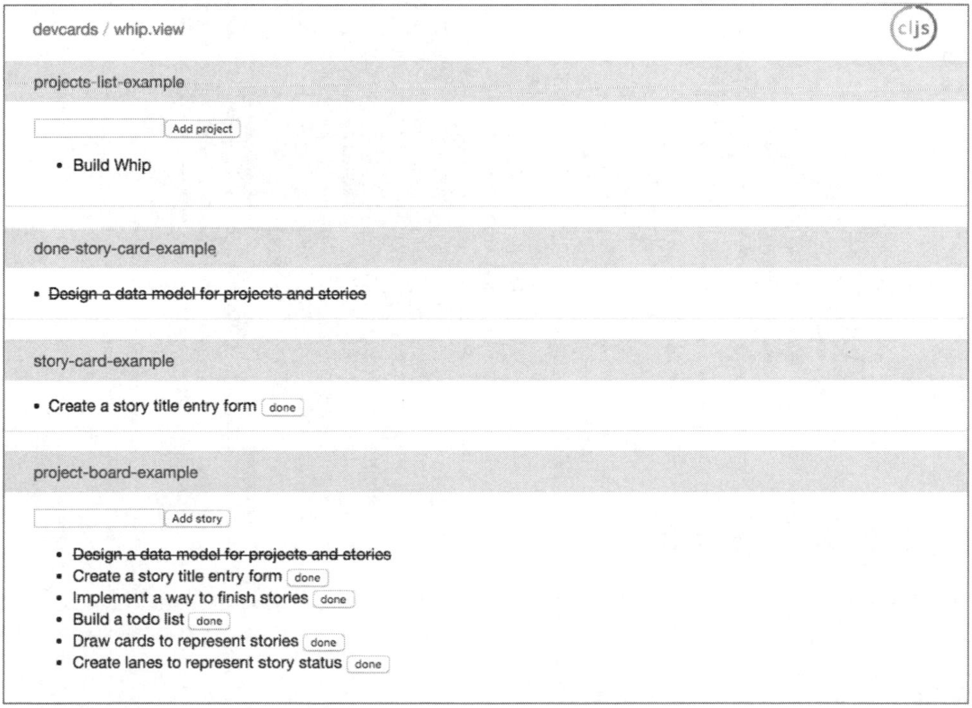

FIGURE 5-16

Let's make a card with a complete board (see Figure 5-17).

Devcards presents cards and tests that occur in namespaces, so you can see what the components will look like in predefined states. You are presented with a visual history and specification of how everything should look and behave.

> **TIP** *ClojureScript and ClojureScript libraries get updated regularly. Add* [lein-ancient "0.6.8"] *to your ~/.lein/profile.clj dependencies so that you can stay up to date easily by executing lein ancient upgrade and lein ancient upgrade :plugins. These commands will rewrite the versions in your project.clj to the latest release. Ancient will run all tests and only save the new project.clj if they are passed.*

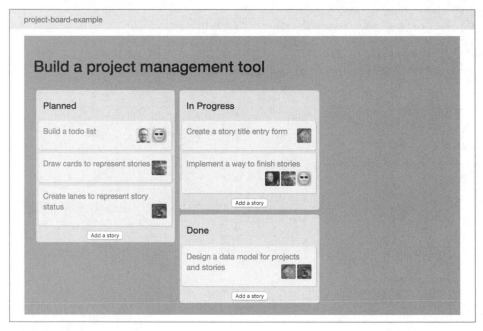

FIGURE 5-17

INTEROP WITH JAVASCRIPT

Interop with JavaScript from ClojureScript is similar to interop with Java from Clojure.

```
(.method object arg1 arg2)
(. object method arg1 arg2)
(.. object method1 (method2 arg1 arg2))
```

JavaScript has a global root object. To access the global root in ClojureScript, use the special js prefix.

```
  js/window
  (.setEventListener js/window (fn [e] (prn "hi")))
  (js/window.setEventListener (fn ...)))
```

To access properties, ClojureScript differs from Clojure slightly in that you must use a dash to indicate property access. JavaScript does not distinguish properties from methods, so the dash is required to explicitly designate property access.

```
  (.-property object)
  (. object -property)
  (.. object -property1 -property2)
  (set! (.-property object) value)
```

You may notice that properties can be accessed another way. The below form is a quirk and will fail advanced compilation, so avoid using it.

```
  object.property         ;; bad, don't do this
  object/property         ;; bad, don't do this
```

Array access is done with aget and aset.

```
  (aget array index)
  (aget array index1 index2 index3)
  (aset array index value)
  (aset array index1 index2 index3 value)
```

Note that you can chain access forms together.

```
  (set! (.-foo (aget array index1)) value)
```

Object constructors are the same as Clojure, but note that you can use constructors from the global JavaScript root.

```
  (js/THREE.Vector3. 0 0 0)
  (new js/THREE.Vcctor3 0 0 0)
```

Modules can be referenced and imported from the Closure Library.

```
  (ns example
    (:import [goog.event KeyCode]))
```

Creating JavaScript objects can be done with js-obj or by using the special #js reader literal. These forms are not recursive. So for nested objects, be sure that the children are specified as literals also.

```
  (js-obj ...)
  #js {"key" "value"}
```

Be cognizant about when to use JavaScript objects and when to use ClojureScript data structures. We recommend using ClojureScript data literals as much as possible, and only using JavaScript objects for interop with third party libraries.

There are transformation functions to convert from ClojureScript data structures to JavaScript objects. These are both recursive.

```
  (clj->js)
  (js->clj)
```

You can optionally specify `:keywordize-keys` true, but keep in mind that not all strings can be keywords.

There is a penultimate escape hatch form `js*` that takes raw JavaScript.

```
(js* "some(javascript);")
```

JavaScript allows anything to be thrown, so the ClojureScript catch form has a special term `:default`, which will match anything. Use this to catch unexpected values being thrown.

```
(try
  (/ :1 2)
  (catch :default ex))
```

You can annotate your functions with `:export` to prevent them being name-mangled during advanced compilation. They will then be easily consumable from JavaScript.

```
(defn ^:export f []
  (+ 1 2))
```

To take advantage of advanced compilation, most popular JavaScript libraries have wrappers available. Wrapping additional libraries is not difficult. Wrapped libraries are easy to depend on, and you benefit from code shrinking. The best source of pre-wrapped libraries is CLJS (`http://cljsjs.github.io`), which also provides instructions on how to create your own wrappers.

ONE LANGUAGE, ONE IDIOM, MANY PLATFORMS

Clojure/ClojureScript realizes the dream of being able to write your frontend code and backend code in the same language, using the same idioms, data structures, and abstractions. Staying in the same language is good, and it goes beyond syntax.

You can even share code directly. Files with the cljc extension are used in any platform. You can specify platform specific code with #clj+.

```
#?(:clj     Double/NaN
   :cljs    js/NaN
   :default nil)
(defn build-list []
  (list #?@(:clj  [5 6 7 8]
            :cljs [1 2 3 4])))
```

THINGS TO KNOW ABOUT THE CLOSURE COMPILER AND LIBRARY

ClojureScript uses the Closure Compiler to produce JavaScript. In the same way that Clojure programming is augmented by some knowledge of the Java ecosystem, it is useful to know a little bit about the Closure Library. There are many opportunities to leverage the platform.

The most impactful feature of the Closure Compiler is that it can do advanced compilation. Advanced mode compilation does aggressive renaming, dead code removal, and global inlining, resulting in highly compressed JavaScript. This power comes with some restrictions. Advanced compilation mode makes assumptions about the code that it optimizes, and breaking these assumptions will result in errors. For the most part you are one layer away from those assumptions, until it comes to interop with JavaScript libraries. JavaScript libraries must be accompanied by extern definitions, or the aggressive renaming will not be matched to your interop calls. Fortunately, many popular libraries are readily available from CLJSJS with extern definitions as a packaged dependency.

Most project templates configure a development build using no optimization, and a production build using advanced mode compilation. Development tools like figwheel can only be used with no optimizations, and these builds are very fast (typically under one second). Advanced mode production builds on the other hand are too slow for an interactive development cycle (typically between 15 seconds to a full minute).

The Closure Library is a rich source of helper code. The library is rigorously cross browser compatible. This is a big win. You took advantage of this when you added the history listener in the navigation and routing section of this chapter. Instead of relying on browser specific code, use `goog.History` instead. As a rule of thumb, if you find yourself accessing browser features directly via interop, consider looking for an abstraction for it in the Closure Library documentation. There are helpers for the DOM, files, events, keyboard handling, form handling, components such as date pickers, and many more. The library is comprehensive, and well worth perusing to familiarize yourself with what is available.

MODELING STATE WITH DATASCRIPT

DataScript is a database implementation in ClojureScript designed to be a replacement for the `app-state` of your application. It goes beyond storing your application state and stores the history of changes to the state as well. Having a database as your `app-state` centralizes state access and modification around a powerful abstraction. You can create queries to view the data in different ways. DataScript is built on the same principles as Datomic, which is explored in depth in Chapter 6. Datascript stores data as datom tuples (entity, relationship, entity, time), which provide a history of all changes. The main advantage of Datascript comes from flexible Datalog queries.

Queries are expressed as data.

```
(def q-player
  '[:find ?s ?attrs (pull ?e [*])
    :where [?a :coach "Coach"]
    [?a :player "William"]
    [?a :attrs ?attrs]
    [?e :name "William"]
    [?e :somedata ?s]])
```

To use DataScript in a reactive website, you can take advantage of the ability to watch transactions. You use the `listen!` function to be notified of transactions. Inside the handler you respond to changes in the database. Re-query the database whenever the data changes:

```
(defn bind
  ([conn q & args]
```

```
(let [k (uuid/make-random)
      ratom (reagent/atom (apply d/q q @conn args))]
  (d/listen! conn k (fn [tx-report]
                      (reset! ratom (apply d/q q (:db-after tx-report)
                        args))))
  (set! (.-__key ratom) k)
  ratom)))
```

Here `bind` creates a ratom that the application can use for reactive rendering. When the database changes, the ratom is updated, and when the ratom is updated the component re-renders, and when the component re-renders the DOM diff occurs to update the browser elements.

```
(defn player []
  (bind conn q-player))
```

One major difference from Datomic is that DataScript does not require an upfront schema. This makes it very approachable, because you can dive right into transactions and queries without defining your attributes. However, a schema is necessary in order to nominate non-defaults such as the cardinality of one to many.

GO ROUTINES IN YOUR BROWSER WITH CORE.ASYNC

Core.async is your get out of callback hell card. Let's take a look at the standard example of callback hell; a nested chain of asynchronous function calls.

```
getData(function(a){
    getMoreData(a, function(b){
        getMoreData(b, function(c){
```

This situation arises frequently in JavaScript applications because JavaScript is single threaded and avoids blocking for operations like remote service calls. The common interface presented by the browser for blocking actions is to return from the function call immediately, while the browser manages the request. When the request is fulfilled there is no way to return control to the original call site. So when a blocking action is requested, the caller must specify a callback function to be invoked when the action is completed. This allows you to get around the single threaded model with asynchronous calls. But, as the number of callbacks increases, it quickly becomes difficult to reason about the order of execution of our code, and how failures should be treated.

Callback hell is the eventual state of any complex callback oriented asynchronous program where the management of callbacks gets so hard that your code becomes extremely hard to understand, reason about, and maintain.

The problem is more than just having nested function definitions. The real rub comes when changing application state inside those callbacks. Consider a text input that you want to populate with a list of completions. Fire off a request to the server with some user input, but by the time the result arrives, it may not be relevant anymore, because the user has since replaced the text in the input. The difficulty using an asynchronous expression goes beyond syntax. How can you express state and error handling in a way that is clear, logical, and testable?

Callbacks close over state and raise events, which are consumed from a queue. The state is in the processing code. To handle all the possible interactions of the callbacks, build a state machine that encompasses all of the possible state transitions.

Core.async provides you with an option to trade where the state lives. It presents a model of short-lived variables in a sequential process, and allows concurrent sequential processes to communicate with each other. The implementation of core.async is actually a bunch of sophisticated macros that build state machines to provide the execution models written as sequential processes. While it isn't important to understand the implementation details, it helps to remember that in ClojureScript these expressions are executing in a single thread in an interleaved fashion controlled by a generated state machine.

Let's look at a basic example where you make a web request.

```
(let [ch (http/get "//whip/projects")]
  (go (hello (<! ch))))
```

Here http/get returns a channel. The go block defines a concurrent process that will pull the result of the web request from the channel and use it. Blocking can only occur inside a concurrent process defined by a go block. The result of a go block is a channel, which will deliver the last value in the go block. In this example the result is ignored. Channels can accept and deliver values. <! is the operator to take a value from a channel. Notice that there are no locks, no condition variables, and no callbacks required for these kinds of expressions. They look like a thread that can block while other threads continue.

Core.async plays well with existing JavaScript libraries. If you have an interface that requires a callback, just pass a callback that only puts the arguments onto a channel, and you can reframe your logic as a sequential process consuming from the channel.

SUMMARY

ClojureScript has many compelling features that position it as the leading option for reactive web-page development. Interface definitions are concise, the reactive model is robust, there are solid abstractions to build on, and there are many helpful libraries to leverage.

This chapter stepped through all of the important aspects of building a ClojureScript application, developing an interactive project tracking webpage, and using several useful libraries. You saw how ClojureScript has a unique and compelling development workflow.

A lot of ground was covered, from getting started through to advanced techniques. You may be feeling a little overwhelmed by the breadth of topics covered in this chapter. The good news is that this knowledge is widely applicable. ClojureScript opens up fundamental computation abstractions that provide the leverage necessary to build large and robust web pages. But you don't need to use all of ClojureScript's special powers. You can start small and build up with the confidence that those special powers are there when you need to reach for them.

You now have a template for building out a ClojureScript project. With this knowledge you are ready to build any interface that a browser can support, using comfortable idioms and powerful abstractions.

The Datomic Database

WHAT'S IN THIS CHAPTER?

➤ Introducing the Datomic Database

➤ Modeling domain data in Datomic

➤ Using Datomic from Clojure

➤ Leveraging Datomic to solve common problems in database-backed applications

Datomic is a new database that offers developers new ways to think about building traditional database-backed applications, and exciting features that make it possible to build entirely new types of applications. It has a modern, cloud-focused design that is easy and flexible to both develop on and deploy. To top it off, it's built by the same people that brought you Clojure.

Just as working with Clojure changes the way you think about programming, Datomic will change the way you think about databases. It is definitely not just another variation on SQL or another narrowly focused NoSQL system. Datomic embodies new ideas about how you think about data and what it is like to work with a general-purpose transactional database.

In this chapter, you'll explore how Datomic works, starting from the fundamentals like its data model, and working up to its high-level APIs. Using examples, you'll look at how to build an application backed up by Datomic, ways to think about modeling domain data in Datomic, and how to tap into the powerful Clojure API.

CHAPTER EXAMPLES AND SOURCE CODE

You can access the examples and source code for this chapter on the Wiley website at www.wiley.com/go/professionalclojure or via Github at https://github.com/backstopmedia/clojurebook.

DATOMIC BASICS

The idea for Datomic was hatched when Rich Hickey started thinking about what it would look like when some of the big ideas that went into the design of Clojure were applied to a database system. With concepts like immutable data, design focused on decomposition, and the importance of value-oriented semantics, the idea grew into a collaboration between Rich Hickey, Stuart Halloway (cofounder of Cognitect and Clojure core committer), and a small group of developers at Cognitect. It was first released in 2012.

Datomic doesn't fit cleanly into a single category. Multiple labels fit it, including NoSQL, graph database, distributed database, transactional store, analytics store, and logic database. It took inspiration from multiple sources, but its basic goal is to be a drop-in replacement for the main cases where you would otherwise use a relational database as a transactional store. Stuart Halloway says that it's targeted at the ninety-six percent use cases of relational databases, leaving off the top four percent of high write-volume users like Netflix, Facebook, etc.

This raises the question: why use Datomic instead of SQL? This section examines some of the ways that Datomic sets itself apart from this traditional and venerable technology. You'll learn about Datomic's data model, query language, data-focused transaction syntax, and its design and deployment architecture.

Why Datomic?

Datomic is a powerful alternative to relational SQL-based databases that's suitable for the vast majority of systems currently built on these more traditional databases. It represents a re-thinking of the role, model, structure, and nature of a database system, incorporating modern concepts of cloud deployment, cheap storage, distributed systems, and persistent data structures/immutable data. It offers a number of key advantages over relational databases.

➤ **Deployment flexibility.** In contrast to monolithic relational databases, Datomic has a pluggable storage backend, which can use many different backing databases to store its data. This means that, when deploying applications, you can use whatever system is most convenient for the deployment environment and your operations infrastructure. For instance, for AWS deployments it's simple and natural to use the DynamoDB backend. If your organization already runs a Cassandra, Riak, Couchbase, Infinispan, or even a SQL database, you can use any of those as the storage backend.

➤ **Data-oriented design.** When learning functional programming there's often a series of "a-ha!" moments as the elegance and simplicity of the data-oriented approach click into place, and the advantages over models that emphasize mutation and data hiding become clear. Datomic is animated by the same kind of mathematical beauty. Once you grasp the data model and how to work with it, using Datomic has a liberating freedom and power. It's a stark contrast to relational databases, with their mutate-in-place semantics and the feeling that you are working with data while wearing bulky and unwieldy gloves.

➤ **Entity orientation.** The central idea of relational databases is tables, but outside of very simple toy applications it's very rare that a table has a one-to-one correspondence with the entity it represents. Typically it takes multiple tables to represent a single entity in realistic relational data models. This represents a real impedance mismatch with the way developers think of entities, and has cost untold numbers of man-years in developing ultimately awkward and unsatisfying solutions like ORMs and query generators. By contrast, the structure of data in Datomic's entity model more closely matches the structure of data as a developer would model it and work with it in an application. Datomic's query and pull APIs also provide powerful tools for elegantly pulling out complex, nested entities in a simple and declarative way.

➤ **Read scalability.** In Datomic, reads are separated from writes and decentralized. A single Datomic database can power mixed workloads—transactional, analytical, and even batch— while retaining low latency for transactional performance, and high throughput for analytical and batch performance. This is made possible by Datomic's unique architecture, where writes don't block reads, reads don't block one another, and you can horizontally scale your read capability by adding more "peer" systems. Relational databases can only scale vertically without requiring sharding and often fundamental changes to the architecture of your application, and often require you to deploy multiple databases to power different workloads with the increased complexity cost of data synchronization between them.

➤ **Flexibility.** The schema, data model, and query system of Datomic support an incredible range of flexibility. This flexibility means that in practice your queries are rarely tied down to a schema designed to make that specific query performant. It's almost always possible to make changes to queries or add entirely new read patterns while maintaining performance, without changing your application data model. This typically translates to simpler application data models and simpler application architecture. Best practices in relational databases, on the other hand, typically call for entirely different schema designs to power, for instance, transactional and analytical workloads, because the schema and read patterns are much more closely tied together.

➤ **Treat the database as a value.** This is one of the big ideas of rethinking the database that motivated Datomic. Relational databases give you a handle that you treat as an external resource that you can send questions to and get answers. The database and the data it contains are treated as a separate system, and from the perspective of the application, every interaction with the databases is a side effect. Datomic's immutable data model and APIs allow you to treat the database itself and the data it contains as a value for the purposes of reads as well as "speculative" writes. This opens up exciting possibilities for how you think about and design your database-driven applications.

➤ **Point-in-time access.** Since the data in a Datomic database is immutable, you can perform read operations and queries on *historical* versions of your data: you can get a view of your data as it existed at any point in time.

➤ **Upsert.** Admittedly, this might seem like a lower-level detail, particularly compared to the previous points. Upsert is a write semantic that allows you to treat the addition of new entities and changes to existing entities the same way, like a combination of a relational INSERT and UPDATE query. If you've never worked with a database that supported this feature, it's going to forever change your outlook. Upserts elegantly solve a whole class of concurrency and state-related issues with adding data, and allow you to use a single code path for your writes.

It's not all roses, of course. Everything in software is about trade-offs. The first major disadvantage is that it's proprietary software. While there are free-as-in-beer ways to get Datomic, there is no open source version, and for any kind of real production deployment, it's likely that you're going to have to pay for it.

You also need to consider the adoption effort. Datomic is very different from relational databases. Although some of what you know about working with SQL and relational data will be able to translate over to working with Datomic, there is definitely a learning curve. Datomic is going to be unfamiliar territory in many ways, and will involve some of the same kind of transformation in the way you think about databases, as functional programming transforms the way you think about writing programs. Building applications with Datomic requires that you and your team all get on board and really dig in to understand how the system works.

The best way to get there is from the ground up, starting with Datomic's data model.

The Datomic Data Model

One of the most important ingredients in the secret sauce that makes Datomic such an outstanding database is its simple, flexible, yet powerful data model. It's the reason that Datomic is often called a "database of facts," and it closely parallels the way people normally think and talk about information when outside the confines of traditional relational databases. In this section you'll get a complete look at that data model with a focus on the basic building blocks that are used and combined in different ways to power the higher-level APIs covered later in this chapter.

A Relational Example

You're probably already familiar with the data model of relational databases. They represent data in tables, also called "relations" in formal terminology, with a row for each "thing" in the table and a column for each piece of information about the thing. For example, a table of contacts might look like what you see in Table 6-1.

TABLE 6-1: Table of contacts

ID	FIRST_NAME	LAST_NAME	EMAIL	EMERGENCY_CONTACT_ID
101	Jane	Doe	everywoman123@gmail.com	115

As Rich Hickey described in his talk "The Value of Values," this is a model of information that's all about "place." If you want to know Jane Doe's email, you go to the location of Jane Doe's row and retrieve it from the location of the email column. If Jane Doe changes her email, you go back to its location, delete what's there, and replace it with the new one, but the old email lost forever. This model quickly starts to look a lot less like what we as Clojure developers think of as data and more like a pile of mutable references.

Inflexibility is another drawback of the relational model. You must declare the structure of all your data in very strict terms ahead of time, and you must shoehorn the dynamic heterogeneity of the real world into fixed and structured tables. Relationships between things must be carefully modeled in advance, typically requiring multiple extra tables whose sole purpose is to describe relationships between things in other tables, and every query that uses them must be written with explicit joins, while paying careful attention to the specifics of the schema.

Datomic Datoms

With that in mind, let's compare Datomic's data model. Datomic stores a collection of 5-tuples called Datoms, which are its fundamental unit of data. The Datomic documentation describes it as a database of immutable facts, and each one of these facts is expressed as a Datom, which look like this:

```
[e a v t added?]
```

➤ e means "entity". It is roughly analogous to the "id" field in the previous relational table. It contains a Datomic entity id, a Long. Also similar to the way primary keys are typically handled in relational databases is that you don't set entity ids directly when adding data; they are internal to Datomic and are generated automatically by the transactor, Datomic's writer.

➤ a means "attribute." It's a bit like a column in a relational table, or in more familiar Clojure terms it's like the key in a hash map. The attribute part of a Datom contains the Datomic entity id of an attribute entity. You'll see what this means later, in the section on schema and modeling data.

➤ v means "value." It's similar to a cell or field in a relational table. In Datomic, the value part of a Datom contains either an entity id, if the Datom is describing a relationship between the e entity and the v entity, in which case it's called a "reference," or some data value like a string, number, date, and so forth.

Together, entity-attribute-value gives you the basic facts. Before talking about what t and added? mean, let's take a look at what the data from the previous relational example might look like as Datoms with just the [e a v] part. You'll notice that keywords are being used in the a position rather than entity ids (Longs). In the schema section you'll see why this is the case, and how Datomic resolves them to the entities they refer to.

```
[[101 :first-name "Jane"]
 [101 :last-name "Doe]
 [101 :email "everywoman123@gmail.com"]
 [101 :emergency-contact 115]]
```

It's very important to keep this [e a v] pattern in mind when thinking about data in Datomic because Datalog—Datomic's query language—is all about matching these patterns with variables and values. This is covered later in the section on querying.

The t and added? parts of the Datom together are what give Datomic its immutable characteristics, point-in-time query features, and database-as-a-value abstraction. This is also where Datomic departs almost completely from the paradigm of relational databases, because there is no real relational analog for this part of the data model.

t means "transaction." Each write to Datomic contains one or more Datoms bound in a transaction. As part of the write process, the transaction itself is created as an entity, which has an attribute with a timestamp that corresponds to the time of the transaction. Every Datom in the transaction has the transaction's entity id in the t position.

Storing transaction entities in this way as part of the data model means that every fact in the database can be traced back to the exact point in time that it entered the system.

`added?` is a Boolean flag that will be set to `true` if the Datom is an *assertion*, and `false` if it's a *retraction*. Assertion means the fact that a Datom is conveying is true as of the transaction time, retraction means it's no longer true. Let's look at an example using Jane Doe and a new attribute: `favorite-color`. As of the time of transaction `t1`, Jane Doe's favorite color is red. The state of the database looks like this.

```
[[101 :favorite-color "red" t1 true]]
```

We have a Datom for Jane Doe (entity id 101), which was added as part of transaction `t1`, and it's an assertion because the `added?` flag is `true`. Now let's assume Jane Doe is going through a rebellious teenage phase, and as of the time of transaction `t2` she decides that her favorite color is no longer red, but it's now black. Here's the new state of the database after `t2`.

```
[[101 :favorite-color "red" t1 true]
 [101 :favorite-color "red" t2 false]
 [101 :favorite-color "black" t2 true]]
```

You see what happened! Rather than an update-in-place, where you would have completely deleted the idea that Jane Doe's favorite color was ever red, you have added a retraction Datom for that fact since it is no longer true, and added an assertion Datom that tells you Jane's new favorite color.

In the most regular usage of Datomic, you don't directly deal with the complete Datom. Most of the APIs work in terms of `[e a v]`—entity, attribute, and value. The transaction and added flag are typically underneath an abstraction where, given a point in time of a particular transaction value, you only see the entity, attribute, and value parts of Datoms that are true at that time. The transaction and added flag of the Datoms are used to build a projection of the current state of the data as of that time. For example, as of transaction `t1` the state looked like this:

```
[[101 :favorite-color "red"]]
```

Whereas, as of transaction `t2` the state looked like this:

```
[[101 :favorite-color "black"]]
```

This is a very important abstraction to keep in mind, because most of the time you're working in Datomic the `t` and `added?` parts of Datoms are abstracted away from you. There are also numerous ways to powerfully leverage the full Datoms, and understanding the complete Datomic data model is very important in designing systems to use it properly, so you need to be able to think about your data in both ways.

It's an abstraction that fits in powerfully with Clojure's broader view of data and state. As a Clojure programmer, you usually think of state as something to be carefully managed and minimized in your systems, because you realize that much of the most tedious, error-prone, and dangerous aspects of programming revolve around state management. The opinionated design of Clojure works very hard to keep state to a minimum, and places more restrictive semantics around mutable state so that developers know to handle it with care. Whenever possible, data is preferable to state.

Datomic's data model works along very similar lines. It looks at the database as a data structure to which you can only add additional facts, and treats state as a projection of that data structure.

Entity Maps

When using Datomic, one of the common ways that you'll interact with data is as entity maps. There is an API for this, which is covered in more detail in the Clojure API section, but in the meantime let's examine the basic concept. You've already seen how to describe all of the facts about an entity in terms of Datoms. Another way to look at that same data is in an entity map format.

Entity maps are conceptually quite simple. You start the projection of the state of an entity as of a given transaction time—in other words, only the [e a v] parts of Datoms representing facts that are true as of that time. After that, it's a fairly straightforward matter to represent the Datoms about a particular entity as a map. The one catch is where the entity id goes. In Datomic entity maps, the entity id is in a special key called :db/id. Here's what Jane Doe would look like as an entity map.

```
{:db/id 101
 :first-name "Jane"
 :last-name "Doe"
 :email "everywoman123@gmail.com"
 :emergency-contact 115}
```

Querying

Datalog is Datomic's query language. It's related to logic programming and also shares many similarities with SPARQL, the semantic query language for RDF, which was one of Datomic's influences. It can look strange to those more familiar with SQL, but it offers several key advantages.

➤   Datalog queries are datastructures—in fact, they're Clojure collections. This makes Datalog queries far more composable, and allows you to take advantage of all of Clojure's powerful features for working with collections to create and modify them. Manipulating SQL queries, on other hand, requires awkward and error-prone string concatenation and interpolation, heavy-weight parsing and rendering code, or idiosyncratic DSLs or ORMs that limit the expressive power of the queries you can write.

➤   Joins are implicit. To write queries that deal with relationships between different entities, you only need to know that those relationships are expressed. Expressing these relationships is simple, transparent, and follows the natural flow of the relationships in the data. You don't need detailed knowledge of the table schema, and the specific way each table is joined, as you do in SQL. In Datalog, you're working with data directly and at a higher level, rather than with the details of how it's expressed in tables.

➤   Advanced query logic is possible through rules. Datalog includes a declarative language for expressing rules, which allows for arbitrary recursion and highly customized logic inside of queries. Datalog's rules let you do things in your queries that would either be completely impossible in SQL, or would require SQL with such daunting complexity that you'd likely never want to use it in a production system.

Datomic arrives at answers to Datalog queries through unification—a concept from logic programming. For those unfamiliar with this style of programming, it may be helpful to do a bit of background reading so that the concepts are not completely foreign. A fantastic resource for this is

The Reasoned Schemer by Friedman, Byrd, and Kiselyov. It uses the same question-and-response dialectic approach as their prominent book for Lisp beginners, *The Little Schemer,* and provides a fun, easy-to-understand, and approachable introduction to logic programming in a Lisp-like syntax.

Syntax

There are two ways to write Datalog queries: the list form and the map form. They are semantically equivalent, but are typically used in different scenarios. The list form is idiomatically most often what's used for queries written by humans, because many people find it somewhat easier to read and it requires fewer inner lists. Here's a simple query in the list form, which will return the first name and last name of the entity whose email address is everywoman123@gmail.com.

```
'[:find ?first-name ?last-name
  :where [?e :email "everywoman123@gmail.com"]
         [?e :first-name ?first-name]
         [?e :last-name ?last-name]]
```

The map form is more often used when building queries programmatically, because it's much easier to destructure and manipulate the various parts of the query when they're in map keys. This is the same query in the map form.

```
'{:find [?first-name ?last-name]
  :where [[?e :email "everywoman123@gmail.com"]
          [?e :first-name ?first-name]
          [?e :last-name ?last-name]]}
```

The two forms are quite similar, but the map form requires that all of the query components be wrapped in lists. You'll notice that both forms have been quoted—the preceding '. This is required when used in Clojure code, because queries are written using symbols, like ?first-name and ?last-name, which throw exceptions when evaluated.

Since it's more idiomatic for queries written by humans, the list form will be used for the rest of this chapter, except in places discussing how to build and manipulate queries programmatically.

Here is what the equivalent SQL might look like. Notice that, in this simple example, the SQL version has at least a vague resemblance to the Datalog.

```
"SELECT first_name, last_name FROM contacts
 WHERE email='everywoman123@gmail.com'"
```

Let's take a closer look at that simple query example.

Find... What Am I Looking For?

The "find" part of the query—the first line starting with :find—is roughly analogous to the SELECT part of a SQL SELECT query. It says what you want to return, and in what format you want it. In this example, here is the find specification:

```
:find ?first-name ?last-name
```

In Datalog, variables are symbols prefixed with ?, so this find specification is returning the values for the two variables ?first-name and ?last-name, as defined later in the where section of the query. This type of find specification—where the variables are simply positionally listed after the

:find keyword—returns a "relation." This is the most common type of find specification in most queries you'll see and write because it's the most general form, and its behavior is the most similar to that of SQL SELECT.

The result, when run against the earlier sample data, is a set of tuples:

```
#{["Jane" "Doe"]}
```

Returning Collections

The second type of find specification returns a collection of all the matches for a single variable. Collection find specifications are written like this:

```
:find [?first-name ...]
```

When run against the example data again, it returns this result:

```
["Jane"]
```

The equivalent SQL looks much the same as the original, only containing one SELECT column rather than two.

Returning Only One Result

You can also write a find specification that has the same general behavior as the relation semantic, but only returns the first match. This is the "single tuple" specification, and it is written like this:

```
:find [?first-name ?last-name]
```

With this find specification, the query returns the first result tuple it finds, like this:

```
["Jane" "Doe"]
```

The SQL version adds a LIMIT clause to achieve the same behavior.

```
"SELECT first_name, last_name FROM contacts
 WHERE email='everywoman123@gmail.com'
 LIMIT 1"
```

Returning a Single Value

In some cases, it's useful for queries to return one scalar value. For that, use the scalar find specification, written like this:

```
:find ?first-name .
```

This find specification simply returns "Jane." The SQL version retains the LIMIT clause and only the first_name SELECT column.

:where Is Where the Magic Happens

The body of the query, where almost all of the query logic and important structure live, are in the where clauses. This part of the query does almost everything that you'd do in a SQL query–conditions, joins, inner queries, filters. As such, there are probably more features that deal with what you can do in the where part of a query than for any other aspect of Datalog.

There's a great breadth of topics to cover to get a full idea of what is possible in where clauses. Truly, the level of power and flexibility that Datalog gives you in expressing query logic here is amazing, and throughout the rest of the chapter you'll see a more comprehensive set of this functionality.

You can think of the where clauses as patterns that describe what the data in the database needs to look like to satisfy the pattern. These patterns match against the entity, attribute, and value parts of Datoms as of a given transaction-time. Let's first get a basic grasp of what's going on in our simple query. The where clauses look like this:

```
:where [?e :email "everywoman123@gmail.com"]  ;; 1
       [?e :first-name ?first-name]            ;; 2
       [?e :last-name ?last-name]              ;; 3
```

In order to return a solution, these patterns require that three Datoms exist in the database:

1. A Datom with any entity id (which will be bound to the variable `?e`), the attribute `:email`, and the value `everywoman123@gmail.com`.

2. A Datom with the same entity id as the previous Datom—in other words, a Datom that's about the entity that has the `:email` of `everywoman123@gmail.com`—has the attribute `:first-name`, and has any value. The value gets bound to the variable `?first-name`.

3. A Datom with the same entity id as the previous two, the attribute `:last-name`, and any value. The value is, as before, bound to a variable: `?last-name`.

There are a few things to note here. When values are "bound" to Datalog variables, that same value is used for the rest of the solution. In this case that means several things.

➤ If there was no Datom with attribute `:email` and value `everywoman123@gmail.com`, then these where clauses would return no solutions. The result would be an empty set.

➤ The entity id bound to `?e` in the first pattern must also have Datoms that match the second and third patterns. In other words, that entity-id must also have Datoms with `:first-name` and `:last-name`; otherwise the where clauses would again return no solutions.

➤ If there were multiple entities that matched all of the patterns, then multiple solutions are returned.

It's important to understand how this variable binding and solution finding process works. It's possible for patterns to match multiple Datoms and have multiple possible value bindings for Datalog variables, and each one of these bindings is tested against the rest of the patterns in turn. If Datoms exist in the database that satisfy all of the patterns, then that solution is considered "unified" and is returned as part of the results. This process can be recursive, since variable bindings from earlier patterns can be linked to additional variable bindings in later patterns, which must in turn each be tested against subsequent patterns.

Let's go through a somewhat more involved example to see how this process works.

Variables and Joins

The initial example was fairly simple. Let's look at one that involves data with more relationships and a query with more variables. First, we'll extend the data to include more than one contact, and the concept that contacts can have friends. For simplicity, let's keep using only the `[e a v]` part of the Datoms.

```
[[101 :first-name "Jane"]
 [101 :last-name "Doe"]
 [101 :email "everywoman123@gmail.com"]
 [101 :friend 102]
 [101 :friend 103]
 [102 :first-name "Ada"]
 [102 :last-name "Lovelace"]
 [102 :email "firstprogramm3r@steampunk.com"]
 [102 :friend 104]
 [103 :first-name "Robert"]
 [103 :last-name "Heinlein"]
 [103 :email "dareallazarus@long.com"]
 [104 :first-name "Jane"]
 [104 :last-name "Smith]]
```

You still have your old friend Jane Doe, but she has two new friends. Using this data, let's look at a slightly more complex query.

```
'[:find ?first-name ?last-name
  :where [?e :email "everywoman123@gmail.com"]
         [?e :first-name ?first-name]
         [?e :last-name ?last-name]
         [?e :friend ?f]
         [?f :first-name "Robert"]
         [?f :last-name "Heinlein"]]
```

In this query, you are still looking for the first name and last name of an entity whose email is everywoman123@gmail.com, but you have added some more clauses. You now have a join! The entity must also have a friend—another `entity?f`—whose first name is "Robert" and last name is "Heinlein." As it happens, "Jane Doe" is friends with "Robert Heinlein," so the result is the same as before: `#{ ["Jane" "Doe"] }`

Let's walk through the execution of this query to help clarify how Datalog works with multiple variables and relationships.

As before, the first three patterns will match Datoms where there is an entity with the specified value for `:email`, which also has `:first-name` and `:last-name`, and as before you bind those to the variables `?first-name` and `?last-name`. The fourth pattern binds any value from a Datom with that same entity-id and the attribute `:friend` to the variable `?f`. This means that `?f` will contain two possible values: 102 and 103.

To satisfy the next pattern, the query will try to find matches where `?f` is 102 or 103. Trying 102 will not return a solution, because there is no Datom where 102 is the entity, and the `:first-name` is "Robert." But the second value, 103, will return a solution because it matches both of the last two patterns.

This query can still be written in SQL, although it begins to look more unwieldy.

```
"SELECT e.first_name, e.last_name FROM contacts AS e
 INNER JOIN contacts AS f
 ON e.friend_id = f.id
```

```
    AND e.email = 'everywoman123@gmail.com'
    AND f.first_name = 'Robert'
    AND f.last_name = 'Heinlein'"
```

Going Deeper

To help you understand this more fully, let's look at an even more complex query that shows some more of the power of logic programming, and the use of variables across joins.

```
'[:find ?first-name ?last-name
  :where [?e :first-name ?first-name]  ;; 1
         [?e :last-name ?last-name]    ;; 1
         [?e :friend ?f]               ;; 2
         [?f :friend ?g]               ;; 3
         [?g :first-name ?first-name]] ;; 4
```

This query returns the same solutions as the previous queries—#{ ["Jane" "Doe"] }, but why? In words, what this query is looking for is:

1. The first name and last name of anyone

2. Who is friends with someone

3. Who is friends with another person

4. Who has the same first name as the first person

In the data, "Jane Doe" is friends with "Ada Lovelace" who is friends with "Jane Smith," so "Jane Doe" is returned as the solution. Here you start to see the magic of logic programming. You did not have to delve into any of the mechanics of how to traverse the data, or the structure and storage of intermediate results, or explicitly call out any joins between different entities. In this query you declaratively describe the data pattern at a high level, so the constraints and relationships you are interested in for the solution, and the Datalog engine, finds all of the answers that match.

The SQL equivalent for this query is left as an exercise to the reader.

However, with great power comes great responsibility. This particular query does almost nothing to narrow down the possible set of matches, so as the number of contacts and size of the friends graph in our data grows, this query will have to churn through more and more possible solutions to find the one that matches. In production systems this can become unfeasibly expensive, so exercise caution and try to write queries that are as selective as possible, as you saw in earlier queries that required a matching email.

Kaboom! A Combinatorial Explosion

Just as in SQL, it's possible to write queries that will result in combinatorial explosions. Here's one such query.

```
'[:find ?first-name ?last-name
  :where [?a :first-name ?first-name]
         [?b :last-name ?last-name]]
```

Notice how the two patterns in the where clause are disjointed. This query returns every combination of first and last name in the database.

Transactions

Now that the basics of queries in Datomic have been covered, let's look at how you write data. Writes are sent to Datomic in the form of "transactions," which are data structures following certain rules. All transactions are expressed as lists containing data to be added or retracted.

There are two basic syntax options for how to write transactions: a lower-level list-based form that hews closely to the format of Datoms themselves, and a higher-level map-based form. The map-based form is essentially syntactic sugar that translates into the lower-level list-based form, so let's first look at the list syntax.

Low-level List Syntax

The list form follows this format:

```
[command e a v]
```

➤ command is either `:db/add` or `:db/retract`—the first means that this fact should be added to the database, the second means it should be retracted. This will map directly to the `added?` part of the Datom.

➤ e is an entity reference, which is an extended version of the e part of the Datom. This is covered in greater detail in the section on using Datomic in Clojure. For now, let's simplify this and say that it is either the entity id of an existing entity, or it's a temporary id structure that Datomic translates into a permanent entity id as part of the transaction.

➤ a and v are the same as in the previous examples.

Perhaps you're wondering, "I see e a v and `added?`, but where's t?" The answer is that it's generated for you. Datomic automatically creates a transaction entity and attaches it to all of the Datoms in the transaction as part of the transaction process.

For example, a transaction in list form to add the data about "Jane Doe" to the system for the first time might look like:

```
[[:db/add jane-temp-id :first-name "Jane"]
 [:db/add jane-temp-id :last-name "Doe"]
 [:db/add jane-temp-id :email "everywoman123@gmail.com"]]
```

This adds an entity for Jane with her first and last name, and email, assuming you have generated a temporary id for her with the Datomic API and bound it to `jane-temp-id`. Now suppose you want to add some friends for Jane. First, you need to find Jane's actual entity id with this query.

```
'[:find ?jane-id .
  :where [?e :email "everywoman123@gmail.com"]]
```

Then you can add her friends with a transaction like this:

```
[[:db/add heinlein-temp-id :first-name "Robert"]
 [:db/add heinlein-temp-id :last-name "Heinlein"]
 [:db/add heinlein-temp-id :email "dareallazarus@long.com"]
 [:db/add jane-id :friend heinlein-temp-id]
 [:db/add lovelace-temp-id :first-name "Ada"]
 [:db/add lovelace-temp-id :last-name "Lovelace"]
 [:db/add lovelace-temp-id :email "firstprogramm3r@steampunk.com"]
 [:db/add jane-id :friend lovelace-temp-id]]
```

Again, let's assume you have generated temporary ids for the two new entities being added, and you've bound Jane's permanent id from the previous query to `jane-id`.

All of these transactions are assertions, so let's take a quick look at what a retraction looks like. Let's assume that Jane Doe, having read some of Heinlein's later works, is shocked by his views on morality, and decides that she no longer wants to be his friend. First, you need to look up Heinlein's permanent entity id using a query—left as an exercise to the reader—quite similar to the above query to find Jane's permanent id. The transaction to retract the friendship looks like this.

```
[[:db/retract jane-id :friend heinlein-id]]
```

You can see that the list form is somewhat verbose and unwieldy. It does offer the advantage of having direct, low-level control over the transaction and, unlike the map form, allows you to retract individual Datoms. However, you will almost always end up using the higher-level map form for all your transactions, with higher-level APIs to handle things like retraction. So let's take a look at the map form.

Map Syntax

The map syntax is, as mentioned before, higher-level than the list syntax and it's also generally considered more idiomatic. It represents transaction data as maps, where attributes are the keys, and entity ids are represented by a special `:db/id` key, just like the format of entity maps. Let's take a look at the Jane transaction from before expressed in this syntax.

```
[{:db/id jane-temp-id
  :first-name "Jane"
  :last-name "Doe"
  :email "everywoman123@gmail.com"}]
```

In this form, as with entity maps, the entity id is represented by the `:db/id` key. Under the hood, Datomic translates this into the list form, exactly the way it was in the previous section, before transacting. But you can see that this is a much more concise, convenient, easy-to-read way of expressing that transaction data.

You can also do something really nifty that would take quite a bit more work to do using the other syntax: add Jane and her friends at the same time. Watch this:

```
[{:db/id jane-temp-id
  :first-name "Jane"
  :last-name "Doe"
```

```
:email "everywoman123@gmail.com"
:friend #{{:first-name "Robert"
           :last-name "Heinlein"
           :email "dareallazarus@long.com"}
          {:first-name "Ada"
           :last-name "Lovelace"
           :email "firstprogramm3r@steampunk.com"}}}]
```

That's right, the map syntax supports nesting for related entities! One thing you'll notice is that Mr. Heinlein and Ms. Lovelace don't have temporary ids. That's because Datomic will generate them for you when building a transaction this way.

There are a few caveats to this. Don't worry, you won't understand them until you read about Datomic schema, but they're included here in case you're reviewing this section later and want this information all in one place. When you use the nested map syntax this way, if you don't provide temporary ids, then the nested entities must either be related to the containing entity via an isComponent attribute, or they must have an identity attribute. Also, their generated ids will be in the same partition as the containing entity's id.

Set Semantics

One thing to keep in mind: Datoms have set semantics. In other words, asserting the same [e a v] more than once is a no-op; the Datom will only exist in the database once. As a quick example, if you transact this data:

```
[{:db/id jane-id
  :first-name "Jane"
  :last-name "Doe"
  :email "everywoman123@gmail.com"}]
```

And then transact this data:

```
[{:db/id jane-id
  :first-name "Jane"}]
```

The second transaction will succeed and it will add a transaction entity, but it will not add another Datom about Jane. This is covered in greater detail in the section about the Clojure API.

Indexes Really Tie Your Data Together

So far the discussion has been about the data in Datomic in terms of collections of Datoms, which is true but incomplete. To understand the way Datomic really stores data, you must go deeper. You also may need to let go of some preconceptions that are often carried over from experiences with relational databases and their storage model.

Generally, you don't have to worry too much about Datomic's indexes or how it stores data. In most cases, straightforward use of Datomic's high-level API without any consideration of these lower-level details will have acceptable results. However, when doing detailed data modeling or thinking about performance, it's very important to be familiar enough with Datomic's indexes that you have a good general idea of how they will be used and how they impact what you're doing.

In a relational database, data is represented in tables and these tables generally map closely to the way data is stored on disk. The rows are generally stored in order, with a struct-like representation of their contents. Indexing is typically managed separately, where each index is created manually over one or more specific columns, with some sort of tree structure managing the indexed data with pointers to the corresponding rows. In other words, indexes are effectively separate from the record-level data.

In Datomic, the indexes are the only representation of the data in the system. The term for that is "covering index," which means that the index contains all of the data, rather than a limited subset as in relational databases. These indexes allow Datomic to quickly access data from different lookup patterns, and enables the powerful and flexible query system. Datomic stores data in four indexes, plus the transaction log.

Each index is sorted and stored in a tree representation. The key distinction between the different indexes is their sort order.

eavt Index

The eavt index represents data in a way that is conceptually similar to the way relational databases store rows. Datoms in this index are first sorted by entity id, so Datoms about each entity are grouped together and then by attribute, then value, then transaction id. Datoms in this index would be stored quite similarly to the way we've been representing them so far, using a dummy transaction id:

```
[[101 :email "everywoman123@gmail.com" 'some-t]
 [101 :first-name "Jane" 'some-t]
 [101 :friend 102 'some-t]
 [101 :friend 103 'some-t]
 [101 :last-name "Doe" 'some-t]
 [102 :email "firstprogramm3r@steampunk.com" 'some-t]
 [102 :first-name "Ada" 'some-t]
 [102 :last-name "Lovelace" 'some-t]
 [103 :email "dareallazarus@long.com" 'some-t]
 [103 :first-name "Robert" 'some-t]
 [103 :last-name "Heinlein" 'some-t]]
```

Since facts about each entity are grouped together, it's easy to retrieve all of the data about a given entity quickly. For obvious reasons, the entity API that's used to retrieve entity maps uses this index. This API is covered in more detail in a later section.

All Datoms are stored in this index.

aevt Index

The aevt index groups all Datoms about an attribute together, allowing for the quick determination of which entities have values for that attribute and, secondarily, what those values are. As the Datomic docs point out, this index is somewhat similar to a columnar store, and is one of the ways that Datomic enables flexible querying that supports mixed workloads. For this example data, the index looks something like this:

```
[[:email 101 "everywoman123@gmail.com" 'some-t]
 [:email 102 "firstprogramm3r@steampunk.com" 'some-t]
```

```
[:email 103 "dareallazarus@long.com" 'some-t]
[:first-name 101 "Jane" 'some-t]
[:first-name 102 "Ada" 'some-t]
[:first-name 103 "Robert" 'some-t]
[:friend 101 102 'some-t]
[:friend 101 103 'some-t]
[:last-name 101 "Doe" 'some-t]
[:last-name 102 "Lovelace" 'some-t]
[:last-name 103 "Heinlein" 'some-t]]
```

One thing to note here is that we are making a slight oversimplification. Attributes are not stored and sorted based on their keyword name, but rather on their underlying attribute entity id. This doesn't make a huge amount of difference in practice, but it's something to keep in mind.

All Datoms are stored in this index.

avet Index

The avet index is subtly different from the aevt index, in that it's designed to very quickly retrieve attributes with specific values. It's also, as the Datomic docs point out, the most expensive index to build and maintain. For this reason it's optional on a per-attribute basis, whether or not Datoms are stored in this index. Assuming indexing is enabled on all of the example attributes, here is what the data looks like in this index:

```
[[:email "dareallazarus@long.com" 103 'some-t]
 [:email "everywoman123@gmail.com" 101 'some-t]
 [:email "firstprogramm3r@steampunk.com" 102 'some-t]
 [:first-name "Ada" 102 'some-t]
 [:first-name "Jane" 101 'some-t]
 [:first-name "Robert" 103 'some-t]
 [:friend 102 101 'some-t]
 [:friend 103 101 'some-t]
 [:last-name "Doe" 101 'some-t]
 [:last-name "Heinlein" 103 'some-t]
 [:last-name "Lovelace" 102 'some-t]]
```

The decision about whether to enable the avet index for a given attribute involves a similar tradeoff to the decision about what columns to index in a relational database. It adds cost to writes, but depending on the kinds of queries you're doing, it may be essential. Any query that relies on the specific value of an attribute, without knowing anything about which entity it belongs to, will be enormously sped up by this index. Best practices here are similar to those in the relational world: if you think you'll query against the attribute's value, then enable indexing.

Fortunately, if you miss out on adding an attribute to this index that you end up needing later, you can always enable indexing on that attribute with a run-time schema update.

vaet Index

The vaet index is for representing reverse references. That is, when you have a reference-type attribute, which means it represents a relationship between two entities, this index stores that relationship in the opposite direction. Naturally, this index is only enabled for reference type attributes. For this example data, the vaet index might look like the following:

```
[[102 :friend 101 'some-t]
 [103 :friend 101 'some-t]]
```

You can grasp the general idea. The other indexes can be used in various ways to easily find outgoing entity references, but the vaet index is required to efficiently determine incoming references.

The log

The log is structured somewhat differently from the indexes. The Datomic docs put it quite simply: the log is an ordered collection of transactions, each of which contains an unordered set of Datoms. Queries do not directly use the log; rather it's accessed via several specialized APIs that can be used as part of queries or to examine the history directly in your application.

Index structure

The above means that every Datom is stored in at least 3 and as many as 5 copies. In the past, this kind of data replication may have been cause for concern or perhaps it was even infeasible. Indeed, the idea that storage is scarce motivated many of the original design decisions that are now deeply embedded in relational database designs. Today this is a rather antiquated assumption: storage is cheap and fast. Datomic's design makes time vs. space trade-offs in the direction of optimizing for speed, because modern hardware and system architectures make data replication and storage size a much lesser concern.

The indexes themselves are stored as shallow (3-level) trees, with an extremely high branching factor. The structure looks like what is shown in Figure 6-1.

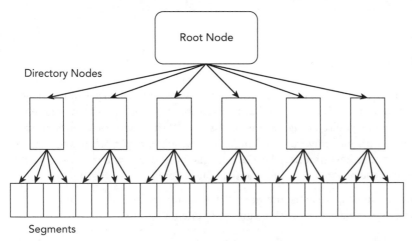

FIGURE 6-1

It's structured as a root node, directory nodes, and segments. Datomic optimizes read performance by keeping the root node and as many of the directory nodes in the memory of the peers and the transactor possible to minimize the number of trips to storage.

Each of the segments contains up to approximately 50Kb of Datoms, which have been serialized to binary using the Fressian format and then gzipped. Depending on the size of the values, each segment can contain many thousands of Datoms. This is the most important thing to grasp about how Datomic stores data: to get at a single Datom in a given segment, the entire segment must be transferred, unzipped, and deserialized into memory. Thus, when thinking about performance, the biggest factor is going to be the number of segment accesses required to complete any operation.

Datomic's Unique Architecture

One of Datomic's main advantages is its de-constructed architecture. Traditional databases are monolithic, performing all of their functions as part of one system running on one computer. Datomic splits these functions up into their own components, which can be run on different systems and even swapped out with different options.

1. **Reads.** Your application's data reads, including query logic, are performed by a Datomic "peer," which runs inside of your application's process. There can be multiple peers per Datomic database to support different components of your application.

2. **Writes.** Datomic has a single writer, called the transactor. It serializes writes, providing ACID transaction guarantees, and also supports arbitrary transaction logic to enforce data integrity, as you'll see in a later section. The transactor runs as its own process, often on a dedicated system.

3. **Storage.** The data and indexes that comprise a Datomic database are actually stored in *another* database. This part of the system is pluggable: supported storage systems include Amazon's DynamoDB, Cassandra, Riak, a SQL database, and others.

4. **Optional cache.** With the Datomic Pro edition, you can incorporate memcached as a cache layer. Datomic's immutable data structures are a natural fit for caching since they never have to be invalidated.

After starting up the transactor, peers connect to it over a message queue and also establish a connection to the storage system and memcached if present. To do a read, the peers access storage directly—no coordination with the transactor is required. Peers send data to be written to the transactor, and as writes are completed the transactor pushes a stream of the newly written data to all peers.

The peers and the transactor have two pools of memory devoted to Datomic data. The first is called the "Object Cache," which is a hot cache of recently and frequently accessed database data. You can independently set the size of the Object Cache on each peer and the transactor. This setting is important when configuring Datomic for production and involves some tradeoffs, so it's a good idea to take a look at the Datomic documentation section on capacity planning for more information.

The second is called the "memory index." This is where newly transacted data is stored after it has been written, but not yet added to the indexes. The transactor is responsible for rebuilding the indexes, and it only does so after a configurable threshold of new data has been added. Newly added data is always immediately persisted to the transaction log, but the indexes are only updated periodically, since this is an expensive operation. This data exists in the memory index of the peers and the transactor until it's been added to the indexes. Reads therefore go against a *merger* of what is in the indexes and what is in the memory index.

The Life and Times of a Transaction

To get a clearer understanding of the process of how data gets into Datomic and how the different parts of the system are involved, let's walk through the life and times of an example transaction.

1. A peer submits a transaction to the transactor.

2. The transactor processes transactions one at a time order of receipt, and the transaction waits in line until its turn.

3. The transaction is processed by the transactor, transaction functions run, temporary ids resolved, etc.

4. The transactor persists the transaction to the transaction log in the storage layer.

5. The transactor adds the new Datoms to its memory index, and sends the new Datoms to *every* connected peer.

6. Some time later, the transactor begins a re-indexing job, incorporating all new Datoms into the indexes.

MODELING APPLICATION DATA

Datomic's schema provides a flexible, descriptive, and easy-to-use system for describing your application's data. In contrast to the schema of relational databases, in which you build fixed tables containing column definitions that can be used only in that table, Datomic schema is primarily concerned with defining attributes that can be used with any entity. Although best practices indicate that you should group your attributes based on the kind of entity, they are used within the application.

Like in many other databases, schema elements in Datomic need to be loaded before they are used by the application. In order to do this, you need to build transactions containing the required parts of each attribute entity, and then write those transactions.

Example Schema for Task Tracker App

In previous chapters, you've looked at various aspects of building a task tracker system. Let's look at how to build a schema for that in Datomic. The system will have several different types of data. It will have the tasks themselves (users), and as in every other task tracker system, you'll want to be able to charge money for it so it will have accounts with charges and payments.

There are some details that aren't covered here in the same depth as they are in Datomic's documentation, so you should review the Schema section of that documentation before moving past this section. There is a wealth of information there.

Let's look at the schema section by section.

Schema Basics

Let's take a look at what a basic schema transaction contains. First, we'll create the schema attributes for the tasks. The first thing a task needs is a description.

```
[{:db/id #db/id[:db.part/db]
  :db/ident :task/description
```

```
    :db/cardinality :db.cardinality/one
    :db/valueType :db.type/string
    :db/doc "description of the task"
    :db.install/_attribute :db.part/db}]
```

The first key assigns the attribute a `:db/id`, which is the entity id that's required for every entity in the system, including attributes. The value is a reader macro implemented as part of the Datomic API, which creates a temporary entity id in the `:db.part/db` partition. All attribute entities are required to be in the `:db.part/db` partition.

A `:db/ident` keyword is required for all attribute entities. It provides a universal identifier that can be used to refer to the attribute in queries and in transactions. In general an ident can be used anywhere an entity id is accepted. You can also give `:db/ident` values to data entities, in addition to attribute entities. Be careful of abusing this feature, though, because all the `:db/ident` values in the database are loaded on startup into every Datomic peer.

This attribute has the `ident` of `:task/description`. The best practices laid out in the Datomic documentation recommend that you use namespaced keywords for all your attribute idents, to organize them into categories, and to prevent name collisions. If you haven't read through the best practices section of the Datomic documentation, you should probably take a few minutes and do so now. It's an immensely useful document that's been distilled from the experience of nearly four years that Datomic has been in production.

Attribute cardinality is specified using the required `:db/cardinality` attribute. There are two possible values for this attribute: `:db.cardinality/one` or `:db.cardinality/many`. If it's `:db.cardinality/one`, every entity can only have one value true at any given time for this attribute—if you try to assert a different value, then the previous value will be retracted and replaced with the new value. Otherwise for `:db.cardinality/many` there is no restriction. Since tasks should only have one title, `:db.cardinality/one` is the right choice.

Every attribute needs to have a `:db/valueType`, which specifies the type that its v value must have. There are two broad categories of valueTypes: reference, which means that the value must be an entity ID, or some data type, such as string, float, integer, URI, and so forth. You want your titles to be strings, and `:db.type/string` is Datomic's string type.

One optional attribute that you can use with both attribute and data entities is `:db/doc`. This is broadly equivalent to a Clojure docstring or simple Javadoc, but there are no hard-coded ways in which it is used, so you can adapt it to whatever purposes suit the needs of your application. Here, we'll treat this attribute as a docstring-like annotation, which is only meant to be used by developers and other internal users.

Finally, there's the somewhat confusing `:db.install/_attribute` key. Whenever you see a Datomic attribute where the name part of the keyword begins with an underscore, you know you're seeing a reverse reference. Reverse references are where the entity and value parts have been swapped.

```
{attribute-temp-id :db.install/_attribute :db.part/db}
```

What this really means is this:

```
{:db.part/db :db.install/attribute attribute-temp-id}
```

The `:db.install/attribute` attribute is a special Datomic attribute used to add attributes to Datomic's schema, and attributes always need to be installed in `:db.part/db`.

Partitions

Datomic best practices call for creating some partitions specific to your app, rather than using the built-in `:db.part/user` that's intended more for development and experimentation. Creating partitions is simple: just create an entity with a `:db/ident` and the partition install command. Let's create two partitions: one for the tasks, and one for accounts that will contain data about users, their accounts, and their payments and charges.

```
[{:db/id #db/id[:db.part/db]
  :db/ident :db.part/task
  :db.install/_partition :db.part/db}

 {:db/id #db/id[:db.part/db]
  :db/ident :db.part/account
  :db.install/_partition :db.part/db}]
```

Fulltext Indexing

Datomic supports fulltext indexing on specific attributes using a Lucene index, and supports fulltext search on those attributes as part of queries. This can be very useful if you have one-off needs for fulltext searching that are limited enough to not call for a dedicated search database. Let's add a task title attribute that is fulltext-indexed.

```
[{:db/id #db/id[:db.part/db]
  :db/ident :task/title
  :db/cardinality :db.cardinality/one
  :db/valueType :db.type/string
  :db/doc "title of the task"
  :db/fulltext true
  :db.install/_attribute :db.part/db}]
```

Use the `:db/fulltext` attribute to enable fulltext indexing for the title attribute. By default, it's disabled, but there are a few things to bear in mind about fulltext indexing.

➤ The underlying Lucene indexes are not ACID, but they are eventually consistent and will be updated during transactor re-indexing. If your app requirements include fulltext search that's immediately available after data is added, then you need to use an external system for search and your app needs to pipe searchable data into it, perhaps using Datomic's transaction report queue.

➤ The decision about whether an attribute is fulltext indexed is final. It is not currently possible to enable or disable fulltext indexing on an attribute after it's been installed.

Enums in Datomic

Many relational databases support the concept of an enum datatype to create columns that require one of a specific set of enumerated values. Datomic emulates this function using reference types and enumeration entities. Let's take a look at an example schema, and add a task status attribute that takes an enum.

```
[{:db/id #db/id[:db.part/db]
  :db/ident :task/status
  :db/cardinality :db.cardinality/one
```

```
:db/valueType :db.type/ref
:db/doc "task status - an enum"
:db.install/_attribute :db.part/db}]
```

There is nothing particularly special required to create an enum attribute. Here the `valueType` is set as `:db.type/ref`, because the enumerated values are entities, and a note was added in the attributes doc to make it clear that it is specifically enum entities that you want to use as the refs for this attribute.

For task status values, it would be nice if they had an attribute that provided some kind of display label that could be used when showing the status. Let's add an attribute that can be used to add a label to any entity.

```
[{:db/id #db/id[:db.part/db]
  :db/ident :label
  :db/cardinality :db.cardinality/one
  :db/valueType :db.type/string
  :db/doc "display label of an entity"
  :db.install/_attribute :db.part/db}]
```

Now, let's create the enumeration values for the task status. It's quite simple to do: just create an entity with a `:db/ident`. You need to add task statuses for "To Do," "In Progress," and "Done."

```
[{:db/id #db/id[:db.part/task]
  :db/ident :task.status/todo
  :label "To Do"}

 {:db/id #db/id[:db.part/task]
  :db/ident :task.status/in-progress
  :label "In Progress"}

 {:db/id #db/id[:db.part/task]
  :db/ident :task.status/done
  :label "Done"}]
```

You'll notice a few things here. First, since these are not schema attributes, you can't put them in the `:db.part/db` partition, so put them instead in the `:db.part/task` partition that was created for the tasks earlier. Next, you'll notice that the namespace of their ident keywords is "task.status," corresponding to the name of the attribute that they're to be used with. This corresponds with the best practice recommended for naming enumerated values in Datomic. Finally, you can give them some display-friendly labels that the app can use, avoiding any hard-coding in the app about what specific status values should be called, or about how to translate the ident keywords into something for display.

Identity Attributes

Next, let's look at identity attributes. These are attributes whose values are meant to be external keys, and can be used to refer to the entity they belong to. In this way, they're somewhat analogous to primary keys in the relational world, although an entity can have more than one of them. It's very important to include identity attributes in the data model for your key domain entities.

It's considered an anti-pattern to use Datomic's entity id to refer to an entity, except in cases where you just have queried for it, and it's a particularly bad practice to ever store entity ids outside of

Datomic. Entity ids are meant to be internal references inside the database, and they are not guaranteed to remain the same if you do a backup and restore.

Let's give the tasks in the app an identity attribute that represents their "issue id," which is sort of like the ticket numbers you often see in other task and bug tracking systems.

```
[{:db/id #db/id[:db.part/db]
  :db/ident :task/issue-id
  :db/cardinality :db.cardinality/one
  :db/valueType :db.type/string
  :db/doc "task's issue ID, for external reference"
  :db/unique :db.unique/identity
  :db.install/_attribute :db.part/db}]
```

This is marked as an identity attribute by setting the `:db/unique` attribute to `:db.unique/identity`. Setting something as an identity attribute has several effects.

➤ The attribute must be cardinality-one.

➤ Values of an identity attribute have enforced uniqueness—two entities can't have the same value for an identity attribute.

➤ The value of this attribute can be used to transparently look up the entity to which it belongs, and using an identity attribute as part of a transaction makes that an upsert transaction.

Identity attributes are covered in more detail later in the Datomic's Clojure API section.

Many-to-Many and Hierarchical Relationships

One of the biggest benefits of Datomic's data model is the flexibility and simplicity of expressing relationships between entities. Datomic's model of many-to-many relationships, in particular, is a welcome relief to those used to the relational way of modeling them. Here are four little words that are music to the ears of every developer who has struggled with many-to-many in SQL: "no more join tables."

To show how many-to-many is done in Datomic, let's create some attributes for adding tags to tasks. This will allow users to tag tasks with things like "Home," "Work," "Shopping," "Family Vacation," and so forth. Let's add the task to tag relationship, and then add a tag attribute that allows us to give tags names.

```
[{:db/id #db/id[:db.part/db]
  :db/ident :task/tag
  :db/cardinality :db.cardinality/many
  :db/valueType :db.type/ref
  :db/doc "task tags"
  :db.install/_attribute :db.part/db}

 {:db/id #db/id[:db.part/db]
  :db/ident :tag/name
  :db/cardinality :db.cardinality/one
  :db/valueType :db.type/string
  :db/doc "tag's name, used as identity"
  :db/unique :db.unique/identity
  :db.install/_attribute :db.part/db}]
```

You see how doing many-to-many in Datomic is as simple as adding a reference-type attribute with cardinality-many? Since you're not constrained by the fixed number of columns in relational tables, it's simple to model the kind of data that typically requires specialized extra tables in SQL databases.

Also, notice that you've made the name of tags an identity attribute. This makes them upsertable, and will make it easier to reuse tags in multiple tasks.

Let's next look at how to create an entity relationship that represents a hierarchy. In the task app you want to create subtasks, which are children of the parent tasks. And perhaps those subtasks can in turn have subtasks of their own, and so on... Some people have very complicated lives, after all, with activities that have deep dependencies on other things being completed. Since subtasks are often attached to parent tasks, moved around, and reorganized, let's model the relationship on the child side.

```
[{:db/id #db/id[:db.part/db]
  :db/ident :task/parent
  :db/cardinality :db.cardinality/one
  :db/valueType :db.type/ref
  :db/doc "parent of the task, establishing arbitrary hierarchy"
  :db.install/_attribute :db.part/db}]
```

This is a fairly straightforward attribute. It says that a task can have at most one parent, and the parent is a reference. Thus, tasks can have parents tasks, which can in turn have parents, allowing for hierarchies of arbitrary depth.

Datomic allows you to model relationships in either direction, so this can be modeled as :task/subtask and be an attribute of the parent, rather than the subtask. The decision largely depends on how you prefer to think about the relationship, and how your application will use it. In this case, the deciding factor was that one of the key operations you want to support is assigning an existing task to be a subtask of some other task, possibly removing it as a subtask from another task. Modeling it this way allows this operation to be done very easily: asserting a new parent for the subtask will automatically remove any existing parent relationship, since this is a cardinality-one attribute.

Let's take a moment to consider something interesting about Datomic that particularly distinguishes it from SQL. In this case we have named the parent relationship attribute such that it appears to be task-specific, but there's no reason that it has to be—Datomic won't enforce that constraint. With a single attribute, you could say that tasks can have "idea" entities as parents, and subtasks or comments or any number of differently structured entities as children. The flexibility of Datomic makes these kind of heterogeneous relationships much simpler to model.

Identity versus Unique

Let's create a simple model for users. It's quite similar to what you might see in a relational schema, but it has a few important differences.

```
[{:db/id #db/id[:db.part/db]
  :db/ident :user/login
  :db/cardinality :db.cardinality/one
  :db/valueType :db.type/string
  :db/doc "user's login name and display name"
```

```
    :db/unique :db.unique/identity
    :db.install/_attribute :db.part/db}

{:db/id #db/id[:db.part/db]
 :db/ident :user/password
 :db/cardinality :db.cardinality/one
 :db/valueType :db.type/string
 :db/doc "crypted pasword"
 :db.install/_attribute :db.part/db}

{:db/id #db/id[:db.part/db]
 :db/ident :user/email
 :db/cardinality :db.cardinality/one
 :db/valueType :db.type/string
 :db/doc "User's email address"
 :db/unique :db.unique/value
 :db.install/_attribute :db.part/db}

{:db/id #db/id[:db.part/db]
 :db/ident :user/account
 :db/cardinality :db.cardinality/one
 :db/valueType :db.type/ref
 :db/isComponent true
 :db/doc "The account linked to the user"
 :db.install/_attribute :db.part/db}]
```

This model adds four attributes: the user's login, an encrypted password, an email address, and a link to an account that will be modeled in a moment. For this system, separate logins are used instead of email addresses to allow people to choose their own clever nicknames like "weavejester" and "hyPiRion," or more pedestrian ones like "rhickey." We do, however, want to store people's email addresses and only allow one user per email address.

Notice that login is an identity attribute, and email address is modeled as a `:db.unique/value` attribute. They have slightly different semantics. Identity attributes, as discussed before, enforce uniqueness, but also allow for `upserts`: if you assert new data that contains an identity value that already exists in the database, then that data updates the entity to which that identity belongs. That means you can refer to your users by their login everywhere, and Datomic will resolve that to the correct entity.

The other type of uniqueness is set with `:db.unique/value`: if you assert new data that duplicates an existing `:db.unique/value` Datomic will throw an exception and the entire transaction will fail.

It's generally bad practice to have more than one identity attribute for a single type of entity, unless they correspond to external keys for different systems. If you need additional unique attributes for a type of entity, you should usually use `:db.unique/value` attributes.

Component Relationships

An attribute can also define a "component" relationship. This describes a relationship where the component entity is owned by the parent entity, and it isn't meant to exist independently. Datomic retracts component entities when you retract the parent entity, and will also return data about component entities when you fetch data about the parent in several key parts of the API.

Let's set up an account system for users that will handle paid accounts and keep track of charges and payments. First let's add an account type attribute, modeled as an enum.

```
[{:db/id #db/id[:db.part/db]
  :db/ident :account/type
  :db/cardinality :db.cardinality/one
  :db/valueType :db.type/ref
  :db/doc "account type (eg paid, free), an enum"
  :db.install/_attribute :db.part/db}

 {:db/id #db/id[:db.part/account]
  :db/ident :account.type/free
  :label "Free account"}

 {db/id #db/id[:db.part/account]
  :db/ident :account.type/paid
  :label "Paid account"}]
```

This is just like the enum covered earlier in this chapter: a cardinality-one reference type attribute, with entities with appropriately named idents as the enumeration values. Now let's add in the charges and payments, which are called "transactions" here against the account.

```
[{:db/id #db/id[:db.part/db]
  :db/ident :account/transaction
  :db/cardinality :db.cardinality/many
  :db/valueType :db.type/ref
  :db/isComponent true
  :db/doc "transactions (payments and charges) against the account"
  :db.install/_attribute :db.part/db}

 {:db/id #db/id[:db.part/db]
  :db/ident :transaction/type
  :db/cardinality :db.cardinality/one
  :db/valueType :db.type/ref
  :db/doc "transaction type (eg charge, payment, adjustment) - an enum"
  :db.install/_attribute :db.part/db}

 {:db/id #db/id[:db.part/db]
  :db/ident :transaction/amount
  :db/cardinality :db.cardinality/one
  :db/valueType :db.type/bigdec
  :db/doc "amount of the transaction"
  :db.install/_attribute :db.part/db}

 {:db/id #db/id[:db.part/account]
  :db/ident :transaction.type/charge
  :label "Charge"}

 {:db/id #db/id[:db.part/account]
  :db/ident :transaction.type/payment
  :label "Payment"}

 {:db/id #db/id[:db.part/account]
  :db/ident :transaction.type/adjustment
  :label "Adjustment"}]
```

You can see the addition of three more attributes. The last two should be familiar. The first is an enum for the transaction type—either charge, payment, or adjustment for those times when you need to correct mistakes. The second is an attribute for the transaction amount. Datomic includes support for a decimal type corresponding with `java.math.BigDecimal` objects, which you've used earlier to model the transaction amounts so as not to worry about any stray precision errors from floats.

The first attribute, `:account/transaction`, models transactions as components of accounts. You do this by setting `:db/isComponent` to true. It has implemented here because these transactions completely depend on the account for them to have any meaning, and if the account entity is retracted it makes no sense for them to remain.

Disabling History

While Datomic is designed around the idea that data is immutable and the complete history of your data should be available, there are some cases where you don't want that to happen. For example, if you have attributes with a high churn rate or represent calculations that are materialized for the sake of convenience, sometimes it's just not worth it to keep a history of every single value the attribute has ever had.

Fortunately, Datomic allows you to disable history on a per-attribute basis. Let's add an attribute that will represent the current balance of the account. This is a value that will change every time there's any transaction, and furthermore it's something that you cancalculate at any point by summing up all of the transactions. It can be convenient to have this value materialized, because then it's easier to do queries about, for example, accounts that have more than a certain balance. Here's how that is modeled in a Datomic schema:

```
[:db/id #db/id[:db.part/db]
 :db/ident :account/current-balance
 :db/cardinality :db.cardinality/one
 :db/valueType :db.type/bigdec
 :db/doc "current balance of the account"
 :db/index true
 :db/noHistory true
 :db.install/_attribute :db.part/db}]
```

By setting `:db/noHistory` to true, you have disabled history. What this means practically is that during every indexing job, the transactor will drop both retraction Datoms and assertions that have been retracted for this attribute, keeping only the most recently asserted value. You can see then that it's possible for some history data about this attribute to be present between indexing jobs, so you shouldn't write your application logic to depend on there never being any history present for the attribute.

Entity ids and Partitions

The creation of Datomic partitions for your application data have been discussed. This is in addition to Datomic's built-in partitions.

➤ `:db.part/db` is the partition for attributes and other schema-related data.

➤ `:db.part/tx` is the partition for transaction entities.

➤ `:db.part/user` is a partition for your use in development.

In addition to providing logical groupings, partitions also have a useful purpose in providing physical groupings. Remember that Datoms are ordered in the indexes, and reducing the number of index segments that are retrieved as part of an operation is key to improving performance. Therefore it's beneficial to have entities that are related and often retrieved together stored in the same segment if possible, which means their entity ids need to be close together. Partitions give you a way to help make that happen.

As discussed earlier, entity ids are Longs. The higher-order bits of the entity id come from the partition, which means that entities inside a partition are grouped together in the indexes as well. If your application is going to create a large number of entities, particularly in one-to-many relationships, it can be beneficial to create multiple partitions and split these entities up logically.

To take an example from the task tracker schema, let's say that later on you extend the system to include enterprise support with various types of metered charges for accounts. This could result in a large number of charge and payment transactions for the account entities. If all of the account and transaction entities remain in a single partition, as they are in the current schema, then the performance might suffer. Since charges and payments are added across time, you could have a situation where it requires many segment fetches to get all of the transactions for an account.

You can solve this problem by creating multiple partitions for your accounts and distributing account entities across these partitions. When adding charge or payment transactions, make sure to put them in the same partition as their account. This will greatly improve the data locality when accessing accounts and their related transactions, because it will both reduce the maximum possible number of required segment fetches, and increase the chance of related transactions being collocated in a single segment.

DATOMIC'S CLOJURE API

Datomic includes a first-class Clojure API that makes it natural and easy to work with when building applications. In this section, you'll learn about how to set up a project and a Datomic database, how to use the API, and how you can write the data access layer for the example task system.

Basic Setup

You can bring in the free-as-in-beer version of the Datomic peer library, which includes an in-memory database you can use for development, as a normal dependency in your project.clj file. Here's your basic project.clj file, including a dependency atom for the current version that is datomic-free.

```
(defproject chapter-6 "0.1.0-SNAPSHOT"
  :description "Code for Professional Clojure, Chapter 6: Datomic"
  :license {:name "Eclipse Public License"
            :url "http://www.eclipse.org/legal/epl-v10.html"}
  :dependencies [[org.clojure/clojure "1.7.0"]
                 [com.datomic/datomic-free "0.9.5344"]
                 [crypto-password "0.1.3"]]
  :profiles {:dev {:source-paths ["dev"]}}})
```

You'll notice a few extra things here, in addition to the basic project.clj file from `lein`, that are new with the Datomic dependency. The crypto-password library is included so user passwords can be encrypted. There are also an extra property defined for the dev profile: the dev folder has been added to the source paths, so you can add some code to support your development process that won't conflict with the production code.

Schema and Example Data

First, let's put the schema that was created in the previous chapter in a file in the resources folder of the project, called schema.edn. This way you can easily work with it in the project.

Next, add some example data in resources/example-data.edn. You can use this data to help you while exploring the Datomic API, developing the data access code, and later it can even form the basis of test cases for testing.

```
;; A test user, with account and charges
[{:db/id #db/id[:db.part/account]
  :user/login "janed"
  ;; bcrypted "totalanon"
  :user/password "$2a$11$W2juQqRpaxVqXt4u..4qz.asyhbfR53K1a3stjQ3wpUYOCcagH8VK"
  :user/email "everywoman123@gmail.com"
  :user/account
  {:account/type :account.type/paid
   :account/transaction
   #{{:transaction/type :transaction.type/charge
      :transaction/amount 7.99M}
     {:transaction/type :transaction.type/payment
      :transaction/amount -7.99M}
     {:transaction/type :transaction.type/charge
      :transaction/amount 2.55M}}
   :account/current-balance 2.55M}}]


;; A couple of tasks
[{:db/id #db/id[:db.part/task]
  :task/title "Write to Robert about Number of the Beast"
  :task/description "He should know the first part was meandering and slow, and the
                     ending was just self indulgent. \"Meet Lazarus, live happily
                     ever after.\" Please!"
  :task/status :task.status/todo
  :task/issue-id "HOME-11"
  :task/tag #{{:tag/name "Home"}
              {:tag/name "Writing"}}
  :task/user {:user/login "janed"}}

 {:db/id #db/id[:db.part/task]
  :task/title "Disappear into anonymity"
  :task/description "Jane Doe can't be a public figure."
  :task/status :task.status/in-progress
  :task/issue-id "WORK-1"
  :task/tag #{{:tag/name "Work"}
              {:tag/name "Important"}}
  :task/user {:user/login "janed"}}

 ;; Add a subtask
 {:db/id #db/id[:db.part/task]
  :task/title "Pack clothes"
```

```
  :task/description "Focus on neutral colors, hoodies."
  :task/status :task.status/todo
  :task/issue-id "WORK-2"
  :task/user {:user/login "janed"}
  :task/parent {:task/issue-id "WORK-1"}}]
```

A test user, "janed," has been created, so you can continue the saga of Jane Doe. Her password is "totalanon," but it's been encrypted with bcrypt. She has an account with some transactions, and a few tasks including one that's a subtask.

Setting Up for Development

While developing you often want to quickly iterate and experiment with an in-memory database. Let's create a dev namespace that lets you do just that. Create a dev folder in the project root (remember dev was added to the source-paths) and add a file called dev.clj to that folder, which looks like this:

```
(ns dev
  (:require [clojure.java.io :as io]
            [clojure.pprint :refer (pprint)]
            [datomic.api :as d])
  (:import datomic.Util))

(def dev-db-uri
  "datomic:mem://dev-db")

(def schema
  (io/resource "schema.edn"))

(def example-data
  (io/resource "example-data.edn"))

(defn read-txs
  [tx-resource]
  (with-open [tf (io/reader tx-resource)]
    (Util/readAll tf)))

(defn transact-all
  ([conn txs]
   (transact-all conn txs nil))
  ([conn txs res]
   (if (seq txs)
     (transact-all conn (rest txs) @(d/transact conn (first txs)))
     res)))

(defn initialize-db
  "Creates db, connects, transacts schema and example data, returns conn."
  []
  (d/create-database dev-db-uri)
  (let [conn (d/connect dev-db-uri)]
    (transact-all conn (read-txs schema))
    (transact-all conn (read-txs example-data))
    conn))
```

```
(defonce conn nil)

(defn go
  []
  (alter-var-root #'conn (constantly (initialize-db))))

(defn stop
  []
  (alter-var-root #'conn
                  (fn [c] (when c (d/release c)))))
```

You can see the usage of the Datomic API, conveniently called datomic.api as a dependency. The entire Clojure API for Datomic is in this namespace, so you will be seeing this dependency quite a bit. The other import is `datomic.Util`, which includes a handy static method for reading schema and other Datomic data from files.

Next, configure the URI for the in-memory Datomic db, `datomic:mem://dev-db`. The format of URIs for a Datomic DB varies based on the type of storage medium in use, but the general format is `datomic:<type>://<connection params specific to the storage>/<db name>`.

We have two utility functions, `read-txs` and `transact-all`, that deal with reading transaction data from a file and writing a collection of transactions. We also have a function, `initialize-db`, that sets up the database for development, adding both the schema and the example data. Let's return to these in a moment.

The two main functions used in our example are `go` and `stop`. The `go` function initializes the in-memory database and connects to it, binding the Datomic connection object to the `conn` var. The `stop` function drops the in-memory database and releases the connection.

This provides a nice development workflow: set up a database, work with it in the REPL, and reset it to the starting state.

Experimenting in the REPL

Start up a REPL in the project, switch to the dev namespace, and initialize the development db.

```
user> (require 'dev)
nil
user> (in-ns 'dev)
#namespace[dev]
dev> (go)
#object[datomic.peer.LocalConnection 0x2117de53
        "datomic.peer.LocalConnection@2117de53"]
```

Connections and dbs

The Datomic connection object represents Datomic's connection to both the transactor and the storage layer. Since you're using an in-memory database, both of these are in-process. You can get a db value from a connection with the `d/db` function of the Datomic API.

```
dev> (def db (d/db conn))
```

So, what's the difference between a connection and a db? The connection is a handle, and it's used when you are sending writes to the transactor. A db, however, has value semantics. It represents the state of the database at a particular time. When you call d/db you get the latest state of the database that the Datomic peer in your application knows about. You can use the db to do all kinds of different reads.

Highlight Tour of the Read API

You can examine attributes with attribute:

```
dev> (d/attribute db :task/title)
#AttrInfo{:id 67 :ident :task/title :value-type :db.type/string
          :cardinality :db.cardinality/one :indexed false
          :has-avet false :unique nil :is-component false
          :no-history false :fulltext true}
```

You can see the transaction number, or t value as the Datomic docs describe it, of the most recent transaction in a db with basis-t:

```
dev> (d/basis-t db)
1021
```

You can retrieve the transaction entity id for a given t value with t->tx.

```
dev> (d/t->tx 1021)
13194139534333
```

You can get low-level access to the Datoms in a specific index with datoms.

```
dev> (first (d/datoms db :aevt))
#datom[0 10 :db.part/db 13194139533312 true]
dev> ;; or seek to specific parts of the index
dev> (first (d/datoms db :aevt :db/doc :task/title))
#datom[67 62 "title of the task" 13194139534313 true]
```

You can then get the entity id for a given ident with entid.

```
dev> (d/entid db :task/title)
67
```

And then back again with ident:

```
dev> (d/ident db 67)
:task/title
```

The Entity API

One of the most commonly used features in Datomic is the entity API. It gives you access to entity data in a convenient, idiomatic way for Clojure. Let's take a look at Jane Doe. But how do you access her record? She wasn't given an ident, so you can't just use that keyword. You have to access her entity id somehow.

Here you can take advantage of a great feature of identity attributes: they can be used in place of entity ids in every place that accepts them. When used this way, they're called "lookup refs" and the format is:

```
[attribute-name value]
```

We know Jane's login from the example data is "janed," and since login is an identity attribute, you can use that as a lookup ref for her entity. The entity API is accessed with the entity function.

```
dev> (d/entity db [:user/login "janed"])
{:db/id 285873023222776}
```

You might be thinking that this looks strange—there's definitely supposed to be more data about Jane than just an id. Now is a good time to step back and learn a few things about the entity maps returned by Datomic's entity API.

They are lazily loaded. Only the :db/id is present at first.

➤ They work with most of Clojure's map functions.

➤ You navigate to related entities through normal map access.

Here are some examples of how you can treat entities like maps:

```
dev> (def jane (d/entity db [:user/login "janed"]))
#'dev/jane
dev> (keys jane)
(:user/login :user/password :user/email :user/account)
dev> (:user/login jane)
"janed"
dev> (vals jane)
("janed" "$2a$11$W2juQqRpaxVqXt4u..4qz.asyhbfR53K1a3stjQ3wpUYOCcagH8VK"
 "everywoman123@gmail.com" {:db/id 285873023222777})
dev> (into {} jane)
{:user/login "janed", :user/password "$2a$11$W2j ...<snip>",
 :user/email "everywoman123@gmail.com", :user/account {:db/id 285873023222777}}
dev> (get-in jane [:user/account :account/type])
:account.type/paid
```

The Datomic API also includes a function that loads in all of the entity's attributes, as well as every component entity, touch. Here it is used on Jane's account entity.

```
dev> (d/touch (:user/account jane))
{:db/id 285873023222777, :account/type :account.type/paid,
 :account/current-balance 2.55M,
 :account/transaction #{
  {:db/id 285873023222779, :transaction/type :transaction.type/payment,
   :transaction/amount -7.99M}
  {:db/id 285873023222778, :transaction/type :transaction.type/charge,
   :transaction/amount 7.99M}
  {:db/id 285873023222780, :transaction/type :transaction.type/charge,
   :transaction/amount 2.55M}}}
```

You see how the results contain all of the attributes of Jane's account, plus all of the related transactions since they're components.

The Query API

There are two ways to access the query API: the more traditional q function, and a query function that takes arguments in a slightly different format and supports setting a query timeout. Let's use the q function here, as it's considered more idiomatic for most types queries.

Here's a simple example, adapted from the earlier section on queries.

```
(d/q '[:find ?login :in $ ?email
       :where [?user :user/email ?email]
              [?user :user/login ?login]]
     db "everywoman123@gmail.com")
#{["janed"]}
```

This query looks up the login of the user with a given email. You see that q takes the query as the first parameter. After that, there are some new things here. First, you see this :in form that wasn't in the previous queries. This is used to specify the inputs to the query, in the same positional order as they are passed to q.

Here the db is the first argument, and it's called $ in the inputs. This is how you refer to the db or dbs—it's possible to query against more than one db!—that the query is targeting. Much like the reader-macro syntax for Clojure anonymous functions, if there's only one input db you can just call it $, and it's used as the implicit database for all of your where patterns. If there are multiples, you need to delineate them with $db1 $db2, for example, and each pattern needs to begin with the data-source it's targeting.

The second argument is an input binding that can be used anywhere in the query. In this query you're passing in the email address that you're looking for. You can have an arbitrary number of these inputs. You can also pass in collections, in which case you need to slightly change the format of the input binding. Here is the same query, except this time you're looking for a number of email address logins.

```
(d/q '[:find ?login :in $ [?email ...]
       :where [?user :user/email ?email]
              [?user :user/login ?login]]
     db
     ["everywoman123@gmail.com" "john.doe@nowhere.com" "postmaster@google.com"])
```

Notice how this uses ?email as the binding form. This is the required format for bindings where you're binding a collection.

The Pull API

Often you want to find some specific entities with a query, and then retrieve more information about those entities. You can do this with the entity API, but that can get somewhat verbose and isn't very declarative and elegant, particularly when compared to the queries. To solve this problem, Datomic introduced the pull API. This let's you describe the "shape" of data you want to return about an entity or entities, and you can even integrate it directly into your queries.

When you use the pull API, normal Clojure data structures are returned: vectors for collections of results, maps for data about entities, and sets for cardinality-many relationships. Let's look at an example, building on the previous query, but returning the user's login and some information about their account.

```
dev> (d/q '[:find (pull ?user [:user/login
                               {:user/account [{:account/type [:db/ident]}]}])
            :in $ ?email
            :where [?user :user/email ?email]]
```

```
                    db "everywoman123@gmail.com")
       [[{:user/login "janed", :user/account
         {:account/type {:db/ident :account.type/paid}}}]]
```

In pull specs, vectors specify lists of attributes to return, and the maps specify relationships. Here you are specifying that you want the :user/login, and then in the account via the :user/account relationship, you want the :db/ident of the :account/type.

Using pull specs as part of queries is often the best way to retrieve data that's meant to be returned to an external system, since the results can be directly serialized as edn and sent over the wire without any further transformation.

Transactions

You can perform transactions with the transact function. It accepts a connection and the transaction data, and returns a future containing a transaction result map. Let's take a look at an example, and what the various parts of the result map mean.

```
dev> (pprint @(d/transact conn [{:db/id (d/tempid :db.part/user)
                                 :task/title "Hello world"}]))
{:db-before datomic.db.Db@c7f1e174,
 :db-after datomic.db.Db@d62413b7,
 :tx-data
 [#datom[13194139534349 50 #inst "2016-02-06T20:22:19.369-00:00"
         13194139534349 true]
  #datom[17592186045454 67 "Hello world" 13194139534349 true]],
 :tempids {-9223350046623220340 17592186045454}}
```

The result map contains a :db-before key that contains the db value from immediately before the transaction, and a :db-after key that contains the db value immediately after it. You can pull either of these dbs directly out of the map and work with them as with any other db value. Using the :db-after in particular is quite common.

The :tx-data key contains a collection of all of the Datoms written during this transaction. Here you see there are two: one for the :task/title Datom that was asserted, and another for the transaction entity.

Finally, the :tempids key contains a mapping from the tempids created for the transaction to the actual entity ids written in the database. In this case the entity created has an id of 17592186045454. Let's see what happens when you try to assert a duplicate Datom for this entity.

```
dev> (pprint @(d/transact conn
                          [[:db/add 17592186045454
                            :task/title "Hello world"]]))
{:db-before datomic.db.Db@d62413b7,
 :db-after datomic.db.Db@10110222,
 :tx-data
 [#datom[13194139534351 50 #inst "2016-02-08T20:27:16.653-00:00"
         13194139534351 true]],
 :tempids {}}
```

You tried to add the Datom [17592186045454 :task/title "Hello world"], but that Datom already existed. Notice that the transaction succeeds, but the :tx-data key only has the

Datom about the transaction entity. You can see that the Datom assertion is idempotent. If you did the same experiment in the other direction—that is, we retracted the same Datom twice—you'd see a similar result: only the first transaction would have had that retraction Datom in its `:tx-data`, and the second would only include the transaction Datom.

Time Travel Will Never Be Impossible Forever

Once confined to fantasy and science fiction, time travel is now simply an engineering problem.

—Michio Kaku

Datomic's treatment of time as first class, and the database as a value, gives you as a developer the power of time travel. Let's look at the more obvious type of time travel in Datomic: journeying to the past.

Let's start by simulating time advancing forward by adding some data. Create a new task with an `issue-id`, and then use the `issue-id` to upsert several new values of the task's description. Each time you'll capture the resulting `db` value.

```
dev> (def db1 (:db-after @(d/transact conn [{:db/id (d/tempid :db.part/user)
                                             :task/issue-id "Hello"}])))
dev> (def db2 (:db-after @(d/transact conn [{:db/id (d/tempid :db.part/user)
                                             :task/issue-id "Hello"
                                             :task/description "First description"}])))
dev> (def db3 (:db-after @(d/transact conn [{:db/id (d/tempid :db.part/user)
                                             :task/issue-id "Hello"
                                             :task/description "Second description"}])))
```

It's time to introduce another Datomic API function: `as-of`, which takes a `db` value and a `t` value—the result of calling `basis-t`, a transaction id, or a date—and returns a new `db` value that is of that point in time. Now let's see how you can travel back in time.

```
dev> (def now-db (d/db conn)) ;; get the most current db
dev> (:task/description (d/entity now-db [:task/issue-id "Hello"]))
"Second description"
dev> (:task/description (d/entity (d/as-of now-db (d/basis-t db2))
                                  [:task/issue-id "Hello"]))
"First description"
```

You can use the `db` from the past anywhere in the Datomic API that expects a `db`: even queries.

```
dev> (def description-query '[:find ?i . :in $ ?desc
                             :where [?i :task/description ?desc]])
dev> (d/q description-query now-db "Second description")
17592186045446
dev> (d/q description-query (d/as-of now-db (d/basis-t db2)) "First description")
17592186045446
```

What's perhaps more unexpected is that you can travel into the future—at least, into a speculative possible future like the kind that Ebenezer Scrooge was brought to in *A Christmas Carol*. This is done with the somewhat innocuously named `with` function in the Datomic API. It takes a `db` and some transaction data, and returns the result of what would occur if the data were transacted, including a :db-after key with a new db value. This lets you chain multiple simulated transactions together, like so:

```
dev> (def future-db (-> now-db
                        (d/with [{:db/id (d/tempid :db.part/user)
                                  :task/issue-id "Hello"
                                  :task/description "Third description"}])
                        :db-after
                        (d/with [{:db/id (d/tempid :db.part/user)
                                  :task/issue-id "Hello"
                                  :task/title "Hello world"}])
                        :db-after))
dev> (d/touch (d/entity future-db [:task/issue-id "Hello"]))
{:db/id 17592186045446, :task/description "Third description",
 :task/title "Hello world", :task/issue-id "Hello"}
```

BUILDING APPLICATIONS WITH DATOMIC

Let's take a look at how to create the data access layer for the task tracker app.

User Functions

Start with the user code. In the application source folder, create a user.clj file with these initial contents:

```
(ns chapter-6.user
  "Database functions for user operations"
  (:require [datomic.api :as d]
            [crypto.password.bcrypt :as password]))

(defn entity
  "Returns user entity from :db/id, string login, or arg if already
   an entity."
  [db user]
  (cond (instance? datomic.query.EntityMap x) user
        (string? user) (d/entity db [:user/login user])
        :else (d/entity db user)))

(defn id
  "Returns :db/id for a user when passed an entity, login, or long id."
  [db user]
  (:db/id (entity db user)))
```

This sets up our namespace declaration, including the bcrypt functionality from the crypto.password library that we'll use to encrypt our passwords. You can also see there are two utility functions intended to help support more flexible APIs. The entity function will coerce several types of arguments into a Datomic entity for the user. If it's already an entity, it will return what's passed. If it's a string, it assumes it's a user login and creates an entity using the lookup ref. Otherwise, it assumes it's an entity id or something that can be passed directly to Datomic's entity function.

The id helper function returns the :db/id of a user passed in any of the forms that entity accepts.

Now let's create a function to check if a login and password are correct. This function can take advantage of the login as a lookup ref since it's being passed in, use that to retrieve the user entity and its encrypted password, and check the submitted plaintext password against the crypted one.

```
(defn check-login
  "Checks if login and password are correct, and if so returns the
   user entity."
  [db login password]
  (when-let [user (d/entity db [:user/login login])]
    (when (password/check password (:user/password user))
      user)))
```

Often in user registration forms, you want to quickly check if the user's login or email address is already taken, and if so give a message to the user that they're not available. Let's write two simple functions to perform those availability checks.

```
(defn login-available?
  "Checks if a login is available. Returns false if already used by a
   user."
  [db login]
  (nil? (d/entity db [:user/login login])))

(defn email-available?

  "Checks if an email address is available. Returns false if already
   used by a user."
  [db email]
  (nil? (d/q '[:find ?user .
               :in $ ?email
               :where [?user :user/email ?email]]
             db email)))
```

The login availability check is somewhat simpler to do since you can use login as a lookup ref. The email check is a little more involved, since you have to perform a query. It's a simple query, however, that will return either a single user id matching the email, or nil if none is found.

Ensuring Data Integrity with Transaction Functions

Next, let's add the function that creates users. Since this function needs to perform a transaction, it will take a Datomic connection rather than db. However, there's one nagging problem here. Since user logins are upsertable, you need a way to ensure that the user you're creating doesn't have a login that's already in use.

You could try using the availability check function to see if it already exists. This would cover most of the cases, but if you have a lot of experience with databases you might already see the problem with this approach. Whenever you do a read and then a write in this way, you open yourself up to a race condition where, in this case, a user with that login gets created by someone else between the read and the write.

Relational databases solve this with transactions spanning both reads and writes and complicated locking semantics. Datomic doesn't need that because it solves the problem with transaction functions.

Transaction functions are run by the transactor as part of transaction processing. Datomic comes with two built-in funtions: a compare-and-swap operation, and an entity retraction operation. But neither of these functions quite meets our needs. What is needed is a transaction function that will look to see if the ident value exists at the time of the transaction.

In Datomic, functions are represented as entities with a `:db/fn` attribute that has the value of a Datomic function object. You can create function objects by calling the Datomic API's function method with a map of information about that function, or with the `#db/fn` reader literal with a map in that same format. The map describes what language the function is in (either Java or Clojure), what parameters it accepts, a string containing the function body, and optional import and require lists.

Another nifty feature of Datomic function objects is that they are callable as regular Clojure functions. Here's a simple example that adds two numbers:

```clojure
(def add
  (d/function {:lang "clojure"
               :params '[x y]
               :code "(+ x y)"}))

(add 1 2) ;; => 3
```

Transaction functions are a special type of Datomic function. They have some additional requirements:

➤ The first argument is a Datomic `db`.

➤ They should return transaction data, or throw an exception to fail the transaction.

Let's create a transaction function that will ensure that an identity value for a given attribute doesn't exist, and add it to the schema file.

```clojure
{:db/id #db/id[:db.part/task]
 :db/ident :add-identity
 :db/fn #db/fn{:lang "clojure"
               :params [db e ident-attr value]
               :code "(if (d/entity db [ident-attr value])
                        (throw (ex-info (str value \" already exists for \"
                                             ident-attr)
                                        {:e e
                                         :attribute ident-attr
                                         :value value}))
                        [[:db/add e ident-attr value]])"}}
```

This function takes a `db` value, an entity id to add the identity for, the identity attribute, and the value. The function looks to see if that identity value already exists, and if so it throws an exception. Otherwise, it returns transaction data that adds the identity to the entity id. Give it an ident, `:add-identity`, so you can refer to it in transactions.

You can make use of this in the function to create users.

```clojure
(defn create
  "Attempts to create a new user entity with given login, password,
```

```
and email. If paid? is true, creates a paid account and link to the
user, otherwise creates a free account. Returns the transaction
data if succesful. Will throw an exception if the login or email
already belong to another user."
([conn login password email]
 (create conn login password email false))
([conn login password email paid?]
 (let [tempid (d/tempid :db.part/account)
       user-tx [{:db/id tempid
                 :user/email email
                 :user/password (password/encrypt password)
                 :user/account {:account/type (if paid?
                                                :account.type/paid
                                                :account.type/free)}}
               ;; db function ensures login doesn't exist already
               [:add-identity tempid :user/login login]]]
    @(d/transact conn user-tx))))
```

You can see how the calling syntax for database functions is fairly close to the way the list-syntax for transaction data works. The first list element is the transaction function name, the following elements are the arguments. You didn't need to use this transaction function for emails since the email was made with a unique value attribute, and Datomic throws an exception that aborts the transaction if there's a duplicate.

Account Functions

Let's take a look at some functions that deal with the charges, payments, and balance of the users' accounts in our app. The account model maintains two sources for an account's current balance: the sum of all the charges, payments, and adjustment transactions against the account; and the :account/current-balance attribute. Keeping those in sync can be a challenge.

Here is another place that transaction functions can be helpful. Instead of manually calculating and asserting the new balance each time you add a transaction, and opening up the risk of another possible race condition, you can let the transactor handle this for you. Here are two choices: you can use Datomic's compare-and-swap function, which will fail the transaction if the current balance has changed since the time it was read, or you can create our own transaction function that automatically adjusts the balance by applying the transaction amount.

Using compare-and-swap has the advantage of being built-in, but the disadvantage is that it will be failing transactions when you really don't need to. If you want to use it in the transaction, be sure to add something like this:

```
[:db.fn/cas account-id :account/current-balance
            expected-current-balance new-balance]
```

Writing your own transaction function for this gives you something like:

```
[{:db/id #db/id[:db.part/account]
  :db/ident :account/update-balance
  :db/fn #db/fn{:lang "clojure"
                :params [db a amt]
                :code "(let [acct (d/entity db a)
```

```
                    balance (or (:account/current-balance acct) 0)]
            [[:db/add a :account/current-balance
                (bigdec (+ balance amt))]])"}}]
```

If you use this approach, here is the function to add a new transaction:

```
(defn add-transaction
  "Takes a conn, user or account entity, transaction type (ident of
   the enum), and amount, and adds the transaction to the user's
   account. Returns the transaction data."
  [conn user-or-account trans-type amount]
  (let [account (or (:user/account user-or-account) user-or-account)
        amount (bigdec amount)
        charge-tx [{:db/id (d/tempid :db.part/account)
                    :transaction/type trans-type
                    :transaction/amount amount
                    :account/_transaction (:db/id account)}
                   [:account/update-balance (:db/id account) amount]]]
    @(d/transact conn charge-tx)))
```

Youo can also add helper functions for each transaction type, such as add-charge, add-payment, and add-adjustment.

Task Functions

Here now is coverage of the heart of the system: tasks. Let's start with the basics of task creation in a new namespace for the task database functions. Create a new file in the project's source folder called tasks.clj and add the basic namespace declaration, along with a few dependencies that are needed.

```
(ns chapter-6.task
  (:require [clojure.string :as str]
            [datomic.api :as d]
            [chapter-6.user :as user]))
```

For the task creation API, the function needs to accept a connection, some reference to the user that is creating the task, and various data for the task: a title, description, status, issue-id, tags, and the parent task if it's a subtask.

To keep the number of required data to the minimum, let's say only the user and the title should be required. The rest you can either leave empty, have a useful default, or generate ourselves.

You'll definitely need an issue-id, since that's the identity attribute. If one isn't supplied, let's write a function that will generate it from the issue's title. It will take the first word of the title, capitalize it, and try incremental numeric postfixes until it finds one that doesn't yet exist in the database.

```
(defn issue-id-from-title
  "Takes a db and task title, returns an issue-id using the first
   word in the title with a numeric postfix that does not already
   exist in the db."
  [db title]
  (->> (range)
       (map (partial str (.toUpperCase (first (str/split title #"\s"))) "-"))
       (remove (fn [issue-id] (d/entity db [:task/issue-id issue-id])))
       first))
```

You can also add an entity function as you had in the user namespace to make the API more flexible, for example, by accepting different forms for the parent task.

```
(defn entity
  "Returns task entity from :db/id, string issue-id, or arg if already
   an entity."
  [db task]
  (cond (instance? datomic.query.EntityMap task) task
        (string? task) (d/entity db [:task/issue-id task])
        :else (d/entity db task)))
```

Now you can add the `create` function. Since you're adding an `issue-id` identity attribute, and it may suffer from the same kind of race condition problems that you noticed with user logins, you should make use of the `database` function you created for that.

```
(defn create
  "Takes a Datomic connection, a user entity, and a map with task
   info, and attempts to create a task in the database. Returns
   transaction data. Task info map has keys:

   * :title (required)
   * :description
   * :status - one of :todo, :in-progress, :done [:todo]
   * :issue-id - defaults to the word in title with a numeric
     postfix
   * :tags - a set of strings
   * :parent - task entity, issue id, or :db/id"
  [conn user
   {:keys [title description status issue-id tags parent]
    :or {status :todo}}]
  (assert title ":title is required")
  (let [tempid (d/tempid :db.part/task)
        db (d/db conn)
        status (keyword "task.status" (name status))
        issue-id (or issue-id (issue-id-from-title db title))
        tags (some->> tags
                      (map (partial hash-map :tag/name))
                      (set))
        parent (entity db parent)]
    @(d/transact conn
                 [(cond-> {:db/id tempid
                           :task/user (:db/id user)
                           :task/title title
                           :task/issue-id issue-id
                           :task/status status}
                    description (assoc :task/description description)
                    tags (assoc :task/tag tags)
                    parent (assoc :task/parent (:db/id parent)))
                  [:add-identity tempid :task/issue-id issue-id]])))
```

Notice that since tags are upsertable with `:tag/name`, you don't have to care about whether they exist or not, and you can simply assert them here and Datomic will either create them or wire up the task with the existing ones. The `:add-identity` database function is the one created for user logins, but we made it flexible enough to work with any identity attribute.

Next, you can add a straightforward function that assigns a task a new parent, supporting the operation in the example app where the user is re-organizing their tasks.

```
(defn set-parent
  "Sets parent of task to parent."
  [conn task parent]
  (let [db (d/db conn)]
    @(d/transact conn [[:db/add (:db/id (entity db task))
                        :task/parent (:db/id (entity db task))]])))
```

You can add similar functions to set task's status, and add and remove tags.

```
(defn set-status
  "Sets status of task to status, one of :todo :done :in-progress."
  [conn task status]
  (let [db (d/db conn)]
    @(d/transact conn [[:db/add (:db/id (entity db task))
                        :task/status (keyword "task.status" (name status))]])))

(defn add-tag
  "Adds a tag to task. Tag is the string name of the tag."
  [conn task tag]
  (let [db (d/db conn)]
    @(d/transact conn [{:db/id (:db/id (entity db task))
                        :task/tag #{{:tag/name tag}}}])))

(defn remove-tag
  "Removes tag from a task. Tag is the string name of the tag."
  [conn task tag]
  (let [db (d/db conn)]
    @(d/transact conn [[:db/retract (:db/id (entity db task))
                        :task/tag [:tag/name tag]]])))
```

Now, let's add a query function that returns all of the top-level tasks for a user. You'll add an optional parameter that flags whether the subtasks should be returned. Since you're using the pull API, let's first write the `pull-spec`.

```
(def task-pull-spec
  "Basic pull spec for task info."
  [:task/title :task/description {:task/status [:db/ident]}
   :task/issue-id {:task/tag [:tag/name]}])
```

This `pull-spec` includes the basic fields for the task, the `ident` of the task's status, and the name of all the task's tags. Now you can add your query function.

```
(defn for-user
  "Returns all the top-level tasks for a user. If sub-tasks? is true,
   recursively returns the sub-tasks as well."
  ([db user]
   (for-user db user false))
  ([db user subtasks?]
   (let [pull-spec (cond-> task-pull-spec
                     subtasks? (conj {:task/_parent '...}))]
```

```
        query '[:find (pull ?task spec)
               :in $ ?user spec
               :where [?task :task/user ?user]
                      (not [?task :task/parent _])]]
(d/q query db (user/id db user) pull-spec)))))
```

If the subtasks flag is true, this function adds something interesting to the `pull-spec`. The addition of `{:task/_parent '...}` means that it will apply the entire `pull-spec` recursively using the parent reverse reference. That is, it will recursively pull all of the task's children, and their children, and so forth. The `...` turns it into a recursive spec, or you could have put a number there instead to limit the recursion depth. The result is that the entire subtask tree of a task will be pulled for the app to use or display for the user.

Also notice that you can pass `pull-specs` in as arguments to the query and bind them as symbols without any special prefix.

Finally, let's look at how you can use the fulltext search index added for the `:task/title` attribute, to search for tasks by title. You can reuse the same `pull-spec` created before. The query function looks like this:

```
(defn search-title
  "Searches for tasks using a fulltext search on the title. Returns
   the matching tasks as well as the match score against the search
   string."
  [db user search]
  (d/q '[:find (pull ?task spec) ?score
         :in $ ?user ?search spec
         :where [(fulltext $ :task/title ?search) [[?task _ _ ?score]]]
                [?task :task/user ?user]]
       db (user/id db user) search task-pull-spec))
```

Notice the use of the built-in `fulltext` function in the query. It accepts the `db` source, the attribute to look in, and the search terms, returning a four-tuple of `[?entity ?value ?tx ?score]`. Since the focus is on the entity, and the matching score for this function, we ignored the value and the `tx` with underscores.

Wrapping Up

Notice that it took very little actual code to power a large amount of functionality, as shown in this chapter. Datomic's powerful API, and the investments made in our application data model, really pay off when it comes to building the application and getting a lot of leverage out of concise code.

Testing is something outside of the scope of this chapter, but you can take advantage of the value semantics of Datomic `db`s, and the ease with which you can stand up in-memory Datomic databases to write a thorough automated test suite for your application code with a minimum of machinery.

Deployment

In order to deploy a production Datomic system with a transactor and persistent store, you need to download one of the release downloads. As of this writing, there are three tiers of Datomic license:

➤ **Datomic Free.** It is, as the name implies, free of cost and doesn't require registration. This lets you run a transactor using the "dev" storage and a maximum of 2 peers. The "dev" storage is actually an embedded SQL database that the peers access via the transactor.

➤ **Datomic Pro Starter.** This is also free of cost, although it requires registration and an access code to download and use in your project. It allows you to use any of the storage backends with a limited number of peers.

➤ **Datomic Pro.** This is the paid edition of Datomic, and is licensed by the number of peers. It gives access to all of the features, including all of the storage backends, high-availability transactor mode, and memcached.

Once you have a version of Datomic downloaded, you need to choose your storage backend and set up the transactor. The Datomic documentation section on deployment is an excellent guide to this process, and is available here: `http://docs.datomic.com/deployment.html`.

The Limitations

No system exists that can handle every possible use case and every possible scenario. Every system has tradeoffs, and those tradeoffs impose limitations on how the system can be used. Datomic is no exception. In building Datomic, Rich, Stuart, et al. made design decisions that make Datomic well suited for use as a transactional system for storing domain data, in the way many applications use a relational database today.

Those same design decisions place some limitations on what you can do with Datomic, and it is helpful to know up-front what those are, and what types of use cases are not a good fit for Datomic.

Hard (and Soft) Limits

The most obvious limitation of Datomic is that there is only one writer, the transactor. This means that write scalability is limited to vertical scalability only, and applications built on Datomic can only handle the write volume that the single transactor node can handle. In practice, this is not generally a critical limitation, since it's not difficult to achieve hundreds of sustained writes per second through the transactor, with bursts into the thousand-per-second range.

If your application is working at this kind of data scale, then generally you are already outside the range where you would be able to get good performance out of a relational database without tuning and designing your schema to optimize your read patterns. In other words, you've already given up many of the benefits of a relational database, and one of the other NoSQL databases designed around this kind of data volume might be a better fit than Datomic.

Another limit is the number of "schema" elements. This includes both schema attributes and partitions. There is a hard maximum of 2^{20} of these—a little over 1 million. It is unlikely you'll ever reach this limit—in fact it's likely that something has gone terribly wrong if you have—but it's something to be aware of.

The max number of entity ids in any partition is 2^{42}, which is around 4.4 trillion. This is purely a theoretical limitation, included here just so that you don't worry about it, because it is absolutely impossible to get this many entities into Datomic, period. Principally this is due to the final, most imposing limitation.

There is a *soft* limit on the total number of Datoms in a database of around 10 billion. This includes assertions, retractions, and history. This is a soft limit, because nothing will stop you from adding more, and in fact Cognitect is aware of a production Datomic database with more than 14 billion Datoms. This is a limit to be concerned with just the same for three reasons.

➤ Cognitect's automated testing of Datomic includes database sizes of up to 10 billion Datoms, so there's reason to be confident that Datomic will work at that volume. Above that, however, you are officially in uncharted waters.

➤ The index data structures start to become quite bloated at this size, such that query performance is likely to suffer and there will be increased resource demands on every peer node.

➤ Transactor performance will take a real hit as the number of directory nodes and segments increase, the magnitude of which depends on how varied your write patterns are and how well you have designed your partitions. If the transactor's re-indexing job needs to rewrite an excessively large number of data segments because the indexes have become very large and your writes are spread across many segments, it is possible that it will not be able to complete and your database will simply fall over to the point of requiring a restore from a previous safe backup.

SUMMARY

This chapter covered in detail how Datomic changes the way you build database-backed applications. You can see how Datomic's emphasis on flexibility and expressiveness is enabled by its simple, yet powerful, data model, and innovative ideas about design and immutability. With so many new ideas in one system, you can see how Datomic in many ways represents a fundamental rethinking of the database.

While this chapter aimed to provide enough breadth to see what's possible with Datomic, and enough depth that you're left with the information and understanding you need to begin building applications with it, there is more to cover. The Datomic documentation is immensely valuable, with a huge trove of valuable information. Additionally, there are a number of great presentations, blogs, and videos that cover different aspects of Datomic and case studies.

We hope that you are now aware of the possibilities that Datomic opens up for your applications, and a glimmer of the excitement that we feel about working with it.

7

Performance

WHAT'S IN THIS CHAPTER?

➤ Understanding performance

➤ Choosing the right data structure

➤ Benchmarking is important

➤ Profiling, Parallelism, and Memoization

➤ Using low-level techniques to improve performance

We should forget about small efficiencies, say about 97% of the time: premature optimization is the root of all evil. Yet we should not pass up our opportunities in that critical 3%.

—DONALD KNUTH

In this chapter you will implement tools and techniques to make code execute faster. How fast can a dynamic, lazy, functional, immutable language be, you ask. Pretty fast. You can expect Clojure code to take around 2–5 times the amount of CPU of equivalent Java code. With a little work you can tweak it to be as fast as Java code. In turn, you can expect Java code to perform at around 1.2 times C. This is amazing considering the high-level abstractions you get to leverage from Clojure. Compared to dynamic languages like Ruby, Clojure is blazingly fast.

So, how does Clojure achieve such great performance? The answer is the JVM. Clojure embraces its host platform and relies on its mature byte code optimization. The same holds true for ClojureScript (relies on the Closure Compiler) and ClojureCLR (embraces the .NET runtime). There is an intentional tradeoff made to embrace the underlying platform and not completely abstract it away. The benefit is performance and interoperability. The downside is you have to live with some unsightly details of the underlying platform leaking into your code.

Clojure has several advantages for producing high performance code:

➤ Clojure is data oriented. Choosing the right datastructure is the prerequisite for writing fast code. Clojure encourages usage of `O(1)` and `O(log n)` data structures by providing the map, the set, and the vector literal notation.

➤ Clojure is a concise language, with powerful functional abstractions. Concise expressions aid algorithmic clarity. Being able to express algorithms succinctly is a great advantage in writing correct and efficient algorithms.

➤ Interop allows you to delegate heavy lifting tasks to Java libraries. When you really need every drop of CPU for a task, chances are there is a library for that. If not, you always have the option to create and use your own Java classes for critical bottlenecks in your system.

➤ Clojure exposes a range of options for trading off between high-level dynamic code and annotated bare metal code.

There are also several aspects of Clojure that commonly produce poor performance. Memory allocation is the biggest aspect to be alert to. Reflection in tight loops commonly causes unexpected slowness, and Clojure is often cited as slow due to its terrible startup time, which is a constant and visible tax. There is no way around it, Clojure is just not good at that. If you look past startup time though, you will find it performs great once it is up and running.

High-level abstractions have a cost. But being able to reason with high-level abstractions is very powerful. If you are able to identify bottlenecks, you can split your code into elegant and performant code, and get large speed gains by tuning the performant code. You can always code with algorithmic complexity in mind. There is no point looking up items from a sequence when you can use a map instead. But how do you approach the performance of your code beyond that?

➤ **Think**—Thinking is by far the most important part. Define your performance goals as an implicit functional requirement for systems you build. Be very clear about what level of performance is acceptable, at what point performance becomes irrelevant, and what are reasonable system requirements to achieve the desired performance.

➤ **Measure**

> ➤ Time your suspicious functions, then benchmark, and profile.

> ➤ Check that appropriate data structures and algorithms are used. Use transients where data structures are built. Look for reduce calls, especially for opportunities to use transients.

> ➤ Check your concurrency, especially if the bottleneck involves external resources. Clojure has concise concurrency abstractions; take advantage of them.

> ➤ Memoize judiciously.

> ➤ Use type hint. For interop code that is called very frequently, reflection costs quickly add up and can become significant.

> ➤ Measure memory allocation and garbage collection. Check your use of laziness. This can be a source of memory consumption and garbage collection.

> ➤ **Monitor**—Monitoring is the only way to know that you are allocating system resources effectively. You are unable to reach all the way down to first principles of computation to fully reason about your system because the computation stack is so complex. It is inevitable that your system assumptions will break, so you need to monitor for it and learn from it.

WHAT IS PERFORMANCE?

A basic view of performance is how quickly your program calculates some result. A more sophisticated definition of performance is the ratio of resources your system consumes, relative to how much value it produces. The practical definition of performance might be: "The system is down, CPU usage is at 100%, I need to fix this right now!" It is important to think of performance in a holistic fashion, because all of these definitions hold some truth, and yet in and of themselves are too myopic.

Any system is built making a trade-off between how much time was invested in creating the system, how well it provides value, and the costs of running and maintaining it. Be aware of where the curve pivots, and at what distance from that pivot your activities are wasteful in either direction.

Focusing too deeply on any one aspect of performance can be wasteful and even counter-productive. It is no use spending hours annotating code with types to avoid reflection, when using a different data structure would have given a far better outcome. Even worse, micro-optimizing the wrong thing can be a barrier to refactoring to a better solution.

Examining performance teaches you how your system actually works. Small changes can have huge impacts. Software typically changes often, so it is unlikely that every change will be examined for performance, unless you have measurement and automated tests that produce metrics.

Achieving high performance requires experimenting with code, with libraries, and with analysis tools. Experiments are only effective when measurement is involved. Keep a record of your results as you try new approaches.

This chapter is all about experimenting and measuring. In order to provide some examples of the techniques, we will be measuring the performance of the example project tracking solution used throughout this book. In order to provide self-contained examples, the focus will be on a feature for running Monte Carlo project simulations. The idea is that you will take a project and iterate to a new state in the project with some simple rules. This will give you one possible path that the project could take. If you run many such simulations, you may be able to draw some insights into important variables to control.

CHOOSING THE RIGHT DATA STRUCTURE IS A PREREQUISITE FOR PERFORMANCE

Vectors have $O(1)$ lookup by index. Sets and hashmaps have $O(\log n)$ lookup by key. Sequences by contrast are $O(n)$. Choosing the right data structure usually boils down to not doing combinatorial sequential lookups $O(n^2)$ or higher. Exponential complexity is the primary performance assassin for algorithms.

Checking for the existence of an element in a sequence is usually a built-in feature of a language. In Java you have `indexOf`. But Clojure does not have an equivalent for sequences. This is a case of Clojure purposefully discouraging a common bad choice. When you need to check membership of an element in a sequence, you should not be using a sequence at all. A set is the right datastructure for testing membership.

Consider two possible data models you can design for the project simulation code. The first represents the team as a list of names, and the stories as a list of stories containing details of the story and an id. This sort of data is very much what you might expect as the result of an SQL query.

```
(def project1-bad
  {:title "Build a task tracking solution"
   :team '("Jeremy" "Justin" "Michael" "Nick" "Timothy")
   :stories '({:id "aaa"
               :title "Build a ClojureScript front end"
               :status "Ready"}
              {:id "bbb"
               :title "Build backend services"
               :status "Done"}
              {:id "ccc"
               :title "Tune performance"
               :status "In Progress"})})
```

As soon as the number of stories starts to grow, any use of the list representation will suffer dramatically. It is certain that even if the list representation shows no problems, you will run into a scenario where it just breaks down completely for a larger dataset.

A better choice is to use a set to store the team, and make the stories a map of story id to story details. This sort of data is more like how a database might internally be structured in the sense that using the unique identifier as a key in a map is similar to indexing the stories.

```
(def project1-better
  {:title "Build a task tracking solution"
   :team #{"Jeremy" "Justin" "Michael" "Nick" "Timothy"}
   :stories {"aaa" {:title "Build a ClojureScript front end"
                    :status "Ready"}
             "bbb" {:title "Build backend services"
                    :status "Done"}
             "ccc" {:title "Tune performance"
                    :status "In Progress"}}})
```

Is this really better? At such a small scale, the only difference is semantic. Using a set is explicitly stating that only unique names are allowed in our data model. Similarly ids must be unique, because they are keys in a map. This alone is reason enough to choose the right data structure. It communicates intent.

Keeping a watchful eye for the right data structure is very different from trying to optimize your code statements for best branch first. The latter is highly situational and impossible to do without benchmarking. The former is correct thinking that leads to efficient algorithms. Choosing the right data structure is never a premature optimization. Thinking about the correct data representation helps you think about the problem domain, the data you are storing, and how that data will be consumed. It is always worth spending the time upfront to choose a data model that best represents sensible access semantics. Do not defer thinking about the complexity implications of data representation on some notion of it being an optimization. Choosing the right data structure is the prerequisite for correct and performant code.

BENCHMARKING

You often know roughly what part of your system is not performing at an acceptable level. You might have a clue such as "When the user adds a story with a very long description, the interface hangs." Begin by thinking about why this may be the case, how this part of the system is bottlenecking, and what you can reasonably hope to achieve. We have a plan of attack and some hypotheses in hand. So now it is time to measure, experiment, and try some techniques to improve the situation.

When constructing experiments you should keep in mind that granular measurements are more practical than fine measurements. This is a truth that is easy to lose sight of as you delve into the complexities of computer behavior. When you move down to measuring and tuning operations instead of algorithms, you enter into a battle to optimize a complex stack of layered yet intertwined abstractions.

These algorithms are implemented in Clojure, which in turn relies on Java classes to provide fundamental abstractions, which in turn relies on the Java compiler to create efficient byte code. The JVM goes to great length to execute the code efficiently. The JVM inlines function calls, does hotspot analysis, removes redundant loads, does copy propagation, and eliminates dead code. The byte code is an abstraction around CPU instructions and memory. On the CPU itself further optimization is occurring such as caching and common branch detection. This tall stack of abstractions allows you to be algorithmically expressive, but along the way you sacrifice optimal use of computational resources. There is a tradeoff between precise control over exactly what the hardware does, and the ability to compose abstract concepts to express useful calculations.

Optimizations in one layer may directly counteract optimizations in another layer. So, you are affected by both the complexity of a tall stack of abstractions, and also how those layers interact with each other. Because of these complex interactions, performance is almost never the sum of its parts. Micro-benchmarking operations in isolation will not accurately match the performance of the combination of those operations.

Micro-benchmarks don't compose, so don't micro-benchmark everything. More detail is worse, but making a very small change can have a large impact over a wide scope. So focus on larger scopes, and the most heavily used functions.

Do use benchmarks to reason about performance. Don't randomly try things to improve performance, but instead make educated guesses about how the code can be made to run faster. Just be cautious about any assumptions you make when it comes to overall performance in the context of the code you will be executing in this chapter.

Timing Slow Things

Measuring slow things sounds a little boring, but most of the big performance wins covered in this chapter are going to come from measuring slow things; finding unexpectedly large chunks of sunk time. Slower is better when it comes to finding a scope of code to time. Try to organize your performance experiments in a way that decomposes the time in halves. Binary search is an excellent way to narrow in on the important aspects of your program.

Often you will be surprised that decomposition is nowhere near the midpoint. This surprise is a good thing, since it means that one of the assumptions is wrong. Let's face it, assumptions about performance are very often wrong. The good news is that finding false assumptions presents an opportunity to better understand your system, and will likely reveal a key insight to improving it.

Profiling tools allow you to avoid having to invest heavily in up front binary time-split style timings. Profiling automatically percolates up the scopes of code that you should investigate to discover bottlenecks.

Performance tuning requires a lot of experimentation. So using a REPL to time and adjust functions is convenient. Start a REPL and follow along with the examples in this book, and take some time to stray from the examples as well. Let's time the top level entry point.

```
(time (sim-project project1))
```

You get the final stimulation state returned back to you. Above, the result you can see is a message printed "Elapsed time: 7299.223 msecs". The time macro is great because you can wrap any part of your code in (time ...) to see how long it is taking. You can quickly try wrapping a few suspicious expressions and discover a bottleneck that can be improved. Perhaps you suspect that a lot of time is being spent in standup, so you can check that without changing the behavior of the code.

```
(defn standup [project]
  (time
    (-> project
      (complete-stories)
      (start-stories))))
```

Now you can see dozens of output messages like "Elapsed time: 70.007 msecs." This certainly seems like a good place to investigate. Ad hoc timing is often easier than going to the trouble of profiling execution, but is less direct. Often you can quickly spot something obvious and get some quick wins, so it is always a good place to start. Be aware that this approach has limitations and switch to another approach when ad hoc timing is no longer yielding traction.

Depending on your environment and goals, relying on printed output can be distracting. Sometimes you want the actual time taken as a value. Let's adapt the time macro to return the number of milliseconds as a value, so that you can make some assertions about your performance goals.

```
(defmacro time-msecs
  "Returns the time in msecs taken to evaluate expr."
  [expr]
  `(let [start# (. System (nanoTime))]
     ~expr
     (/ (double (- (. System (nanoTime)) start#)) 1000000.0)))
```

Now you can write a test to describe your goal.

```
(deftest slow-tests
  (is (< (b/time-msecs (sim/sim-project sim/project1))
         1000)
      "A full project simulation should take less than one second"))
```

This approach works great for measuring calculations longer than 10 milliseconds, but breaks down for shorter periods.

Benchmarking external resource access is less susceptible to JVM variance. It doesn't make any sense to worry about nanosecond accuracy when timing web service request round trips. Monitoring is often done at the service level, which is usually perfect. You should rely on monitoring instead of benchmarking for external resources as much as possible.

Use Criterium for Timing Fast Things

Benchmarking code is usually not as simple as calling `(time (some-fn ...))`. The time of execution can vary wildly, depending on how and when it is invoked due to advanced techniques such as adaptive optimization and dynamic recompilation employed by the JVM. This becomes a big problem with trying to time short calculations that take less than 10 milliseconds.

Consider this puzzling case.

```
(time (inc 1))
"Elapsed time: 0.028 msecs"
(time (dotimes [i 1000] (inc 1)))
"Elapsed time: 0.23 msecs"
```

Doing 1000 times more calculations takes only 10 times as long. Clearly there is more going on than meets the eye.

A naïve approach to writing benchmark tests might be something like start a JVM, run bench-mark1, benchmark2, benchmark3, and shutdown. After benchmark1, the JVM is optimized for benchmark1, but wrongly optimized for benchmark2. The name for this order dependent perfor-mance is path dependency. Changing the ordering changes the benchmark results. You need a fresh JVM for each benchmark to isolate them.

The Criterium library (`https://github.com/hugoduncan/criterium`) provides a way to work around most of those issues. It includes a warm-up period, during which the Just-In-Time (JIT) compiler can work its magic. The library also mitigates the effects of garbage-collection (GC) prior to measuring the speed. Finally, it computes not just the mean time, but also upper and lower quan-tiles, and standard deviation. You get a wealth of insightful statistics about your benchmarks to better understand the performance profile of the code.

```
Evaluation count : 18900 in 60 samples of 315 calls.
            Execution time mean : 3,574752 ms
   Execution time std-deviation : 1,127694 ms
  Execution time lower quantile : 2,304367 ms ( 2,5%)
  Execution time upper quantile : 5,652621 ms (97,5%)
                  Overhead used : 3,443486 ns

Found 4 outliers in 60 samples (6,6667 %)
     low-severe     2 (3,3333 %)
     low-mild       2 (3,3333 %)
 Variance from outliers : 96,4221 % Variance is severely inflated by outliers
```

Where and how should benchmarks be run? The easy answer is from the REPL. This has the same advantages and drawbacks as using the `time` macro for ad hoc timing. Keep in mind that Criterium is aimed at CPU/memory bound tasks and is not appropriate for slow functions such as IO bound operations. Trying to get 60 samples of a function that takes 10 second is going to take 10 minutes. That's not very interactive, nor is the additional accuracy valuable in such a scenario.

Consider using Criterium inside tests, because it is good to assert performance to avoid releasing bugs. If you gather this data regularly you can plot performance per source control commit, to see how your system is being affected by changes. You can make assertions using `quick-benchmark`, which returns the benchmarks instead of printing a report.

To gather all of the results into a form convenient for charting, you can use a fixture.

```
(defn add-results! [k results]
  (swap! benchmarks assoc-in [(:time git-commit-info) k] results))

(defn save-gathered-benchmarks [f]
  (f)
  (with-open [w (io/writer (doto (io/file "benchmarks" benchmark-filename)
                             (io/make-parents)))]
    (clojure.pprint/pprint @benchmarks w)))
```

Then, create a macro to define a benchmark to be recorded.

```
(defmacro bench-press [title acceptable-time & form]
  `(deftest ~(symbol (kebab/->kebab-case title))
     (testing ~title
       (let [results# (assoc (cr/quick-benchmark ~@form nil)
                        :acceptable-time ~acceptable-time)]
         (add-results! ~title results#)
         (is (< (first (:mean results#)) ~acceptable-time))))))
```

Now you can very concisely express benchmarks that will be run in continuous integration builds.

```
(use-fixtures :once b/save-gathered-benchmarks)

(b/bench-press "Remove 1 done story" (* 1000 b/nsecs)
  (remove-done-stories project1))
```

The fixture produces a file containing the full performance results relative to source control commits, suitable for charting. With this information on hand, finding out what change introduced a performance bottleneck is easy.

```
{#inst "2016-02-01T08:37:59.000-00:00"
 {:git-commit-info
  {:id "d2cbd0ded4b16300d76231b6d553edbfc3fb1668",
   :message "namespacing and adding some example improvements" ...}
  "Bug?"
  {:mean
   [3.4741639538209525E-6
    (3.3825290092479442E-6 5.5348896790521507E-6)],
   :final-gc-time 95103961,
   :execution-count 38459,
   :variance
   [1.2185041088601622E-14
    (3.4091764724026322E-15 2.3422252112283815E-14)] ...}}}}
```

Criterium is the de facto standard library for benchmarking CPU/memory bound calculation. It addresses many of the challenges to accurately measuring the time taken for code to execute, and how variable the time span is over many runs. Use it to measure fast things.

Use Test Selectors for Performance Tests

Tests and namespaces should be labeled to limit benchmark execution to only occur in continuous integration test runs, or when you explicitly request them in development. Prevent benchmarks from running in development test by default; they are too slow for interactive development. To label a namespace or test, attach a metadata flag.

```
(deftest ^:perf slow-tests ...)
```

Attaching a metadata flag to the namespace is equivalent to labeling all of the tests in the namespace.

```
(ns ^:perf mush.simulation-test ...)
```

You can configure test selectors in the project.clj file. Let's set up a selector for the :perf label, and make the default be everything except :perf tests. The default occurs when no selector is specified.

```
:test-selectors {:perf :perf
                 :default (complement :perf)}
```

When you execute lein test :perf, only the tests labeled with :perf are run. If you execute lein test, only the tests not labeled with :perf are run. There is a special selector :all, which you don't need to specify in the configuration. If you execute the lein test :all, then all of the tests are run regardless of labels. Test selectors work with lein-test-refresh as well. With this configuration in place, you can have your CI server execute lein test :all to include your performance tests, but not be bothered by them during interactive development.

PARALLELISM

Say that you identified that calculating completion-rate is a major bottleneck, which in turn is spending the most wall clock time in member-info.

```
(defn member-info [member]
  (let [history (fetch-history member)
        profile (fetch-profile member)]
    (merge history profile)))
```

Here you see how two external services are being queried for data. These requests will be made sequentially; the history will be fully fetched before the profile is requested. You can instantly improve this by starting both requests immediately, and only returning the combined result when both are available. One way to express this is making both requests inside a future, and deref them for the final result.

```
(defn member-info-better [member]
  (let [history (future (fetch-history member))
```

```
      profile (future (fetch-profile member))]
(merge @history @profile)))
```

Now instead of waiting 21 milliseconds to get all of the data, it arrives in 11 milliseconds! Clojure has very concise and expressive abstractions for dealing with concurrency. See `pmap`, `pcalls`, `future`, and `core.async`.

MEMOIZATION

Caching is the wildcard of performance optimization. If your program is slow, just remember the answers instead of recalculating them! Caching is very effective at improving performance.

Clojure's memoize function takes a function and returns a function that does exactly the same thing as the original function, but remembers the results per input arguments it has previously calculated. Let's see it in action by defining a function `f` that prints a message and returns the increment of its argument.

```
(defn f [x]
  (println "Calculating...")
  (inc x))
```

Now define `g` to be the memoization of function `f`, and call the function `g` with the same input twice.

```
(def g (memoize f))
(g 1)
(g 1)
```

Notice that the message "Calculating..." is only displayed once. The second time that you call `g` it does not execute the body of the function, because `g` was able to look up the answer in its map of already calculated results. When the calculations occurring in the body of the function are intensive, looking up the answer is far faster than re-calculating it.

Returning to completion-rate you will observe that this function is called many times per step, but the return value never changes for the entire simulation. Using memoization provides a massive improvement.

```
(def completion-rate-better (memoize completion-rate))
```

Memoization enables you to write expressively without concern for the cost of repeatedly calling a function. With some care you can organize code according to intensive, but useful calculations, or slow IO requests that front load work and remember the answers.

Beware! Caching can subtly change the logic of your system. Imagine if completion-rate was affected every step. Clearly if that is the case you should then only memoize it per step. This is easy to accomplish in this case since you can see that you only need to call the function once.

```
(defn complete-stories-alternative [project]
  (let [rate (completion-rate project)]
    (reduce (fn complete-story [acc story]
```

```
      (update-story-status acc story "Done"))
    project
    (take (rand-int (int (* rate 2)))
          (stories-by-status project "In Progress"))))))
```

But say, instead you were relying on data fetched from the `member-info` function in several paths of your simulation. Ensuring that `member-info` is only queried once per step would be much more challenging. In this case you can avoid messing with the code by using a new memoization of the function for every step. Thus, your code can remain free of the concern of resource access cost. One way to express this is to wrap the sim-week step with a redef of `member-info` as a memoization. Redundant calls are eliminated.

```
(defn sim-week-alternative [project]
  (with-redefs [member-info (memoize member-info)]
    (sim-week project)))
```

The important thing is to have a good grasp on what is both correct and fast. There are many other ways to do small scope memoization, such as passing a memoized function to other functions to use, so be alert for opportunities.

Beware! Memoizing everything is going to eat up more memory than you have available, resulting in an Out of Memory failure. The domain of inputs must be bounded to some reasonable size.

The `core.memoize` library provides time-to-live and least-recently-used memoization, which are well proven strategies for trading off time and memory. Most long-lived service applications will have opportunities to cache, but need to carefully control the extent to which the cache can grow. Think about how the cache should be controlled when you use memoization. As a rule of thumb, most long-lived memoized functions should be created with `core.memoize`.

INLINING

The shape of your code can have unexpected performance implications. The Just-In-Time compiler (JIT) will try to inline frequently called functions to avoid the overhead of invocation. The heuristic it uses depends upon how often the function is called and how big it is. As well as removing the function call, inlining enables other optimizations by reorganizing execution.

Extracting functions can lead to better performance. Functions that are too big can't be inlined without bloating the call sites. Thus, smaller functions are often faster because it helps the JVM find the most efficient inlining.

This may seem counter intuitive at first. If function calls have a cost, many smaller functions should cost more, right? Thinking this way is reasonable, but wrong. It highlights the dangers of making assumptions about how written code actually executes at the nanosecond scale. The only real way to know is to benchmark it.

Check for deeply nested function calls in hot code paths because there are depth limits to where the JIT can apply inlining. For example, Ring handlers often have many middleware wrappers, which may be preventing optimization that would otherwise occur.

To go deep into the impact of code shape on the byte code produced, you can use the `nodisassemble` library to discover what byte code is being produced from your source code.

When you discover a hot bottleneck, it is worth experimenting with rearranging your code scopes, because it will affect the ability of the JVM to optimize your calculations. Always do this guided by a benchmark, and avoid assuming that a very reasonable rule of thumb actually results in the performance impact you expect.

Persistent Data Structures

Amazingly, the cost of immutability is low. So low that immutability is a good default. The low cost of updates to Clojure's collections is achieved through an implementation of ideal hash trees. Clojure data structures use shared structure to allow efficient creation of new values. If you start with a map of data and add a new key value, you are returned a new map. But that map is not a naïve copy of the original map. Instead it is a new data structure that shares the original data, and provides novelty.

Clojure's built in collections perform in a wide range around half an order of magnitude slower than their mutable counterparts. For most usages this is blazingly fast. So, they make an excellent default because of the strong safety guarantee that immutability brings. However, if you are really searching for speed, you need to be willing to use mutable collections where warranted.

Clojure programs tend to have many small maps/vectors/sets. There are small version maps (array-maps) and vectors and sets (custom classes) that are even more efficient. These get converted if they expand. Generally you can be comfortable relying on Clojure to do the right thing. If these costs are significant, you can avoid them by carefully managing the types used.

Nested maps are also very commonly used in Clojure programs. This is a good thing. But there can be occasions where nested map operations such as assoc-in and get-in may be improved by unrolling. `(get :a (get :b (get :c (get :d m))))` is not the same thing as `(get-in m [:d :c :b :a])` in terms of the byte code produced. The latter is implemented as recursive function calls.

The ultimate way to manage the types in your program is to use protocols and records. These constructs make no compromises in relation to the host platform. They are literally as fast as Java classes. You do not need to leave Clojure to get the highest performing data structures possible.

A datatype is created using deftype, defrecord, or reify with explicit fields. They provide access to the highest-performance primitive representation and polymorphism mechanism of the host. Accessing fields in these types is faster than using maps. Records behave like maps for undefined fields, so you can check whether your Record has accumulated unexpected key values during use by examining the __extmap field.

SAFE MUTATION WITH TRANSIENTS

The best way to make use of mutation safely is to limit the scope they exist in. So long as they don't escape into your program at large, they can't cause trouble. Clojure has an explicit mechanism for defining well-scoped mutation called transients.

The function `transient` returns a new, transient version of a collection, in constant time. The function `persistent!` returns a new, persistent version of the transient collection, in constant time. The transient collection can't be used after it is persisted. Any such use will throw an exception. Consider this example for constructing a set.

```
(persistent! (reduce conj! (transient #{}) coll))
```

Clearly this is the safe use of mutation, because the mutation is limited to building up a collection, and only an immutable version of that collection is returned for use by the rest of the program. Clojure uses transients for creating its collections, so you don't need to do this yourself, but you can use the same pattern where you may otherwise be doing many modifications in a well-scoped way.

The secret formula to using transients is:

1. Identify looping code that is using immutable datastructures.

2. Inside the scope of the function use a transient accumulator.

3. Change modifying functions to their transient equivalents.

   `assoc!, conj!, 'dissoc!', 'disj!', 'pop!'.`

4. Persist before returning the result.

Let's apply this formula to create a transient version of a function that will remove all "Done" stories from a simulation.

```
(defn remove-done-stories-with-transient [stories]
  (persistent!
    (reduce
      (fn [acc story]
        (dissoc! acc (:id story)))
      (transient stories)
      (filter #(= (:status %) "Done") stories))))
```

PROFILING

Profiling is observing the runtime characteristics of a program, such as time spent by function or memory consumption, in order to better understand and optimize them. The main question profiling seeks to answer is "Where does the program spend most of its time?" Even experienced programmers are often surprised by the results—performance is a complex matter. Performance problems and opportunities hide in unexpected places.

The JVM has a solid selection of excellent profilers, all of which work great with Clojure programs. The widely used profiles are:

➤ Java Flight Recorder and Java Mission Control

➤ YourKit

➤ VisualVM

Ultimately the most useful thing they produce is a table of where the time is spent in your program. But they also have a bunch of features such as measuring memory allocations, which are extremely useful for understanding how your code is performing. Clojure programs are especially susceptible to memory allocation and garbage collection, so be sure to look beyond just the timing results (see Figure 7-1).

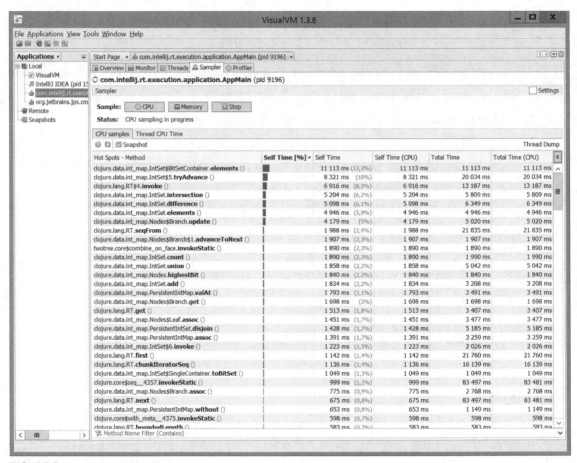

FIGURE 7-1

AVOIDING REFLECTION WITH TYPE HINTING

Reflection is the inspection of classes, interfaces, fields, and methods at runtime. Clojure is a dynamic language in the sense that code gets compiled at runtime, but Clojure code is always compiled. You rarely have to deal with types in Clojure, and generally eschew them, but the compiler will take advantage of types that it knows about. Type hinting is a special syntax to tell the compiler precisely what methods and fields are being used when doing interop. Where interop is ambiguous, the compiled code will use reflection to discover at runtime the method or field and call it.

Let's take a look at an example. Imagine part of your simulation algorithm involved counting how many stories were bugs. The definition of what a bug is might be to check for the string bug in the title of a story.

```
(defn bug? [s]
  (not (neg? (.indexOf s "bug"))))
```

The intention is that the input parameter s is a string, and you will use the Java method indexOf to see if it contains the substring "bug". The result of indexOf is -1 when the substring is not found. The compiler has no way to know that s will be a string. So it will compile byte code that will use reflection to work with any input. But reflection has a cost.

You can bind the global var *warn-on-reflection* to true in order to have the compiler notify you that it is producing reflection code. The easiest way to do this is to specify it in your project.clj file.

```
:global-vars {*warn-on-reflection* true}
```

Now, if you restart your test-refresh or repl session, you will see in the output console a reflection warning.

```
Reflection warning, mush/simulation.clj:150:3 - call to method indexOf can't be
  resolved (target class is unknown).
```

So let's make a type-hinted version to benchmark against. Annotate s with ^String to indicate to the compiler that you want to call the String instance indexOf method on s.

```
(defn bug?? [^String s]
  (not (neg? (.indexOf s "bug"))))
```

And now you benchmark both approaches to see the impact.

```
(def stories
  ["When the user clicks new story, the app crashes. (bug)"
   "Add a team member profile page. (feature)"
   "Build a backend service to store stories."
   "Every second story created splits into three stories. (bug)"])

(criterium.core/quick-bench
  (count (filter sim/bug? stories)))
=> Execution time mean : 739.032651 ns

(criterium.core/quick-bench
  (count (filter sim/bug?? stories)))
=> Execution time mean : 18.578044 µs
```

Look very carefully at the time units. 18.578 µs is 18578 ns. The type hinted version is 25 times faster! Clearly, reflection can have a big impact on your simulation if the bug? function is called many times over many stories over many steps.

There is an additional benefit to type hinting. Type hinting makes inlinable byte code. The JVM can further optimize execution beyond simply avoiding reflection.

Annotating types can be quite effective for bottleneck code. But it is a good style to be minimalistic about type hinting. Avoid annotating unnecessarily, as it makes your code noisy and does not provide a benefit. Even worse, an incorrect type hint can be extremely confusing. When type hinting, focus on input parameters, and try to avoid returning something that needs a type hint. This will help limit the amount of hinting necessary.

JAVA FLAGS

Leinigen sets the `-XX:+TieredStopAtLevel=1` flag set by default to optimize for startup time. You can remove this flag by using the `^:replace` metadata on your `:jvm-opts` setting.

```
:jvm-opts ^:replace ["-server" ;; maximize peak operating speed
            "-Xms256m" ;; heap minimum
            "-Xmx256m"  ;; heap maximum
            "-XX:+AggressiveOpts" ;; point performance compiler optimizations
            "-XX:+UseCompressedOops"] ;; neutralize penalty imposed by 64 bit JVM
```

There is widespread disagreement about what flags are the best to use for Clojure and Java applications. Many flags are situational and get a good or bad reputation from specific instances of them being useful or horrible in a particular scenario.

MATH

Clojure's numeric stack is much more forgiving than Java's numeric stack. Arithmetic operators are much more powerful, but they are slower. In Java if you add two integers together that combine to a number greater than can fit in a result integer, you get an exception. In Clojure you get the result upcast to the next biggest type that can hold your result. Generally this is very convenient, but for some applications you may want to take direct control over numerical behavior for best performance.

When dealing with numbers, things that can make for faster math are:

➤ `unchecked-add` and `*unchecked-math*`.

➤ Avoiding boxing, using primitives by casting `(int x)` and hinting `^int`.

➤ Using Java arrays.

One especially interesting library for math is `core.matrix`, which provides several different implementations of the same matrix abstractions with different tradeoffs.

SUMMARY

The performance of a computer program or system depends on many factors. Fortunately, Clojure and ClojureScript have great answers to those considerations. Clojure is an abstraction of the host platform, but there are many facilities to reach down to lower levels.

General solutions are difficult when it comes to performance. You should keep an open mind to narrowing the scope of your solution. Define your performance goals and think about what is possible and what is acceptable. You have many tools at your disposal for optimization, so creating a plan of attack is useful. Be ready to change your hypothesis as assumptions become invalidated, and send your experiments in a different direction where necessary.

Be wary of making assumptions about performance based on the results of micro-benchmarks. Fast operations are not the sum of their component operations. Focus on measuring larger scopes of code that are important to your system. Measuring slow things is usually more valuable than measuring fast things.

Think, measure, and monitor.

INDEX

ring.util.response helpers, 57–58
ROI (Return On Investment) calculator, 104, 123–125
routes, creating named set of, 28
routes function, 65
routes library, 28
routes namespace, 76
routing, 89–94
  in ClojureScript, 145–147
  DELETE/links/:id, 92–93
  GET/links, 93–94
  GET/links/:id, 91–92
  and middleware, 69–70
  path variables, 68–69
  POST/links/:id, 90–91
  principles, 147
  PUT/links/:id, 92
  writing routes, 65–68
routing library, 64
running application, reloading, 44–46
running tests, automatically, 48–49
runtime error, 138

S

same-origin policy, 147–148
schema elements, limit on number, 214
schema for task tracker app, 188–196
  basics, 188–196
  fulltext indexing, 190
  partitions, 190
search filter, 143
secure-api-defaults, 78
Selenium, webdriver API, 123
Sente library, 149
separation, of namespaces, 75
sequences, 154–155
set
  of numbers, infinite, 12
  semantics, in Datoms, 183
  for testing membership, 220
shared state, storing and accessing, 13–14
shortener-routes, 90
Sierra, Stuart, 94
Slager, Derek, 130
slurp function, 61–62
Software Transactional Memory (STM), 14
sort order, of indexes, 184
source code
  automatically reloading, 43–49
  measuring quality, 112–118
  reloading, 40–51
  style, 158–159
  writing reloadable, 49–51
source maps, enabling, 139
SPARQL, 175
Speclj framework, 119–120
SQL
  vs. Datomic, 193
  defining queries, 28

stack overflow, 5
state, modeling with DataScript, 165–166
state change, handling, 136–137
state management, 143
  and user inputs, 145
static analysis, with kibit and bikeshed, 114–116
storage
  constructor for implementation, 82
  costs and design, 186–187
  in-memory, 79, 81–83
storage protocol
  creating, 79–80
  for web services, 78–83
style, for source code, 158–159
sum-of-squares function, 3
SVG image tag, 156
swap! function, 13
System/getProperty method, 72

T

tail recursive style, 6
task functions, 210–213
task tracker app
  data access layer for, 206
  schema, 188–196
    basics, 188–196
    fulltext indexing, 190
    partitions, 190
tasks, query function for, 212
:task/subtask, 193
:tempids key, 204
test driven development (TDD), 99
testing, 99–127
  for app-routes, 66
  clojure.test library for, 100–104
    are macro, 102–103
    deftest macro, 101–102
    with-test macro, 101
  components with Devcards, 159–162
  with fixtures, 103–104
  framework alternatives, 119–127
    Cucumber, 120–126
    Expectations framework, 119
    Kerodon, 126–127
    Speclj framework, 119–120
  for handler_test.cli, 84
  JSON request and, 71–72
  for middleware, 76
  mocking/stubbing using with-redefs, 108–110
  for protocol implementations, 80–81
  reloading, 46–49
  Ring handlers, 58–59, 106–108
  running automatically, 48–49
  strategies for, 104–112
    against database, 104–106
time, Datomic treatment of, 205–206
time macro, 222
today function, :dynamic decoration for, 110

241